New Gaelic Speakers in Nova Scotia and Scotland

Histories of the Scottish Atlantic
Series Editors: S. Karly Kehoe and Chris Dalglish

This series showcases new research into the history of Scotland's relationship with the Atlantic World and promote understanding of the present-day legacies of this past. It analyses how interactions between diverse Atlantic communities influenced the development of particular landscapes and regions, both in Scotland and on the other side of the ocean. It interrogates the ways in which these past interactions and developments continue to resonate with people today, as an aspect of their identity and a factor influencing their lives and life chances.

Histories of the Scottish Atlantic reveal and explore the legacies of a complex past and advance understanding of how this at-once positive and negative heritage might be harnessed for the future development of communities on both sides of the Atlantic.

Available titles

Reappraisals of British Colonisation in Atlantic Canada, 1700–1930
Edited by S. Karly Kehoe and Michael Vance

Scottish Highlands and the Atlantic World: Social Networks and Identities
Edited by S. Karly Kehoe, Chris Dalglish and Annie Tindley

New Gaelic Speakers in Nova Scotia and Scotland: Heritage, Motivation and Identity
Stuart S. Dunmore

Forthcoming titles

Mohawks and Highland Scots: Life in the St. Lawrence River Valley after the American Revolution
Peter Cook and Katie Louise McCullough

The Men who Killed Chatoyer: Scots and their Enslaved Families in the Ceded Islands, 1763–1834
Désha Osborne

Transatlantic Threads: Scottish Linen and Society, c. 1707–1780
Sally Tuckett

edinburghuniversitypress.com/series/has

New Gaelic Speakers in Nova Scotia and Scotland

Heritage, Motivation and Identity

STUART S. DUNMORE

EDINBURGH
University Press

Airson Finn agus Flò.

Edinburgh University Press is one of the leading university presses in the UK. Publishing new research in the arts and humanities, EUP connects people and ideas to inspire creative thinking, open new perspectives and shape the world we live in. For more information, visit www.edinburghuniversitypress.com.

© Stuart S. Dunmore, 2025, under a Creative Commons Attribution-NonCommercial-NoDerivatives 4.0 International licence

Edinburgh University Press Ltd
13 Infirmary Street
Edinburgh EH1 1LT

Typeset in 10/13 Giovanni by
Cheshire Typesetting Ltd, Cuddington, Cheshire

A CIP record for this book is available from the British Library

ISBN 978 1 4744 9163 1 (paperback)
ISBN 978 1 4744 9162 4 (hardback)
ISBN 978 1 4744 9164 8 (webready PDF)
ISBN 978 1 4744 9165 5 (epub)

The right of Stuart S. Dunmore to be identified as author of this work has been asserted in accordance with the Copyright, Designs and Patents Act 1988 and the Copyright and Related Rights Regulations 2003 (SI No. 2498).

Contents

List of Figures		vi
List of Tables		vii
Acknowledgements		viii
1.	Gaelic and Gaels in Scotland and Nova Scotia: A Historical and Contemporary Account	1
2.	Language, Ethnicity and Identities: A Conceptual Frame	20
3.	Gaelic Language Ideologies in Scotland and Nova Scotia: An Ethnographic Introduction to the Research Sites	38
4.	New Gaelic Speakers' Language Acquisition and Use	50
5.	Contrasting Gaelic Identities: Heritage, Language Ideologies and Motivation	97
6.	Quantitative Perspectives on New Gaelic Speakerhood in Scotland and Nova Scotia	141
7.	New Worlds: Transatlantic Gaeldom and Twenty-first-century Linguistic Practice	163
Bibliography		173
Index		182

Figures

6.1	Location of respondents	142
6.2	Age of respondents	143
6.3	Gender	143
6.4	Socio-economic class	144
6.5	University attendance	144
6.6	Ability in Gaelic	145
6.7	Age of first Gaelic acquisition	147
6.8	School exposure to Gaelic in childhood	148
6.9	Language use in childhood home	149
6.10	Language use in community	149
6.11	Overall frequency of Gaelic use	150
6.12	Language use at home	151
6.13	Language use at work	151
6.14	Language use with friends	152
6.15	Language use with partner/spouse	153
6.16	Language use with son/daughter	153
6.17	Language use with mother	154
6.18	Language use with father	154
6.19	Language use with brother/sister	155
6.20	Language use with grandparents	155
6.21	Attitudes to the regional importance of Gaelic	157
6.22	Attitudes to the national/provincial importance of Gaelic	157
6.23	Responses to 'Gaelic is important to my personal identity'	158
6.24	Attitudes to potential language and identity loss	158
6.25	Responses to 'Gaelic is dying out'	159
6.26	Reported identities in Scotland	160
6.27	Reported identities in Nova Scotia	160

Tables

1.1 Gaelic speakers in Scotland 1806–2022   4
6.1 Reported linguistic abilities in Gaelic and English   146
7.1 Key to transcription conventions   171

Acknowledgements

I am very grateful to the series editors, and particularly Dr S. Karly Kehoe, for the invitation to contribute a title to their ground-breaking *Histories of the Scottish Atlantic* book series. The research on which this book is based was generously funded by the British Academy with a postdoctoral fellowship (grant number PDF160055) held at the University of Edinburgh from 2016 to 2019. It was also developed greatly over the course of a Fulbright scholarship held at Harvard University in 2022, and I am grateful to the US–UK Fulbright Commission and Royal Society of Edinburgh for their support. A sincere thank you is owed to my family, colleagues past and present, and to all of my research participants, without whose insight and kind input this monograph would have been impossible – *tapadh leibh uile, a chàirdean còire*.

ONE

Gaelic and Gaels in Scotland and Nova Scotia: A Historical and Contemporary Account

In the twenty-first century, ever greater numbers of individuals are engaging with Scottish Gaelic as a second ('L2') or additional language on both sides of the Atlantic, whilst communities of first language ('L1') speakers persist in spite of ongoing language shift within the Highlands and Islands of Scotland and in Cape Breton, Nova Scotia (National Records of Scotland 2024; Statistics Canada 2022). This chapter provides an overview of the key questions the monograph will address, linking the relevance of the research to a diverse audience of scholars, educators and policymakers. It will contextualise the key themes of the book within the sociological and historical settings of Gaelic in Scotland from the sixth century CE, and in Nova Scotia from the eighteenth century, before discussing the theme of language revitalisation and current initiatives to develop and renew minority languages internationally. Previous research has suggested that whilst new Gaelic speakers' language use in both countries is by definition substantial, their numbers are small, and crucially, their social identities and language learning motivations vary widely.

Recent years have witnessed a resurgence in Gaelic language learning activity using various methods, in diverse settings internationally. Conversely, in Scotland, Gaelic has now been in decline for almost a thousand years, since at its zenith it was the dominant tongue over a large majority of the country's territory. The most widely accepted historical account holds that Gaels (Old Gaelic: *Goídil*; Latin *Scotti*) in north-eastern Ireland settled the western seaboard of northern Britain from around the early sixth century, and possibly much earlier (Ó Baoill 2010; Clancy 2011). As the Gaels (or 'Scots') extended their dynastic and cultural influence across the mainland of Alba over the next five centuries, their language expanded over most parts of the northern third of Great Britain, as previously Pictish- and Brythonic-speaking societies were absorbed within the Kingdom of Alba (Dumville 2002; Ó Baoill 2010). Whilst Woolf (2007: 17) has cautioned that written evidence for the social history of Scotland is 'appallingly slight' in the early medieval era, the incidence of Gaelic place names over the south of modern Scotland, and into northern England, nevertheless clearly indicates the furthest extent of the Kingdom of Alba. Notably, Gaelic names are sparsest in the far south-east, an area predominantly settled by 'Inglis'-speaking people, whilst the Gaels continued to expand their kingdom from the west (Barrow 1989; Woolf 2007; Clancy 2011).

The Gaelic foundations of the Kingdom of Alba were increasingly replaced from the early twelfth century by those of the ascendant Anglo-Norman aristocracy (Barrow 1989: 70; MacKinnon 1991: 34). The combination of a largely French-speaking nobility and the increasing economic importance of market burghs in Lowland areas (where 'Inglis' varieties predominated) motivated an inexorable sociocultural shift among inhabitants 'from membership of a Gaelic-speaking essentially kin-based society to that of a Scots-speaking feudal society' (Barrow 1989: 70). Gaelic was increasingly replaced by 'Inglis' as the language of social prestige and vernacular communication in Lowland Scotland, the latter variety being increasingly referred to as 'Scottis' from c.1500, while Gaelic became known as 'Erse' ('Irish'; MacGregor 2009: 37). The notional Highland–Lowland divide was thus first expressed in terms of a primarily ethnolinguistic distinction, a result of language shift to Scots-English varieties in the Lowlands (MacKinnon 1991; Withers 1984, 1988).

After the mid-sixteenth-century Scottish Reformation, hostility to Gaelic on the part of the Scots crown became explicitly connected to the elimination of resistant elements from the kingdom. Starting with the 1609 Statutes of Iona, developments throughout the seventeenth century are regarded by Withers (1988: 157–8) as constituting an early wave of 'improvement' and Anglicisation which instigated language shift from Gaelic to English in much of the Highlands and Islands. The Statutes consisted of a series of measures to undermine the effective autonomy of the clan chiefs (*cinn cinnidh*). Gaelic chiefs' heirs were required to be educated in Lowland or English schools, with the express intention that they should then be able to speak, read and write in English (MacGregor 2006: 145).

Consequently, the deep-set, kinship-oriented linkages between the clan chiefs, their middle class client tacksmen and dependent followers were fatally disrupted. Explicit policy to bring about cultural transformation thus began even a century before the formal onset of 'improvement' in the eighteenth century. After the 1707 Union, policy in this connection was heavily influenced by notions of civilisation and 'enlightenment' (Withers 1984, 1988). A central concern of eighteenth-century philosophy was the supposed relationship of reason and culture as the distinguishing features of humanity, and of these notions' very basis in human language (Glaser 2007: 37). For example, the Romantic view of the nation emphasised the importance of a people's 'shared spirit' (*Volksgeist*) manifested in their language and culture (Reicher and Hopkins 2001: 8). Yet the conception of language that Romantic philosophers privileged in their theses pertained to varieties that were perceived as beneficial for wider communication, such as French, German and English. The English philosopher John Stuart Mill (1991 [1861]: 431) insisted that

> [n]obody can suppose that it is not more beneficial to a Breton, or a Basque of French Navarre, to be brought into the current of ideas and feelings of a highly civilised and cultivated people ... The same remark applies to the Welshman or the Scottish highlander [sic] as members of the British nation.

Gaelic was perceived as an implacable barrier to the economic, moral and cultural development of Highlanders, and its replacement with English was seen as imperative to realising wider goals of the drive for improvement (Withers 1988: 58). Processes and ideologies of improvement in the Highlands came into fierce conflict with indigenous notions of *dùthchas* ('heredity', 'tradition', 'heritage') and Gaelic understandings of how society should operate (MacKinnon 1991: 64–5). The cultivation of industry in the Highlands was actively encouraged by Enlightenment thinkers such as Adam Smith, who denounced Highland society as characteristic of the very worst excesses of patriarchal feudalism (Withers 1988: 58).

Landowners became increasingly concerned with economic reorganisation in the belief that harnessing markets would bring civilisation and development to Highland Scotland (Withers 1988; Macleod 2010). The clan chiefs were increasingly absorbed within the British aristocracy and took an ever greater interest in making their estates more profitable, exacting higher rents from tenants and developing large-scale livestock farming (Glaser 2007: 65). Faced with increasing economic pressures and loss of traditional livelihoods, Highlanders began to emigrate en masse as early as the 1730s (Devine 1994: 16). Harvest failures in the late eighteenth and early nineteenth centuries exacerbated hardships for middle-class tacksmen and rural workers alike, and drove ever greater numbers to emigrate to the urban Lowlands, England, or colonial North America and Australia (Glaser 2007: 65). Hunter (1976) has estimated that in 1803 alone up to 20,000 people may have left the Highlands for North America. Gaelic-speaking Highlanders were increasingly encouraged (later compelled) to emigrate in processes of land reorganisation and mass displacement that became known as the Clearances (Withers 1984; Glaser 2007; Richards 2007).

McLeod (2005: 178) observes of the relationship between the Clearances and language shift to English that 'the dislocation and disruption caused by clearance ... seem to have contributed to longer-term trends by which Gaelic was devalued and gradually abandoned'. The activities of the Gaelic Schools Societies and particularly the Society in Scotland for Propagating Christian Knowledge (SSPCK) in the area of Gaelic-medium elementary tuition tended only to accelerate general trends toward bilingualism in the Highlands (Durkacz 1983: 219–22; MacKinnon 1991). With the passing of the Education (Scotland) Act 1872, which made no mention of Gaelic, responsibility for education that had previously been administered by SSPCK, church and Gaelic Schools Societies was transferred to local school boards (MacLeod 2007; Macleod 2010; McLeod 2005). Whereas certain schools had thus previously made some provision for Gaelic instruction, its use declined as a direct consequence of the Act (Durkacz 1983: 223–4; MacKinnon 2009: 588). The 1918 Education (Scotland) Act required education authorities to make adequate provision for Gaelic teaching 'in Gaelic-speaking areas' but neglected to specify what such teaching should entail, or which areas were to be considered Gaelic-speaking (MacLeod 2007: 1). The First World War had a particularly major impact on Gaelic-speaking communities in the Highlands and Islands, Macleod (2010: 29) noting losses of especially high proportions of young men who never returned from France and Flanders. Such losses severely exacerbated and rapidly hastened the decline of Gaelic in many such communities.

Various researchers have juxtaposed the emergence of Gaelic revitalisation initiatives from the 1960s with the ongoing decline of Gaelic in its former heartlands (MacKinnon 1977; Dorian 1981; Macdonald 1997; Oliver 2002; McEwan-Fujita 2003, 2010c; Macleod 2010; McLeod 2020; see Table 1.1, below). Alongside numerous other commentators, Macdonald (1997: 6) has referred to greater institutionalised provision for Gaelic since the early 1980s, as well as a general 'growth of interest' in the language in Scotland, as a 'Gaelic renaissance'. McLeod (2014; 2020) relates this growth both to greater perception of Gaelic as a national language and marker of cultural distinctiveness in general since the Scottish Parliament was (re)established in 1999.

Notwithstanding various cultural and political developments related to the Gaelic renaissance, the language enjoyed no legislative protection prior to the Scottish Parliament's unanimous passing of the Gaelic Language (Scotland) Act 2005 (Dunbar 2006; McLeod 2020). *Comunn na Gàidhlig* (the Gaelic Language Society) had campaigned for legislation since the passing of the Welsh Language

Table 1.1 Gaelic speakers in Scotland 1806–2022

Date	Total Gaelic speakers in Scotland	% of total Scottish population
1806	297,823	18.5
1891	254,415	6.3
1951	95,447	1.9
1981	79,307	1.6
1991	65,978	1.3
2001	58,652	1.2
2011	57,602	1.1
2022	69,701	1.3

(Source for 1806–1991: MacKinnon 1993; 2001–2022: National Records of Scotland 2013; 2024)

Act 1993, which stipulated that Welsh and English should be treated on 'a basis of equality' in Wales (Jones and Williams 2009: 697). The MacPherson Taskforce was established in 1999 to investigate potential legislation for Gaelic, whilst in 2001 the Ministerial Advisory Group on Gaelic (Dunbar 2006: 16) was established. The latter group's recommendations included the establishment of a civil service unit dedicated to Gaelic affairs, along with a language board and the passage of a language act conferring official status. These broad recommendations were followed up with the enactment of the Gaelic Language (Scotland) Act 2005, which established the national, executive public authority Bòrd na Gàidhlig on a statutory basis (MacKinnon 2009: 644). Under the Act, the Bòrd has been required to produce a National Gaelic Language Plan every five years and is conferred authority to require public bodies to produce their own institutional Gaelic language plans, with a view to securing the status of Gaelic as 'an official language of Scotland commanding equal respect with the English language' (Walsh and McLeod 2008: 35).

McLeod (2014: 6) describes this expression of the language's position in Scottish society as the 'most significant formal statement of Gaelic's status as a national language', though noting that legal requirements involved in securing 'equal respect' were intended to be less demanding than those in Welsh Language Act 1993 (Walsh and McLeod 2008: 35). Dunbar (2006: 17) argues that it was rather unclear where the status of 'equal respect' derived from, especially since it is by no means obvious that the Act itself conferred such status. The 2005 Act has nevertheless been seen as a 'historic step forward for the language', even though in international terms it has been seen as a 'relatively weak' enactment (Walsh and McLeod 2008: 35). At the time of writing (May 2024) the Scottish Languages Bill is completing stage 1 committee scrutiny in the Scottish Parliament. It is unclear at this point exactly what form the final Act will take on completion of its passage through parliament. Its key provisions include establishing areas of linguistic significance using various criteria, replacing the statutory preparation of a national plan with a new national strategy to be published by the Scottish Government, the institution of a system of language standards, and introduction of substantial new reporting responsibilities for Bòrd na Gàidhlig (Scottish Parliament 2024).

As Walsh and McLeod (2008: 24) have observed, the goal of stimulating language use via legislative provision relies ultimately upon 'aspects of identity and ideology' impacting on speakers' linguistic practices (see Dunmore 2019). While Gaelic has long been regarded as a facet of an expressly Highland (and Island) identity, positive attitudes to the language's relevance for Scottish identity have been revealed in surveys undertaken in recent years. For example, the 2021/22 Scottish Social Attitudes Survey found that 79% of a representative sample of the Scottish population (n = 1,365) regarded Gaelic as important to Scotland's cultural heritage, while 88% saw it as important to that of the Highlands and Islands (Dean et al. 2022: 43; cf. Paterson et al. 2014). Meanwhile, 55% agreed that some Gaelic should be taught to all schoolchildren in Scotland (as against 38% in 2012), while 70% agreed that all children should learn about Gaelic culture and history (Dean et al. 2022: 50–2). With regard to immersion education, 37% indicated they were in favour of Gaelic-medium education in Scottish primary schools, with 38% neither in favour of nor against the system (Dean et al. 2022: 53).

Whilst public attitudes to Gaelic have clearly improved, widespread (if sometimes rather superficial) general support for the language in Scotland is not a new phenomenon in itself (McLeod 2020). Macdonald (1997: 256) argued on the basis of ethnographic fieldwork conducted in the 1980s that Gaelic had 'come to be accepted as a symbol of Scotland's distinctiveness' by that time. Gaelic speakers have therefore found themselves to be increasingly regarded as the fountainhead of a valued national resource (Macdonald 1997: 63) and the bounded and quasi-ethnic understanding of Gaelic as the language of the traditional Highlander is seen to have weakened (Oliver 2002, 2006). In the 2022 census, for example, 62% of all Gaelic speakers were reported to be living outside of the Highlands and Islands (National Records of Scotland 2022). Yet the historic perception of the Highlands and Lowlands as embodying essentially distinct cultures still persists in certain quarters (Macdonald 1999: 106; Glaser 2006: 170), and as Macdonald (1997: 131–2) noted over twenty years ago, the link between the language and a specific, local sense of place has long been strong in heartland communities.

Oliver (2002, 2005, 2006) observed that conceptions in Scotland of Gaelic as an ethnoculturally and geographically bounded language had weakened in the later twentieth century, giving way to broader understandings of the language's place at a national level. The contrast was defined by Oliver (2005: 5) in terms of *Gemeinschaft* and *Gesellschaft*, broadly conceived of as a distinction between 'community' and 'society'. Yet Oliver (2006: 161) elaborated that the evolution of the *Gesellschaft* approach was often inhibited by the persistent association of Gaelic with the 'traditional', observing that the language tended more frequently to be perceived as a marker of a specifically Gaelic identity than of Scottish identity in a wider sense (Oliver 2005: 9, 2006: 162).

Two decades on, however, ever increasing numbers of people from a range of different cultural backgrounds have chosen to learn and speak Gaelic as a facet of their daily lives, and the language's role as a marker of identity among different kinds of Gaelic speakers today is seen to be far from straightforward (Glaser 2007; McLeod, O'Rourke and Dunmore 2014; Dunmore 2019; McLeod 2020). The hybrid nature of many learners' and new speakers' identifications with Gaelic has sometimes met with a degree of scepticism in traditional contexts in the Highlands and Islands (MacCaluim 2007: 78–82), whilst being regarded as an advantage for emerging and 'new' Scottish identities in urban Lowland centres (Glaser 2007: 258). Others still have questioned the importance of the language to either Scottish or Highland identity (Rogerson and Gloyer 1995). Nevertheless, Dorian (2011: 468) has argued that revitalisation efforts on behalf of Gaelic have led to the 'revalorization of a language that was once disdained', with benefits for the wellbeing and 'self-regard' of traditional speakers.

Yet in spite of these benefits, Dorian (2011: 468) has observed that the long-term success of efforts to revitalise Gaelic remains to be seen; losses to speaker numbers from older speakers dying 'still far outstrip gains in new speakers via home transmission and Gaelic-medium schools', she argued, observing that 'the relatively favourable current position of Gaelic is very precarious'. Edwards (2013: 13) has similarly argued that a notional distinction may be required between bilingual speakers in Gaelic 'heartland' areas and those 'in Glasgow ... or Edinburgh [who] have more formally set themselves (or been set) to become bilingual' via immersion education programmes. He argues that classifying speakers within these two groups 'under a single "bilingual" rubric' – irrespective of language practices – 'might give a rather inaccurate picture of the state of health of ... Gaelic' in Scotland (Edwards 2013: 14). As such, Scottish policymakers' previous observation that an apparent diminution in the decline of Gaelic speakers in the 2011 census data was 'mainly due to the rise in Gaelic-medium education' (Bòrd na Gàidhlig 2014) must be carefully considered in light of current sociolinguistic theory on language revitalisation (see also Dunmore 2019).

Gaelic in Nova Scotia

The history of Gaelic as a spoken vernacular in Nova Scotia dates back some 250 years (Edwards 1991, 2010). Some scholars have traced an early connection between the Gaelic world and Maritime Canada a good deal further back, in the enslaved Gaelic-speakers Haki and Hekja's reported landings in North America during the age of Norse 'Viking' expansion (MacKinnon 1996, 2001; cf. Mertz 1982; Ó hIfearnáin 2002). Notwithstanding such early contact, Gaelic-speaking Scots' permanent settlement of Atlantic North America started in earnest during the seventeenth century. The survival of Gaelic in Cape Breton Island into the twenty-first century is clearly astounding in terms of local communities' tenacity in the maintenance of their minority language, culture and identity. In spite of this longstanding resilience in the Nova Scotia diaspora, native speaker numbers have now dwindled to a tiny minority (Statistics Canada 2022) and some commentators have suggested that the Gaelic-speaking community may undergo its ultimate demise in future decades (Dembling 1997; Edwards 1991, 2010). As Newton (2014: 141) observes, the 'core Gaelic community in Nova Scotia has reached a critical state' in the twenty-first century.

The name *Nova Scotia* ('New Scotland') was first applied to the historic territories of the Indigenous Mi'kmaq people in 1621, when they were chartered for colonisation by James VI to William Alexander, first Earl of Stirling (Campbell and MacLean 1974: 35; Mertz 1982: 36). The first Gaelic-speaking Scots to immigrate to Nova Scotia arrived as early as 1629, and while Alexander's attempts to establish a sizeable Scottish colony in the region proved unsuccessful, Highlanders continued to migrate in small numbers during the seventeenth and early eighteenth centuries (Ó hIfearnáin 2002: 64). Kennedy (2002: 25–7) even cites evidence that Scots constituted the largest minority group in the Acadian colony of New France after the territory was ceded to the French in 1632 (Campbell and MacLean 1974: 35). Edwards (1991, 2010) has noted that although the earliest records of Gaelic settlement in what became Maritime Canada are scarce, the first large-scale movement of Highland Scots into Nova Scotia accelerated in earnest from the 1770s, as middle-class Gaelic tacksmen sought a new life and livelihood in North America, in response to declining living standards at home (Kehoe 2021, 2022). Often faced with unappealing (and rapidly deteriorating) prospects in Scotland, the first Scottish settlers thus largely migrated to Nova Scotia as a matter of their own choice, in stark contrast to many of those who made the dangerous journey later in the nineteenth century as a result of forced exile and Clearance (Withers 1984; Ó hIfearnáin 2002; Kehoe 2021, 2022).

Peak emigration to Nova Scotia occurred between about 1770 and 1850, when over 50,000 Highland Scots are estimated to have arrived into eastern Antigonish, Victoria, Inverness and Cape Breton Counties (Kennedy 2002: 20–1; Ó hIfearnáin 2002: 65). MacKinnon (2001: 20) notes that Gaelic speakers first settled en masse in Pictou County from 1773, being preceded by migration to Prince Edward Island from 1769, and followed by mass migrations to south-eastern Cape Breton Island between 1791 and 1795, Antigonish County and western Cape Breton Island between 1803 and 1815, and north-western Cape Breton between 1802 and 1843 (see also Campbell and MacLean 1974). Later centres of Gaelic settlement in eastern Canada included Glengarry County, Ontario, as well as parts of eastern Quebec, and also included secondary migration from Cape Breton into south-western Newfoundland (MacKinnon 2001: 20–1).

The settlement patterns that these successive waves of migration produced were diffuse, widely dispersed and overwhelmingly rural in nature, in contrast to the urban settlement of predominantly English speakers who moved into the burgeoning towns of Nova Scotia (Kennedy 2002: 22–3). In sociolinguistic terms, Gaelic-speaking communities thrived as sites for language socialisation in these more relatively isolated contexts, although socioeconomic conditions were often fragile (Mertz 1982, 1989; Kennedy 2002; MacKinnon 1996, 2001). The cultural homogeneity of Gaelic-speaking communities in Nova Scotia was amplified by the chain migration patterns that characterised their settlement in the nineteenth century. Communities that were relatively uniform in terms of their (Gaelic-dominant) linguistic practices and religious observation (whether Catholic, Presbyterian or Episcopal) were frequently transplanted into similarly homogeneous communities in eastern Nova Scotia (Edwards 2010; Kennedy 2002; Ó hIfearnáin 2002; MacKinnon 2010).

Kennedy (2002: 277) remarks that 'the nature of the migrations from Scotland ensured that large, nearly homogeneous communities were established [in Nova Scotia], dominating nearly a third of the province's area'. Lowland settlement was also consistent, with English-speaking Scots forming homogeneous blocks in other communities, as distinct from Highland Gaels in Nova Scotia as in the old country (Campbell and MacLean 1974: 46). As a result, the increasing numbers of Gaelic speakers in Nova Scotia fared somewhat better than their peers back in the Highlands and Islands; Kennedy argues that within this 'richly Gaelic environment', a unique, 'truly Canadian and North American Gaelic community' developed and flourished in the early decades of the nineteenth century (2002: 277).

Chain migration from the Scottish Highlands to Nova Scotia accelerated through the mid-nineteenth century. As a consequence of the mass displacement of Highland families caused by the Clearances, Shaw (1977) estimated that by 1880 over 80,000 Gaelic speakers were present in Nova Scotia. By the time of the 1871 census, Scots were the largest ethnic group in Nova Scotia, having temporarily overtaken English settlers (MacKinnon 2001; Edwards 2010). Furthermore, the majority of Scots to have immigrated into the province were Gaelic speakers, who formed the linguistic majority over large parts of eastern Nova Scotia (Kennedy 2002: 25). Even at this stage, however, Edwards (1991: 273) has reviewed evidence for the weakening of intergenerational transmission of Gaelic, and subsequent language shift to English in Nova Scotian communities settled by Gaels (see also Kennedy 2002: 61). The seeds of language decline may already have been sown at this early juncture, therefore. Nevertheless, at one point in the later nineteenth century the Scots had come to comprise Canada's third largest ethnic group – and Nova Scotia's largest. As MacKinnon (2001: 19) explains:

> The numbers of Gaelic-speaking Scots were very comparable to those of the original French settlers in Quebec, and there were attempts to secure language rights for Gaelic both at dominion and provincial levels in the nineteenth century ... Over the period 1871–1971 Nova Scotia's Scots declined in proportion from the province's largest ethnic group – 32.5% of the whole – to 11.1% in 1991, being overtaken by the English from 1901 onwards. Nova Scotia then became the most English of Canada's mainland provinces ... The Gaelic language likewise entered a terminal state.

At various points in the nineteenth century, Canadian policymakers had considered (if only ever fleetingly) providing formal recognition for Gaelic (Campbell and MacLean 1974; Edwards 1991, 2010; MacKinnon 2001). In fact, legislation was passed to support, in principle, the establishment of Gaelic education in Nova Scotia schools (MacKinnon 2001: 19). Edwards (2010: 156) notes that the Nova Scotia Education Act 1841 even permitted a form of publicly funded Gaelic-medium education in the province (alongside the options of French- and German-medium education), should teachers and parents wish for it to be made available. The Act stipulated (as quoted in Edwards 2010: 156–7):

> Be it enacted, That any school wherein the ordinary Instruction may be in the French, Gaelic or German language … shall be entitled to the like portion of the public money as any school wherein the ordinary Instruction may be in the English language.

Yet demand for the provision of education through Gaelic was minimal and, as in Scotland, when state schools were established in 1864 no provision was made for any form of Gaelic education (Edwards 2010: 156–7; MacKinnon 2001: 19). As a consequence of this oversight in the Nova Scotian education system, Kennedy (2002: 51) remarks that, in effect, Gaelic-speaking teachers were being paid by Gaelic-speaking parents 'to teach Gaelic-speaking students through the medium of English about subjects deemed important in English-speaking society.' Children of Gaelic speakers in the nineteenth century thereafter learned next to nothing – and certainly nothing positive – of their language in schools, and internalised negative attitudes regarding the relevance and importance of Gaelic in Canadian society (Kennedy 20022: 51).

Such attitudes would later be reflected at even the highest levels of Canadian public life. Infamously in the history of Canadian Gaelic, in 1890 the Cape Breton–born senator Thomas Robert MacInnes (representing British Columbia) unsuccessfully proposed a bill to recognise Gaelic as Canada's third official language, after English and French (Kennedy 2002; Edwards 2010). Whilst, on the one hand, a limited official multilingualism was therefore already acknowledged in post-federation Canada, MacInnes's argument that the ancestral language of Irish and Scottish Canadians – whose combined population of 1,657,266 outnumbered the 1,298,929 French- and 881,301 English-Canadians in the 1881 census – was deserving of official recognition was largely treated as a joke in Parliament, and the motion was defeated by forty-one votes to seven (Kennedy 2002: 58). As such, Kennedy (2002: 58–9) argues, senators unwittingly betrayed the superficiality of official accommodation for multilingualism and multiculturalism after federation; Gaels, whether Scots or Irish, were subsumed within a largely imagined, homogeneous Anglophone community – that of the 'British' founder population – in the minds and actions of policymakers, and thereby airbrushed out of the picture of Canadian multiculturalism. This is to say nothing of the many Indigenous languages and cultures to have been largely excluded in the official 'bicultural' dynamic (Kennedy 2002: 27). The fact that thirty-five senators present at the debate, including two future prime ministers, were first-language Gaelic speakers did not aid support for MacInnes's bill.

Edwards (2010: 156–7) states that only in 1921 was Gaelic permitted in the Nova Scotian education system for study as an optional subject 'if the majority of students demanded it', by which time it was unarguably a 'language well in decline'. Again, demand for uptake of Gaelic was limited, partly due to the internalisation of hostile official attitudes in the nineteenth century described above, and partly due to an already declining Gaelic population (Kennedy 2002; Newton 2014). MacKinnon (2001: 19) observes that from a population of over 70,000 in the mid-nineteenth century, Cape Breton's Gaelic population had declined to just 24,000 by the time of the 1931 census (cf. Edwards 1991: 278). Numbers of recorded Gaelic speakers in Nova Scotia continued to decline by around 50% in each subsequent census throughout the twentieth century, until just under 1,500 were recorded in 1971 (MacKinnon 2001: 19; see also MacLean 1978; Mertz 1982, 1989).

Kennedy (2002: 5) draws a direct correspondence between the lack of educational provision for Gaelic and the catastrophic rate of language decline in the twentieth century, arguing that 'the continued exclusion of Gaelic from education ... would have multifarious effects and was probably the single most important cause of the unusually rapid decline of the language in Nova Scotia in the 20th century'. Whilst surely an important contributory factor, however, the lack of Gaelic educational opportunities, as such, can hardly explain the critical disruption of intergenerational transmission that is widely held to have occurred in the early twentieth century. Mertz (1982, 1989) investigated the dynamics of Gaelic language shift in Nova Scotia in great detail, identifying a 'metapragmatic filter' through which Gaels came to attribute relative values to their languages, and which in turn impacted on their willingness to speak and transmit the Gaelic language in the crucial domains of daily life. The 1920s and '30s transformed the prevailing socioeconomic circumstances in Nova Scotia, hastening and enhancing the ideological association of Gaelic with rurality, economic immobility and low social cachet. Mertz (1982: 311–12) argues that the particular metapragmatic filter – that is, the sets of language attitudes, ideologies and 'folk theories' concerning Gaelic – that had the greatest consequence for the future trajectory of the language in Nova Scotia was that prevailing at the time of the Great Depression. She explains:

> The social basis for a difference in metapragmatic views is easily understood if we remember the economic foundation for the linguistic shift of the thirties. Gaelic was a marker of a stigmatized, lower class, rural identity. It was particularly for the members of the community who best exemplified that identity that a repudiation of Gaelic had value. (Mertz 1982: 312)

The harsh economic climate of the 1920s and '30s essentially prompted Nova Scotia Gaels to re-evaluate their relationship with Gaelic, a language they increasingly viewed via the metapragmatic filter of linguistic ideology as an irrelevance to their children's future wellbeing, and at worst a hindrance (Mertz 1982, 1989). When renowned Highland folklorist John Lorne Campbell surveyed the state of Gaelic in Nova Scotia in 1932, he found levels of transmission of the language to children to be very low, even within the shrinking heartland areas of Gaelic settlement in Cape Breton (Kennedy 2002: 84). A linguistic 'tip' had been reached, and language shift to English then accelerated. The situation was compounded as Gaelic-speaking Nova Scotians began once again to migrate in large numbers, this time to the urban centres of Sydney, Antigonish, Pictou and Inverness, or further afield, to Halifax, New England, Ontario or the prairie provinces of the Canadian west (Kennedy 2002: 73; Edwards 2010: 154). As urbanisation gathered pace in the late nineteenth and early twentieth century, and rural eastern Nova Scotia (previously the core Gaelic heartland) became increasingly depopulated, the language started rapidly to retreat. Kennedy (2002: 75) states frankly that, '[t]o a very large extent, rural decline in eastern Nova Scotia was Gaelic decline', describing how the urban environments that were increasingly the destination for Gaels 'proved particularly hostile to the socialization of children in Gaelic … [while] the proportion of the population living in rural communities fell rapidly' (2002: 73–4).

As a result of the linguistic tip that Nova Scotia's Gaelic community experienced in the early twentieth century, language shift accelerated through later decades as older generations, who had ceased to speak the language to children, themselves aged and died (MacKinnon 1996, 2001; Kennedy 2002; Edwards 2010). Declining numbers of Gaelic-speaking teachers, in particular, meant that efforts to secure a permanent place for Gaelic in the education system were sporadic and generally unsuccessful, as had been true in the nineteenth and early twentieth centuries (Cox 1994; Kennedy 2002; MacKinnon 2001; Edwards 2010).

Although, as already noted, Gaelic was available for study subject to student demand after 1921 (Kennedy 2002; Edwards 2010), requests for provision remained limited, and teacher recruitment became extremely problematic as the population of Gaelic speakers continued to decline. Kennedy (2002: 92–3) describes the disappearance of Gaelic as a subject for study in the provincial curriculum as characteristic of the Gaelic language's 'yo-yo like existence in the Nova Scotian educational system'. This portrayal seems particularly apt in light of the growth of tertiary-level Gaelic provision under the professorship of Major CIN MacLeod at St Francis Xavier University in Antigonish from 1958 (Edwards 2010: 158). Hundreds of students enrolled in Gaelic courses at the university during this time and, consequently, unprecedented numbers of potential Gaelic teachers were generated, at almost the very same time that Gaelic 'was dropped as a from the public school curriculum altogether' in 1964 (Kennedy 2002: 92).

In spite of the small overall numbers of reported Gaelic speakers in modern-day Nova Scotia, the provincial Office of Gaelic Affairs (2018) has estimated that at least 230,000 Nova Scotians claim descent from families who spoke Gaelic historically. Contemporary policy to revitalise Gaelic in Nova Scotia can be traced to bottom-up, grassroots efforts to stem the language's decline that started in the 1970s (Dunbar 2008; Edwards 2010). Such grassroots initiatives were joined at the start of this century by 'top-down', institutional supports for the language community. In 2006, Rodney MacDonald, then-Premier of Nova Scotia, established *Oifis Iomairtean na Gàidhlig* (the Office of Gaelic Affairs) as a civil service unit within the provincial government, along with a ministerial portfolio for Gaelic Affairs and modest annual budget for programme funding. *Iomairtean na Gàidhlig* exists, in its own words, for the purpose of helping

> Nova Scotians [to] reclaim their Gaelic language and identity as a basis for cultural, spiritual, community and economic renewal … by creating awareness, working with partners and providing tools and opportunities to learn, share and experience Gaelic language and culture (Gaelic Affairs 2018).

These objectives are in turn to be achieved by

- Creating awareness of Gaelic language, culture and history and its contribution to Nova Scotia's diversity, community life and economy.
- Providing language training, support materials, innovative programming, strategic advice, research, translations and communications services to enable appreciation, acquisition and use of Gaelic language and culture.
- Building partnerships within government to ensure investment in and stewardship of these language and cultural resources that are uniquely Nova Scotian. (Gaelic Affairs 2018)

The aims of Nova Scotian policymakers with responsibility for Gaelic can therefore be interpreted to go beyond generating new speakers, and the principle of promoting the language as an aspect of the province's distinctive identity is clearly discernible in the above extracts. Stimulating awareness and ownership of the language and its associated identity, even among the estimated 230,000 Nova Scotians of Gaelic heritage, is no small task for such a modestly funded unit, let alone among the rest of Nova Scotia's almost one million inhabitants. Yet the emphasis on language training, programming and materials highlights the importance of new speakers to the future of the language in the province. Very little is currently known about either the size or the linguistic practices of the new speaker population. Watson and Ivey (2016: 184) summarised this deficiency in a seminal conference paper, asking, 'Who are these speakers? Why are they learning Gaelic? How fluent are they? And how often do they use it?' (author translation).

The Nova Scotia provincial government supports *Gàidhlig aig Baile* ('Gaelic in the community') and *Bun is Bàrr* ('root and branch') programmes, both of which regularly emphasise the importance of ongoing interaction between native Gaelic speakers and learners. Such interaction is prioritised as a means both of socialising new Gaelic speakers in the language, and of developing their identities as Gaels, to a degree rarely observed in contemporary Scotland. Notably, however, Gaelic educational opportunities in Nova Scotia are limited by comparison with Scotland, where around six thousand children are currently enrolled in Gaelic-medium education. Immersion programmes have been available to Indigenous Mi'kmaq children and to Acadian children in the province of Nova Scotia for some years, and in September 2021 North America's first Gaelic immersion school opened its doors to nine primary school pupils in Mabou, Cape Breton. In general terms, however, 'core Gaelic' second language teaching in high schools, extracurricular immersion programmes and adult language-acquisition initiatives have formed the basis of revitalisation efforts in recent decades (MacEachen 2008; Dunbar 2008; Watson and Ivey 2016). It is interesting to note, in that sense, that the community-centred focus of current Gaelic revitalisation efforts in Nova Scotia may be seen, at least from the perspective of the renowned sociologist of language Joshua Fishman's scholarship (1991, 2001, 2013) as theoretically more sustainable than the school-focused initiatives often emphasised in European settings.

As will be demonstrated over the course of subsequent chapters, the emphasis on ethnolinguistic identity and discourses of cultural distinctiveness currently dominating in Nova Scotia's Gaelic community also closely parallel recommendations advocated by Fishman (1991, 2001, 2010a, 2010b, 2013). As mentioned above, the provincial government–supported *Gàidhlig aig Baile* and *Bun is Bàrr* programmes, in particular, place a strong emphasis on encouraging meaningful interaction between L1 Gaelic speakers and L2 learners for socialising and creating new speakers of the language. MacIntyre, Baker and Sparling (2017) have recently investigated language learning motivations and 'ideal' or 'ought-to selves' among a sample of (more or less advanced) Gaelic learners in Nova Scotia. This notion of the 'rooted' self in second language acquisition is extremely useful and resonates closely with the analysis I outline in later chapters.

In general terms, language shift, loss and revitalisation have become matters of increasingly urgent political attention internationally (Nettle and Romaine 2000; Romaine 2000, 2008, 2013; Fishman and García 2010, 2011; Costa 2017). Efforts to stem the decline of minoritised languages have turned increasingly to second language acquisition – and especially bilingual, 'revitalisation immersion education' (García 2009) – as a strategy for increasing numbers of speakers. In part, this development, observed in such diverse contexts as

Aotearoa/New Zealand, the Basque Country, Hawai'i and the Celtic world, reflects a recognition by policymakers that once interrupted, the organic, intergenerational transmission of languages in the home domain is extremely hard for them to influence or to reinstate.

Gaelic language education in Nova Scotia and Scotland

In Scotland, Gaelic-medium immersion education ('GME') is regarded by policymakers as one of the principal mechanisms for the generation of new Gaelic speakers (cf. Bòrd na Gàidhlig 2014, 2018, 2022, 2023; Scottish Government 2014). Nevertheless, a variety of leading scholars have theorised on the basis of research from the international context that the potential impact of (bilingual) education on language revitalisation initiatives may be undermined by a complex mixture of factors. Evidence from this substantial and variegated literature – and especially that drawing on French immersion education in Canada – provides a mixed picture of target language use by past students after their completion of bilingual schooling (see, for example, Harley 1994; MacFarlane and Wesche 1995; Johnstone 2001).

Prefiguring much of this linguistic research, Fishman (1972, 1991, 2010, 2013) consistently theorised that school-based language policy interventions would ultimately fail without adequate support outside the classroom. He observed that minoritised languages at which RLS ('reversing language shift') efforts are directed require spaces for their habitual use 'before school begins, outside of school, during the years of schooling and afterwards, when formal schooling is over and done with' (Fishman 2001b: 471). Fishman emphasised the importance of securing the minoritised variety as the language of the home – and minority communities' inability to do so as having contributed in large part to the failure of language revitalisation initiatives generally (Fishman 1991: 406). In Nova Scotia, given the very new and limited introduction of Gaelic immersion education, revitalisation efforts in recent decades have tended to focus on second language teaching in high schools, extracurricular immersion programmes and adult language acquisition (MacEachen 2008; Dunbar 2008; Watson and Ivey 2016). As noted above, the community-run *Gàidhlig aig Baile* and *Bun is Bàrr* programmes each emphasise the importance of interaction between native Gaelic speakers and learners for socialising and creating new speakers of the language.

Such initiatives clearly resonate with Fishman's (1991, 2001a, 2001b) recommendations vis-à-vis the reattainment of diglossia and intergenerational interaction at the fundamental, lower-level stages of his model for assessing and reversing language shift, the graded intergenerational disruption scale (GIDS). In that sense, the community-centred focus of current Gaelic revitalisation efforts in Nova Scotia may be regarded as theoretically more sustainable, in

Fishman's view, than developments that may be seen within education systems elsewhere. As I demonstrate over the following chapters of this book, an emphasis on ethnolinguistic identity and discourses of cultural distinctiveness currently dominating in Nova Scotia's Gaelic community also closely parallel recommendations advocated by Fishman.

Yet Fishman's (1991, 2001a, 2001b, 2013) GIDS model and his recommendations on behalf of threatened minority languages rest to a large degree upon a conception of language and ethnic identity which contemporary sociolinguists increasingly regard as problematic, and his paradigm has been questioned by various authors (see Edwards 1984, 2010; Heller 2006, 2010; Romaine 2006, 2013; Jaffe 2007a, 2007b). Fishman's (1991: 394) model rests to a large degree on the 'premises that Xmen are not Ymen and that Xish culture ... is not Yish culture' and that 'ideological clarification' of these fundamental premises must be undertaken and agreed upon by community members if revitalisation initiatives are to succeed.

In recent years, however, research on new speakers of minority languages has frequently demonstrated that individuals who have attained a degree of fluency in a second language (whether through formal schooling or personal effort) tend largely not to claim or exemplify such straightforward ethnolinguistic identifications with the target variety of their acquisition activities (Costa 2015; Hornsby 2015; O'Rourke and Walsh 2020). The term 'new speaker' has become increasingly prevalent in the sociolinguistics of European minority languages relatively recently, having initially been coined within the contexts of Galician and Catalan (O'Rourke and Ramallo 2013; Pujolar and Gonzàlez 2013; O'Rourke, Pujolar and Ramallo 2015). As is now widely recognised, the concept refers to individuals who have acquired an additional language outside of the home setting and, crucially, who continue to make frequent use of it in the course of their daily lives.

At the level of devolved (respectively, national and provincial) government, policymakers in both Scotland and Nova Scotia make frequent reference to the pivotal role that such individuals may play in the future of the Gaelic language. The results of the 2022 Scottish census in relation to religion, language, national identity and ethnicity were released in May 2024, showing substantial growth in the number of individuals reporting skills in Gaelic (NRS 2024). These included 130,161 people in Scotland reporting abilities in any skill in the language (2.5% of the population over age three) and 69,701 reporting speaking ability (1.3%). This is a rise of 12,000 additional speakers compared to the 2011 figure, a growth rate of 21%. Limited as census data are as a source of reliable data on language ability, use or aptitude, this reported growth clearly constitutes an historic point in the social and demographic history of the language in Scotland. Disappointingly for Gaelic language advocates in Nova Scotia, by contrast, the 2021 Canadian census recorded just 635 Nova

Scotians with 'knowledge' of Scottish Gaelic, sixty-five 'mother tongue' speakers and thirty-five who used the language 'most often' at home (Statistics Canada 2022). These recorded declines in Gaelic speaking ability and use underscore the historical significance of both ongoing official support for Gaelic via the provincial Office of Gaelic Affairs, and the establishment of the first Gaelic-medium school outside Scotland in Mabou, Cape Breton in 2021 (Taigh Sgoile na Drochaide 2021).

In Scotland, the 2011 UK census showed a 2 per cent decline in the number of people claiming an ability to speak Gaelic compared to the 2001 census. This constituted a sharp diminution in the rate of decline from ten years previously. In spite of this, the census also showed growth, for the first time, in the proportion of Gaelic speakers under the age of twenty. Although the rate of this growth was just 0.1 per cent compared to the percentage of speakers recorded for this age group in 2001, a great deal was made of its importance in demonstrating the growth of GME in Scotland. The significance attached to the development of GME as a key priority was similarly emphasised in the Scottish Government's (2014) consultation paper on a Gaelic education bill. The previous iteration of Bòrd na Gàidhlig's National Gaelic Language Plan stated in relatively unambiguous terms that

> Gaelic education is central to the ambition of Gaelic growth and for this reason education and learning will remain central to this Plan, as they were to the previous Plan ... Our clear view is that Gaelic education makes an important contribution to the aim of increasing the numbers of those speaking, using and learning the language (Bòrd na Gàidhlig 2018: 32 [National Gaelic Language Plan 2018–23]).

Policy statements of this kind therefore indicate the degree to which policymakers have viewed GME as a mechanism by which not only to increase rates of Gaelic language acquisition in school, but also to generate new speakers who will later carry forward their bilingualism into the domains of home and work. In essence, the intention is that GME will substantially increase the numbers of new speakers of Gaelic in Scotland, equipping students to use the language to a considerable degree throughout their adolescent and adult lives. Yet, while various scholars have observed that the impact of immersion education in other contexts of language revitalisation appears to be limited, research on the long-term outcomes of bilingual programmes has been notable by its scarcity. Although it is the hope and intention of many that bilingual education systems will equip children to lead a bilingual life after school, until recently the long-term effectiveness of such programmes in doing so had not been clearly assessed (cf. Dunmore 2019).

In later chapters of this book (Chapters 3–5, below) I will draw attention to some of the language ideologies that Scottish and Nova Scotian speakers from this study convey when describing their current identifications with Gaelic. I will argue that whilst the language clearly plays an important role in the professional lives of Scottish new speakers, the ideologies that they express tend to militate against their association with the traditionally defined, ethnolinguistic Gaelic community. By contrast, Nova Scotian new speakers seem generally more eager to embrace their heritage identities as Gaels. A clear distinction will be demonstrated between Scottish new speakers' negative perceptions and lack of association with the term 'Gael(s)', and their Canadian counterparts' relative ease in employing that term as an element of their cultural heritage.

Research on new speakers of Gaelic in Scotland has previously examined the nature of such speakers' language learning trajectories, motivations and linguistic practices. In a seminal study of new speakerhood in Gaelic Scotland, McLeod, O'Rourke and Dunmore (2014) employed semi-structured interviews and focus groups to elicit discourse surrounding the phenomenon from an emic perspective, while studies by Nance (2015) and colleagues (Nance et al. 2016) looked further into linguistic productions of Gaelic by new speakers. These studies emphasised Scottish new Gaelic speakers' relatively greater association with the term 'Gaelic community' compared to that with the traditional ethnonym 'Gaels'. Whilst most new speakers, by definition, make frequent and committed use of their second language in the course of their day-to-day lives, in the current research different linguistic behaviours were reported in interviews and survey responses (see Chapters 3–6, below).

This opening chapter has contextualised the key themes of the book within the sociological and historical settings of Gaelic in Scotland from the sixth century CE, and in Nova Scotia from the eighteenth century. It has also discussed the issue of language revitalisation and the relevance of new speakers to current initiatives to develop and renew Gaelic in both countries. Chapter 2 considers the interrelationship of language, culture and identities from a theoretical, sociolinguistic perspective. It then conceptualises the notions of language ideologies, socialisation and acquisition, as well as a number of relevant perspectives from second language acquisition research. Chapter 3 introduces and contextualises relevant Gaelic language ideologies in Scotland and Nova Scotia, situating them within the two research sites by means of an ethnographic introduction to both settings. Using ethnographic vignettes to depict and describe the most salient and relevant ideologies that I observed to operate in Scotland and Nova Scotia through participant observation in both countries, this chapter will in turn introduce qualitative analyses of interview material presented in the following two chapters.

Chapter 4 considers research participants' paths to new speakerhood and Gaelic language learning trajectories in Nova Scotia and Scotland. I examine interviewees' past experiences of acquisition and socialisation in the language, and the relationship between these factors and current practices, as demonstrated using qualitative methods. My analysis unpacks interviewee experiences in their own words, assessing the extent to which interviewees report acquiring Gaelic in the contexts of school, home and community. An initial focus considers how adult immersion education informs Nova Scotian new Gaelic speakers' acquisition of the language. In Scotland, former GME pupils form a sizeable subset of the new speaker universe; in spite of these two key distinctions, however, the importance of university or independent study as an initial impetus for Gaelic learning is clear from interviewees' accounts, as is the status of Sabhal Mòr Ostaig, Scotland's Gaelic college on the Isle of Skye, as a leading context for Gaelic learning and socialisation among new speakers in both countries. My analysis then explores Scottish and Nova Scotian interviewees' varied perceptions of the importance of acquiring a native-like Gaelic accent (or *'blas'*) and of opportunities to acquire such an accent in light of current language policy priorities in both territories. Having thus first examined participants' linguistic ideologies in respect of accent or *blas*, the rest of Chapter 4 explores interviewees' ideologies in respect of 'opportunity' for Gaelic use, and the role of schools and Gaelic immersion education for revitalising the language generally.

Chapter 5 considers contrasting Gaelic identities in the two research contexts, drawing out key perspectives on participants' conceptions of heritage, language ideologies and attitudes. Discussion focuses first on perceptions of heritage, identity and motivation in Nova Scotia and Scotland, whilst subsequent discussions analyse new speaker narratives in relation to language and community change, new speakers and revitalisation objectives generally. My analysis will then addresses the issues of motivation, heritage and language socialisation in new speaker accounts of identity. Chapter 6 presents quantitative analysis of research participants' responses to an online survey, to bring a degree of data triangulation to bear on questions of language acquisition and identity. As I demonstrate, language attitudes, examined quantitatively as responses to several attitudinal propositions, pattern closely with language ideologies identified in the qualitative interview analysis. Taken together, the analyses of attitudes and ideologies strongly indicate rationales underlying current linguistic practice among new Gaelic speakers. Finally, Chapter 7 presents the book's overarching conclusions in respect of transatlantic Gaeldom and linguistic practices of new speakers in the twenty-first century.

TWO

Language, Ethnicity and Identities: A Conceptual Frame

Over the past seventy years linguists and anthropologists have consistently emphasised the deep complexity of the nexus connecting language, culture and society. In the first part of this chapter I will set out a wider theoretical framework surrounding language, culture and identity, reviewing perspectives on these issues from relevant disciplines. I will also address the symbolic value that language may possess, including from the perspective of essentialist conceptions of language and identity, heritage and ethnicity, and the supposed relationship between language and nationalism. Later discussion introduces the notions of language ideologies and socialisation, conceptualising scholarly views of how speakers' culturally constituted beliefs and feelings about language can be seen to impact on the ways speakers use it from day to day. Lastly, the chapter will address relevant perspectives from second language acquisition research, notably the motivational self system, which has assumed an increasingly prominent position in language attitudes and motivation research.

Language, culture and identities: theoretical underpinnings

Researchers in the fields of sociolinguistics, linguistic anthropology and the sociology of language have established that the interplay of language, culture and society is both complex and context-specific. Romaine (2000: 26) famously stated that although there is 'no necessary one-to-one relationship' between language and society, there are unlikely to be any contexts in which the two have no impact on one another. Yet the meanings of either of these terms are far from universally agreed upon in contemporary scholarship. Makoni and Pennycook (2007) have argued that the popular notion of language as a bounded, finite and standardised entity ultimately stems from state attempts to legitimate and consolidate political power and control linguistic practices, and they advocate a less rigid approach to conceptualising language. In this regard, García (2009: 40) has stated that commonly held, persistent assumptions about what we mean by 'language' must be constantly retheorised in light of how speakers use language within social context.

Heller (2007b: 9) has argued that the very idea of language cannot be adequately theorised without reference to the speakers who use it and the social context within which they do so. A more fluid approach to conceptualising language accounts more directly for speakers' linguistic practice, for example, taking account of evidence concerning multilingual speakers' flexible use of linguistic resources across contexts. Academic discourse surrounding such linguistic usages developed substantially after the discussion of bilingualism was at the forefront of theorists' concerns when the field of sociolinguistics first came into existence over fifty years ago (see Trudgill 1974; Hymes 1974). For example, Fishman (1972: 153–4), famously challenged what he regarded as a tendency on the part of many psychologists and sociologists at the time to view multilingualism as an 'unnatural' and transitory occurrence, instead arguing that it was a 'stable and widespread phenomenon in its own right'.

Within the closely related field of linguistic anthropology, researchers often position their work on language and culture within one of three interrelated frameworks, respectively concerning language and identity (Kroskrity 2000, 2004; Bucholtz and Hall 2004) language ideologies (Silverstein 1979, 2000; Schieffelin, Woolard and Kroskrity 1998) and language socialisation (Schieffelin and Ochs 1986a, 1986b; McEwan-Fujita 2010). While the three frameworks have distinct research traditions, there is considerable overlap between them. A large and multidisciplinary literature focuses on language, identity and ideologies. This literature is summarised below, before concepts from the principal relevant literatures are introduced concerning language ideologies and second language acquisition.

Edwards (2009: 15) has observed that studies of identity within the human and social sciences became increasingly prominent partly as a consequence of theoretical models concerning the nature of the 'self', and the impact of these considerations on popular understandings of identity. From an anthropological viewpoint, Glaser (2007: 30) notes that the possession of identities became regarded as an increasingly essential element of an individual's sense of self, following a mid-twentieth-century shift in theoretical orientations, toward approaches tending to privilege symbolic and imagined group membership (Glaser 2007; see also Anderson 1991). In this connection, Reicher and Hopkins (2001: 33) explain social identity theory as a conceptualisation of the processes by which individuals make the 'psychosocial shift' required to integrate their distinctive and idiosyncratic personal identity with a social identity, derived from appreciation of 'our membership of social groups'. Whereas personal identity draws on distinguishing features at the level of the individual, social identity is thus based on differences and similarities across and between groups. La Fontaine (1985) and Krombach (1995) theorised that these processes in turn draw on notions of otherness, with identity formation regarded as the result of overcoming internal and external differences in social life.

The large and wide-ranging literature on the interrelationship of language and identity demonstrates its deep complexity, and debate on the specific nature of the nexus is ongoing. Joseph (2004: 20) stated that language and identity are 'ultimately inseparable', since 'language is central to the human condition, and … many have argued that it is the most salient characteristic of our species'. In relation specifically to ethnic identity, Edwards (2009: 162) has suggested as a working definition an 'allegiance to a group – large or small, socially dominant or subordinate – with which one has ancestral links'. On the relevance of language for ethnic group connection, May (2012: 135) comments that whilst the former is not regarded by contemporary scholars as an 'essential', 'primordial' or 'determining' feature of ethnic identity, a large body of evidence suggests that it nevertheless remains significant in many instances. Indeed, Williams (2008) stated that, as 'one of the chief components of group identity', language had become 'one of the most sensitive issues' in contemporary life. In the first half of the twentieth century, a great deal of anthropological and linguistic investigation was dominated by the Sapir–Whorf hypothesis (also known as 'linguistic relativism'), which proposed that speakers of languages experience the world in fundamentally different ways, according to the limitations of their (linguistic) frames of reference (Makihara 2010: 32–4; Silverstein 2000: 85–6). Whorf (1956 [1940]: 221) summarised this principle, maintaining that speakers of different languages 'are pointed by their grammars toward different types of observations and different evaluations', thereby assuming 'different views of the world'. Whorf arrived at such a conception influenced by his mentor Sapir (1962: 68) who later described language as a 'guide to "social reality" [that] conditions all our thinking' about social processes.

Linguistic relativity subsequently impacted greatly upon scholarly understandings of the relationship between language and identity, but has been treated more critically in recent decades. The possibilities of translation, multilingualism and social diversity among speakers of the same languages tend to indicate that language does not in fact constrain the ways people think or identify as human beings (Kramsch 2004: 239). Rather, Ochs (1993: 288) has argued, the relationship between the two phenomena is in reality 'a sociolinguistically distant one' as language rarely systematically encodes the respective identities of its users. The relationship of language to identity is thus generally regarded as being mediated through speakers' shared understandings of social convention, rather than reflecting a direct association. Ochs (1993: 297) essentially claimed that, as both language and identity are in constant flux, a given language variety or structure 'cannot neatly be assigned to one pure view of one or another social identity'. This conception frames the language-identity nexus in terms of speakers' respective positionality in interaction (Bucholtz and Hall 2004, 2005).

Yet Romaine (2000: 164) states that the 'relative discreteness of languages ... as markers of distinct ethnic identities' can nevertheless have important consequences for the ways in which people conceive of their group memberships. The 'interactional' turn in the sociolinguistic study of bilingualism has increasingly demonstrated how linguistic resources are creatively used 'in the construction of social meaning' and particularly in the display of ethnolinguistic identity (Heller 2007b: 13). Mendoza-Denton and Osborne (2010: 113–14) note of bilingual communities that the social meanings of languages spoken in such contexts may differ substantially, providing multiple resources for speakers to produce and interpret their identities. The role and relevance that speakers attach to spoken varieties in the social life of bilingual communities is therefore frequently controversial and contested.

Fishman (2010: xxiii) observed that identity 'depends essentially on circumstances and contrasts that play upon it, modify it, and create or recreate it'. As such, he states that the dynamic interaction of language, identity and ethnicity 'is an unending process' (Fishman 2010: xxxiv). Edwards (2010a: 4) has stated that societal shifts away from the use of a particular variety must be understood as a 'symptom of social interaction', inseparable from its cultural context. He argues that a shift in the language a community uses in the intimate settings of home and neighbourhood generally implies a substantial shift of 'social and psychological significance' for that community (Edwards 2010a: 26). Concern for the preservation of languages for reasons of sociopsychological cohesion is by no means only felt by minority groups, however. Majority (inter)national languages such as French and English are (erroneously) feared by some to be under threat from migration patterns and multilingual practices in the contemporary, globalised economy (see, for example, Moïse 2007; Schmidt 2007).

A potential reason for this is that a language shared by members of a given group 'serves as a powerful force' in building associations of group identity, especially via the key institutions of modernity, such as education and the media (Makihara 2010: 37). Yet such associations, Makihara (2010: 42) argues, 'are socially constructed and change over time', depending on the linguistic awareness and attitudes of group members. In this sense, and on the basis of diverse perspectives analysed by researchers in the two-volume second edition of his *Handbook of Language and Ethnic Identity,* Fishman (2010: xxix) states that ethnic identity and group consciousness of it 'are not evenly spread' throughout human societies in the twenty-first century.

Rather than conceiving of identities as pre-existing social categories (of which individuals may or may not be conscious), however, social constructivist approaches in interactional sociolinguistics and anthropology have proposed to conceive of identities as being both projected and shaped by group members through language, a principle referred to as *emergence* (Ochs 1993: 289–90; Bucholtz and Hall 2005: 605; Schilling-Estes 2004: 190). In this conception, identity is regarded as a 'product of unfolding talk', which emerges through interaction (Schilling-Estes 2004: 190). Schiffrin (1996: 169) states that an individual's conception of themselves 'neither pre-exists all conversation nor arises just from interlocutors' responses'; rather, conceptions of selfhood are seen to arise within interaction, as our identities are constructed, realised and conveyed through communication. This principle of *practice* is in turn inhibited by the concept of *partialness*, that an identity construction 'may be in part deliberate and intentional, in part habitual', and therefore below the level of consciousness (Bucholtz and Hall 2005: 606). In other words, an individual may at any point be only partly aware of the identities they display in communication. García (2009: 82) notes that language often has 'a rhetorical function' to construct and display identities, concurring with with Bucholtz and Hall's (2004: 380) point that identity is also expressed in language through *performance*, a 'highly deliberate and self-aware social display'. Sociolinguistic performance highlights and exaggerates 'ideological associations of identities with language use' in day-to-day social intercourse (Bucholtz and Hall 2004: 380–1).

In addition to these four concepts, Bucholtz and Hall (2004: 380–1) theorise that an individual's *positionality* in identity constructions can vary from interaction to interaction, depending on the identity of their interlocutor. In this connection Ochs (1993: 290) explains the principle in terms of individuals' linguistic use of 'different kinds of acts and stances' to construct their various identities. Such a conception views identity as 'inherently relational', dependent on social interaction and the individual's position within this. Social constructivist approaches therefore view the communicative functions of language, and the various manners in which they form, inform and display identity in interaction, as key to understanding the 'ebbs and tides' of identity construction from day to day, and across the lifespan (Ochs 1993: 298). Rather than being a fixed, a-priori social category, therefore, a given identity is viewed as being contextually dependent – and constructed through social interaction (Schiffrin 1996: 199). The relation of identity to language in its communicative sense is thus regarded in contemporary sociolinguistic theory as complex, contextual and conditional.

In addition to its communicative function, however, Edwards (2013: 19) has observed that language often serves as a valuable conduit of cultural tradition and 'group narrative'. Apart from the instrumental sense in which language may be used to construct and perform identities in conversation, languages are often instilled with semiotic and symbolic value for human communities' negotiation of group identities (see also Fishman 1991, 2001a, 2001b; Makihara 2010). Elsewhere, Edwards (2010) has even argued that a community undergoing societal language shift will not necessarily experience the associated cultural shift away from the obsolescent language culture. Rather, he suggests, 'the social and psychological cohesion of the group as a unique entity' may in fact outlast vernacular use and transmission of the endangered language; symbolically, the variety may often still play an important role 'in the maintenance of group boundaries' (Edwards 2010: 6).

Edwards (2009: 60) therefore envisages a key distinction between language in its communicative sense, and its symbolic significance for the maintenance of group identity. He argues that it is often possible – and even desirable in many contexts of language shift – for the latter to remain important in the absence of the former. While the instrumental use of a group's language may be intertwined with its symbolic value, Edwards (2009: 56, emphasis original) observes that the 'two aspects of language *are* separable', and may not be interwoven in the same ways in divergent contexts (see also Williams 2008; Rosa 2019).

Yet the relationship between language – in its instrumental, communicative sense – and ethnic identity lies at the core of Fishman's (1991) model for the maintenance of threatened languages or 'reversing language shift' (RLS). He states that RLS efforts are often rooted in a 'sentimental' bond between speakers in terms of ethnicity and kinship, which stresses 'an aspiration toward consciousness and identity (re)formation' (1991: 383). Numerous researchers have identified obstacles to the feasibility of assigning a central and enduring position to language in such contexts, however. In this connection, May (2012: 134) observes that where language is considered crucial to identity, it is the 'diacritical significance' attached to it, rather than the actual language as such, that is often regarded as essential. Where there exists a close association between ethnic identity and a particular language, knowledge of that language is not always considered necessary for the expression of that identity (Edwards 2009, 2010). Yet it is clear the relationship between the two may be more heavily stressed in some settings than others. Edwards (2013: 23) notes that while the connection between the communicative function of language, and its symbolic value for identity work is often seen as benign and simplistic by monolingual, majority language speakers, matters of language and identity are often more immediately problematic for minority language groups.

Fishman's (1991) theoretical model relies on a more straightforward and fundamental association between language and culture in minority language contexts than that hypothesised by the various theorists cited above, necessitating a clear and compelling distinction between the minority language and culture and that of the majority. Although Fishman's paradigm rests in large part on this type of ideological contrast, sharp distinctions of this kind often lack the nuance of much contemporary sociological and anthropological research on language shift (such as in Heller 2006, 2010). He states, for instance, that the fundamental premise that the minority 'Xish' culture 'is not Yish culture must not be skipped over, no more than the premises that Xish culture is worth maintaining' (Fishman 1991: 394).

More recently, Fishman (2013: 473) described this proposition in terms of developing a rationale for the maintenance of a community's 'own language' (that is, Xish), as opposed to the less personal (Yish) language of wider communication. In some respects, Fishman's models of language and ethnic identity clearly sit uneasily with contemporary conceptions which problematise essentialist perspectives in social research (such as Jaffe 2007a). Writers and researchers frequently distance themselves from essentialist positions, which hold that group identity members are 'both fundamentally similar to one another and fundamentally different to members of other groups' (Bucholtz and Hall 2004: 374).

Jaffe (2007a: 58) notes that, from an essentialist perspective, 'both "language" and "identity" and their iconic relationships are seen as fixed, ascribed/natural and unproblematic', in contrast with much contemporary scholarship on language and culture. Conversely, Jaffe (2007a: 74) describes how much research on language revitalisation is conducted within contexts in which 'an essential relationship between language, culture and identity is posited as a given' by community members themselves. Bucholtz and Hall (2004: 376) argue that such essentialist perspectives should not necessarily be discounted as long as they have 'salience in the lives of the speakers we study'. On this point, Bourdieu (1991: 221) comments that contested definitions of identity and the nature of its 'reality' can be understood only if we include in conceptions of reality 'the representation of reality' itself.

Drawing on this conception, Joseph (2010: 12) argues that whilst group identities may 'essentialize what are actually arbitrary divisions among peoples', they become socially meaningful when speakers conceive of them as 'mental representations' of reality. Similarly, Jaffe (2007a: 57) advises against interpreting essentialist outlooks 'as detachable from meaningful practice'. To appreciate the social reality of essentialist perspectives in a given community's conception of language and identity need not entail assuming such a perspective in one's own theoretical approach (Bucholtz and Hall 2004, 2005). Indeed, Dorian (2010: 89) cautions that the situated realities that actually link language and identity are in fact 'rarely so straightforward' as essentialist conceptions envisage.

One reason why essentialist perspectives proposing an unproblematic association between language and identity are often adopted by individuals and communities stems from the perceived usefulness of language in the construction of national(ist) identities within the modern nation state (Makihara 2010: 36). Anderson (1991: 6), for instance, notes that the concept of the nation as an 'imagined political community' relies heavily on nineteenth-century notions of language, an approach that Pujolar (2007: 71) describes as reflecting a notional, Romantic, nationalist ideal of 'one language/one culture/one nation'. Whilst Heller (2007b: 4) states that the imagined centrality of language to national identity 'did not emerge fully-formed' at this time, its enduring relevance to linguistic considerations can be traced to the emergence of the modern nation state (Nairn 1997).

Romantic nationalist philosophers in the eighteenth century regarded language as vital to their theses in two key senses. Firstly, Anderson (1991: 76) argues, the importance of written language in the emergence of print capitalism at that time was key to raising national consciousness among literate elites. Whereas the pre-capitalist aristocracy cohered chiefly around extralinguistic notions of imagined community, both writing and literacy were instrumental to the emergence and imagined solidarities of the developing bourgeoisie in Western Europe (Anderson 1991). The peasantry, on the other hand, were viewed as indispensable in the next stage of national movements' development, being presented as the 'natural repositories' of national language and culture (Hroch 1985: 150). Secondly, Anderson (1991: 144) argues, the supposed 'primordialness' of shared languages was understood to offer a continuous, ancestral connection to an imagined national heritage. This conception of language, he argues, was clearly problematic, since many national languages are shared across multiple nations, while in many other nations only a small proportion of inhabitants actually use a national language in daily interaction (Anderson 1991: 46). Anderson (1991: 133) thus regarded nationalist conceptions of languages 'as emblems of nation-ness' as being far from unproblematic or straightforward.

Gellner (2006: 43) notes of nationalist movements not centred on language (such as Scottish or British nationalism) that they tend instead to allude to arguments of precedent, history and culture in their visions of nationhood. Although language has frequently been invoked as a signifier of national identity, it does not, as McCrone (1998) has argued, define the nation. Yet Romantic nationalist philosophers depicted language as absolutely central to national identity formation in the eighteenth century (Kramsch 2004; Edwards 2009). May (2012: 135) notes that contemporary scholars tend to view 'linguistic nationalism' of this kind as 'little more than sociological (and linguistic) nonsense'. In this connection, Reicher and Hopkins (2001: 8) state that 'the idea that a nation needs its own language doesn't live up to even the most superficial scrutiny', since linguistic definitions often in fact present obstacles to national unity. More generally, Hobsbawm (1992) and Gellner (2006) have critiqued nationalist conceptions of the centrality of nations to social organisation in modern life. Similarly, Smith (2010: 25) suggests that the supposed naturalness of the nation as a basis for the exercise of social power is in fact deeply ideological, while Gellner (2006: 54) states that nations as a means of classifying and differentiating social groups 'are a myth'.

On the role attributed to language in such efforts to classify groups, Hobsbawm (1992: 54) states that national languages, far from being 'primordial foundations of national culture', instead resulted from the deliberate attempt of elites 'to devise a standardized idiom out of a multiplicity of actually spoken idioms'. Kumar (2003: 9–10) traces the problematic relationship of English to national identities, for instance, noting that even when the word 'English' first occurred in varieties of the Old English language, 'it had already lost its etymological sense, "of or about the Angles"'. The term was later used to refer not only to the language spoken by English people, but also to that used in many parts of Lowland Scotland (reflected in the medieval era in the vernacular spelling *Inglis/Ynglis*). In the modern era, the internationalisation of world English(es) tends to count generally against its being regarded 'as a badge of a specifically English national identity' (Kumar 2003: 11).

While Smith (2010: 11–13) considers language an 'objective' factor in the definition of national identities, he suggests that in fact a nation may better be defined as 'a named human community' inhabiting a shared space, and possessing 'common myths and a shared history, a distinct public culture, and common laws and customs for all members'. Yet the allusion here to myth and public culture highlights the way in which ideologically nationalistic rhetoric may be used to 'authenticate' a language variety in respect of national identity, with the result that the language in question 'comes to index particular ways of being in and belonging to the nation-state' (Bucholtz and Hall 2004: 385; see also Makihara 2010: 37–8). In this way, Jaffe (2007a: 58) states, language becomes 'a tool used to naturalize and legitimate political boundaries'. The ideological processes behind these phenomena, particularly in relation to the ideological iconisation of a language as emblematic of identity, are further discussed below.

As emergent national identities were fused through the spread of national (print) languages in the Romantic era, Fishman (1991: 389) describes how writers such as John Stuart Mill 'equated tradition with unhappiness' in their ideas concerning social development. By contrast, as has been seen in Chapter 1, nationalists of the time promoted the use of larger languages on the basis that they offered progress, sociocultural 'improvement' and opportunities for advancement and wider communication. The various dichotomies that have been used to conceptualise this distinction – 'roots/options', 'parochialism/intercourse', *Gemeinschaft/Gesellschaft* – betray the significant attention it has commanded across various disciplines (Edwards 2004, 2010a). Conceptions of ethnic group identity that sat uneasily with nationalist aspirations were criticised by advocates of the latter as inhibitive to the progress of human conditions; Fishman (1991: 393) argues that the concept of ethnicity was consequently regarded frequently as a problem – viewed as 'anti-intellectual, irrational, anti-progressive and anti-civil' (see May 2012). Edwards (2009: 157–62) however, sees close ties between conceptions of ethnic and national identity, viewing nationalism as a kind of 'self-aware' ethnicity, and ethnicity itself as a state of 'pre-nationalism', since both entail the maintenance of essentially arbitrary group boundaries for categorising identities. Languages may serve as emblems of identity for both majority/national and minority/ethnic groups. One reason why Edwards (2009: 205) problematises Fishman's (1991, 2001b) model, with its insistence on the straightforward connection of ethnic identity and language, is that the fluid, changing nature of group language use means there is no necessary connection between the maintenance of a traditional or ancestral language and the continuation of group identity.

Social life and language in contemporary thought

Considerations of language and identity relevant to the foregoing discussions are frequently invoked in sociolinguistic and anthropological research on language ideologies and language socialisation. A large sociological literature on ideology generally tends to address its importance in the exercise of social power. Similarly, in political science, empirical work on ideology tends to address the reproduction of ideologies – as beliefs, myths and doctrines held by different social groups – and the manner in which they are contested by those groups. Yet the use of the specific phrase 'language ideology' has a distinct history within social and language sciences, whilst sharing a focus on the manner in which perceptions and beliefs can influence behaviour. The term has gained increasing currency in linguistic anthropology and the sociology of language particularly since the 1990s (see for example Schiefflin, Woolard and Kroskrity 1998).

Silverstein (1979: 193) first coined the term 'linguistic ideologies' (more frequently 'language ideologies' in later works) which he defined as 'sets of beliefs about language articulated by users as a rationalization or justification of perceived language structure or use'. A wide variety of definitions has since been used to explicate the term 'language ideology', from Kroskrity's (2004: 512) wide-ranging 'beliefs or feelings about languages', to the more precise 'cultural system of ideas about social and linguistic relationships, together with their loading of moral and political interests' (Irvine 1989: 255). The usefulness of the concept for understanding questions of language and identity is reflected in Makihara's (2010: 41) definition of language ideologies as 'cultural sensitivities ... about language, its use, and its users'. In this sense, speakers' ideas about the language(s) they use are seldom culturally neutral; the ways in which people make sense of their own and others' linguistic practices are often, in fact, 'a matter of language ideology' (Heller 2007b: 14–15; see also Rosa 2019 for an exposition of raciolinguistic ideologies in relation to ethnic identity and language use in a US high school). The interrelationship of linguistic practice and language ideologies continues to occupy a central position in much contemporary sociolinguistic (and linguistic anthropological) research.

Cavanaugh (2013: 46) argues that the language ideologies framework 'enables an analytical unpacking of how speakers understand, view, and use language' through a dual focus on speakers' perceptions of language as it is actually used, and the non-referential functions of language, such as its potential symbolic function in identity constructions. Crucially for the considerations of this monograph, Makihara (2010: 44–5) states that language ideologies often have an important role in determining 'the direction of changes in languages and speech ways', whether by motivating language shift and loss, or by acting against them. In somewhat broader terms, Gal and Woolard (1995: 130) define language ideologies as 'cultural conceptions of the nature, form, and purpose of language'. Elaborating further, Boudreau and Dubois (2007: 104) define language ideologies as shared sets of beliefs on language that 'come to be so well established that their origin is often forgotten by speakers, and are therefore socially reproduced and end up being "naturalized", or perceived as natural or as common sense'. This quotation reflects particularly well the systematic processes by which language ideologies are produced and reproduced within a social context.

In a seminal discussion, Woolard and Schieffelin (1994: 58) stated that the construction of language ideologies is 'a process involving struggle among multiple conceptualizations', which may consequently become a source of conflict in social life. Sociolinguists have since investigated the contested nature of language ideologies in various contexts, including the minority language situations of Hungarian German (Gal 1993), Corsican (Jaffe 1999, 2009), Arizona Tewa (Kroskrity 2000c) and Scottish Gaelic (Dorian 1981, 2013; McEwan-Fujita 2010a, 2010b, 2010c, 2020; Dunmore 2019). King (2000: 168) has helpfully distinguished the notion of language attitudes from ideologies, explaining that whilst the former may be elicited 'as a specific response to certain aspects of a particular language', the latter tend to be verbally articulated as complex sets of beliefs. Furthermore, as Kroskrity (2004: 496) notes, beliefs of this kind are often advanced by speakers as attempted rationalisations for their own language practices.

The more attitudinal aspects of the present research project are examined through an online survey (see Chapter 6, below), while the more qualitative focus on ethnographic and interview material (outlined in Chapters 3–5, below) allows for an examination of how informants' language ideologies relate to their actual linguistic practices and Gaelic learning motivations. Importantly for the methodological orientations of the study outlined in this book, Kroskrity (2004: 496) notes that whilst speakers relate language ideologies through explicit assertions, these are also 'embodied in communicative practice'. Language ideologies are thus reflected in the linguistic choices speakers make as well as in the content of what they articulate. When examining speakers' openly articulated language ideologies, therefore, it is also important for researchers to be aware of ideologies that may be inferred from speakers' linguistic usages.

The prevalence of the language ideologies framework within sociolinguistics since the 1990s reflects its perceived usefulness as a means to link linguistic practices with wider sociocultural considerations (García 2009: 84; Cavanaugh 2020: 52). Valdés et al. (2008: 107), for instance, view language ideologies as socially mediated processes that 'enact ties of language to identity', while Woolard (1998: 3) sees language ideologies as central to 'the very notion of person and the social group', and as the means by which the two are linked discursively. Just as sociocultural identities are conceived of as multiple, contested and contextual, language ideologies which enact such ties tend to be viewed within a social constructivist framework. In producing ties between language and identity through daily interactions, speakers attribute values to particular varieties or practices through the related processes of indexicality and iconisation (Pierce 1955; Bucholtz and Hall 2004, 2005).

When linguistic practices become ideologically associated with a particular sociocultural group, they are considered to index that group's social character, while the representation of languages as 'pictorial guides to the nature of groups' is seen to iconise that relationship (Kroskrity 2004: 507). For example, the semiotic relationship of an individual's speaking Gaelic to their identification, whether in Scotland or Nova Scotia, as a 'Gael' can be conceptualised as an indexical one. By contrast, the tradition of aligning language, nation and state within European Romantic nationalism may be seen as example of overt iconisation. Conversely, the tentative iconisation of Gaelic as a symbol of Scottish national identity (see Macdonald 1997; Oliver 2002; McEwan-Fujita 2003; Dunmore 2019) may be viewed as a more covert example. Whereas indexical processes may indirectly envisage and enact ties between language and identity through linguistic practice, iconisation is the ideological representation of a language as 'formally congruent with the group with which it is associated', irrespective of actual practices (Bucholtz and Hall 2004: 380). Ideologies which iconise language varieties are thus regarded by Irvine and Gal (2000: 37) to transform the symbolic relationship between language and group identity, as if the language in question 'displayed a social group's inherent nature' (Bucholtz and Hall 2004: 380).

The relevance of the foregoing considerations to this monograph are apparent in Valdés et al.'s (2008: 108) identification of education as an important site for 'the legitimization of particular ways of speaking', whilst devaluing others. Macleod (2010) argues that the marginal place occupied by Gaelic in Scottish education had a powerful effect on the orientation of language ideologies in Gaelic-speaking communities; the same is undoubtedly true of Gaelic communities in Cape Breton and elsewhere in eastern Nova Scotia. Jaffe (2009) distinguishes between ideological production and reproduction in multilingual educational settings, noting that schools may act to ideologise students' language use by attributing different values to different languages. These concepts are useful for framing the objectives of the research presented in this book regarding how new Gaelic speakers' language ideologies and heritage identities may be shaped by various experiences of language learning and socialisation. These considerations bring us to the next notion to be considered here.

Sociological and psychological literatures on 'socialisation' have tended to focus on the acquisition by children of habitus, which Bourdieu (1990: 59) defines as the 'system of dispositions' and social practices inherited by members of a given community or cultural group. The development of the language socialisation paradigm has its roots in a dual analytic focus on the role of language as the medium through which such practices are produced, and socialisation to use language(s) as such (see Schifflin and Ochs 1986a, 1986b: 163; Garrett and Baquedano-López 2002: 339; Kulick and Schiefflin 2004: 349). Duff (2010: 172) summarises the theoretical premise of the framework, defining language socialisation as the processes of acquisition by language learners of 'the worldviews, ideologies, values, and identities of community members', in addition to the grammar and structure of the language itself. The framework thus constitutes a useful conceptual link from issues of language and identity to the notions of language acquisition discussed below.

In the early days of the paradigm's use, research focused on the socialisation of children by primary caregivers in the home-community context (see Watson-Gegeo and Gegeo 1986; Crago, Annahatak and Ningiuruvik 1993), but the framework has since broadened to take account of socialisation experiences over the life cycle (Bucholtz and Hall 2004; Garrett and Baquedano-López 2002). For example, Garrett (2007: 233) emphasises that the ongoing acquisition of 'communicative competence' (after Hymes 1972) proceeds not only through learners' interactions with older or more experienced persons but also generally through their daily interactions with peers (see also Wenger 1998). The home, school, college and workplace may thus each be viewed as important sites of language socialisation; crucially in such settings, the use of one variety over another often has important consequences for individual socialisation experiences (Garrett 2007). Bayley and Schecter (2003) maintain that young people's experiences in multicultural settings provide a rich research site for investigating cultural and linguistic hybridity, since young multilinguals often define their identities in contrast to fixed, traditional ethnolinguistic categories. In particular, this may have important consequences in minority language settings such as that of Gaelic in either Scotland or Nova Scotia.

McEwan-Fujita (2010b: 30) describes ongoing language shift to English in the Western Isles of Scotland as a phenomenon that is 'perpetuated by linguistic socialization of children and adults' into particular patterns of language use and ideology. The Gaelic classroom, immersion week or *Bun is Bàrr* programme may thus be either undermined or bolstered by language practices outside the formal learning experience, in such social spaces as the home, playground or neighbourhood. Will's (2012) doctoral research with Gaelic-medium schoolchildren in Lewis, for example, documented numerous obstacles to children's wider Gaelic socialisation in that system (see also Dunmore 2019; NicLeòid and Dunmore 2019). Duff (2010: 173) states that as language learners' aptitudes increase through continuing processes of socialisation, they gain insight into 'cultural knowledge about ideologies, identities or subjectivities' specific to the language community. This statement has numerous implications for the study outlined in this monograph generally, and the following sections in particular.

Fishman (1991: 406) has famously emphasised the importance of securing the minority (Xish) language as the medium of home socialisation, and stressed that many communities' inability to maintain the home-community sphere as an Xish-dominant domain contributed in large part to the failure of many language revitalisation efforts. Fishman (1972, 1991, 2010, 2013) has consistently theorised that school-based language revitalisation policies would ultimately fail without adequate support outside the schoolroom. As an example of this, Edwards (2010: 261) notes that, in spite of their greater command in the target language, immersion pupils generally appear not to seek out opportunities to use their second language (see also Dunmore 2019). In this connection, Baker (2011: 265) notes the pervasive possibility that '[p]otential does not necessarily lead to production' of the target language by bilingual students. Fishman's (1991, 2001a, 2001b) recommendations regarding the reattainment of diglossia and intergenerational interaction therefore remain influential, at least among language policy scholars. As previously stated, intergenerational transmission within the home of the endangered (Xish) language is foregrounded at the fundamental, lower-level stages of Fishman's model for assessing and reversing language shift, the GIDS (Fishman, 1991: 395). The implicit suggestion of Fishman's scholarship thus holds that new speakers, generated through schools and formal acquisition activity in adulthood, should not be relied upon for the future revitalisation of endangered varieties (see O'Rourke, Pujolar and Ramallo 2015).

Yet, as also previously noted, Fishman's (1991, 2001a, 2001b, 2013) model and his recommendations generally rely upon a conception of language and ethnic identity which contemporary sociolinguists increasingly regard as problematic, and his emphasis on the straightforward relationship of the minority (Xish) language to its traditionally defined, ethnolinguistic speaker community (Xians) has been widely questioned (see Edwards 1984, 2010; Heller 2006, 2010; Romaine 2006, 2013; Jaffe 2007a, 2007b). Jaffe (2007a: 58), for instance, critiques such interpretations of the language-identity nexus, in which language, identity and their iconic relationships are regarded as immovable and unproblematic. Contemporary sociolinguists tend, by contrast, to distance themselves from essentialist positions which assume a fundamental similarity between group members, and fundamental distinctions from members of other groups (Bucholtz and Hall 2004, 2005; Rosa 2019).

Although Fishman's theoretical stance regarding the importance of the home context to intergenerational transmission remains influential, some of his ideas have been understood to draw to on such an iconicised conception of language and group membership. Fishman's (1991: 394) model rests to a large degree on the notion that Xians and Yians constitute fundamentally different – and oppositional – groups, and that the traditional Xish language contains the source and essence of this key difference. He states, furthermore, that 'prior ideological clarification' of these fundamental issues 'must not be skipped over' if revitalisation initiatives are to succeed in the long term (Fishman 1991: 394). The limited practicability of 'prior' clarification of such complex issues in many contexts of language endangerment, or of such clearly defined ethnocultural distinctions in any modern society, leads us back to the relevance of language ideologies and their role in the development of ethnolinguistic identities.

As previously noted, Silverstein (1979: 193) regards language ideologies as sets of beliefs conveyed by speakers as a 'rationalization or justification' of perceived linguistic structure or usage. Sociolinguists and anthropologists have frequently shown in recent decades that ideologies of this kind are advanced in speakers' discourse as attempted rationalisations for their own language practices (Kroskrity 2000, 2004; Bucholtz and Hall 2004; Boudreau and Dubois 2007; Makihara 2010; Cavanaugh 2013, 2020; Dunmore 2017, 2019). Such considerations regarding the role of language ideologies and cultural identity in speakers' linguistic practices are central to the analysis I present in later chapters of this book.

A number of principles present in the second language acquisition literature are also of particular relevance here, notably those pertaining to Gardner and Lambert's (1959, 1972) 'integrativeness model', and Dörnyei and Ushioda's (2009) 'L2 motivational self system'. Based on long-term examinations of French–English bilingualism in Canada, Gardner and Lambert (1959, 1972) define integrative motivation as the second language learner's sincere desire to adopt and integrate with the culture of the relevant language community. In their studies of Canadian French–English bilingualism, this desire was frequently observed to effect an influence on learners' successful acquisition of the L2. Yet there exist a number of questions as to this model's applicability to the context of heritage language learners of Gaelic in Scotland and Canada (however distant such heritage connections to the historic and contemporary language community may be). A particularly relevant consideration in this connection concerns the various ways in which contemporary notions of emergent, performative and nested linguistic identities may influence this model's applicability in contemporary society. As noted above, Bucholtz and Hall's (2005: 605) emergence principle conceives of identity as a product of unfolding conversation, which emerges through interaction. In such a view, identity arises habitually within interaction, as specific sociocultural identities are practised and negotiated. At the same time, Bucholtz and Hall (2004: 380) view language as being creatively used to construct identities through performance, a 'highly deliberate' and 'self-aware' display of social identity, whilst individuals' performance of their identities largely depends on their positionality in relation to their interlocutors' own identities.

Relatedly, albeit from a sociological perspective, Norton (2013, 2019) builds on Gardner and Lambert's (1959, 1972) theories of L2 motivation to develop the notion of investment, conceived of as L2 learners' commitment to learn an additional language, in light of their own multiple (and changing) identities and future aspirations. Developing Anderson's (1991) concept of imagined communities, Norton (2013, 2019) theorises the existence of an 'imagined identity' which guides L2 learners' sociocultural and linguistic investment in language acquisiton processes.

A possible solution to incorporating a motivational second language acquisition (SLA) approach within such theoretical developments in sociology and sociocultural linguistics was developed by Dörnyei (2005) and Ushioda (2011, 2019; Dörnyei and Ushioda 2009). The concept of the L2 motivational self system proposes that second language learners' acquisition of an additional language is guided largely by their imagined identities in the language in question, conceived of in terms of their ideal and 'ought-to' L2 self. The distinction between these two notional 'selves' is characterised by, on one hand, second language speakers' internal conceptions of their desired identity in the target language and, on the other, the identity they feel they 'ought to' enact externally while interacting with other speakers. Importantly, MacIntyre, Baker and Sparling (2017) conceptualise Nova Scotian Gaelic learners' motivations in terms of the 'rooted' L2 self, distinguishing their heritage-focused orientations from L2 learners without such keenly felt identifications vis-à-vis the target variety.

Noting an analytical distinction between L2 learners and individuals who transcend the learning process to use additional languages with regularity and commitment, O'Rourke and colleagues theorised and disseminated the notion of the new speaker (O'Rourke and Ramallo 2013; McLeod, O'Rourke and Dunmore 2014; O'Rourke, Pujolar and Ramallo 2015; O'Rourke and Walsh 2020). New speakers are defined as 'individuals with little or no home or community exposure to a minority language but who instead acquire it through immersion or bilingual education programs, revitalisation projects or as adult language learners' (O'Rourke, Pujolar and Ramallo 2015: 1). Notwithstanding Fishman's previously stated views on the theoretical sustainability of policy focusing on the creation of new speakers without sufficient home-community support, the new speaker paradigm has most frequently been applied to research from contexts of language endangerment (see, e.g., Smith-Christmas et al. 2018). Problematising a lack of reliable data on new speakers in the context of Gaelic in Scotland, McLeod (2020: 313) remarks that 'new speakers have become a much more obvious presence in the twenty-first century, although there are no reliable data to indicate how numerous they actually are'. Whilst McLeod (2020: 314) notes wide-ranging systemic issues in the limited provision of viable pathways for the creation of 'large numbers of potential learners', he maintains that Gaelic has nevertheless 'widened its social base with the growth of GME and attracted a wide range of new speakers, all of whom find different kinds of appeal and meaning in the language' (McLeod 2020: 330).

Certainly, new speakers of various language-learning backgrounds have become an increasingly important demographic in Gaelic Scotland, and have been been exmained in a series of seminal studies (McLeod, O'Rourke and Dunmore 2014; Nance 2015; Nance et al. 2016). For the purposes of this monograph, these studies emphasise Scottish new Gaelic speakers' association with the term 'Gaelic community'/*Coimhearsnachd na Gàidhlig* in preference to the ethnonym 'Gaels'/*Gàidheil*, an ideology partly reflected in their (L2) pronunciation (Nance et al. 2016). Whilst, on one hand, native speakers were widely viewed as the best model for new speakers' pronunciation and *blas* ('accent/taste'), native speakers' greater use of English loan words tended to be something new speakers tried to avoid (McLeod, O'Rourke and Dunmore 2014: 39; Nance et al. 2016: 181).

A major investigation of adult Gaelic learners in Scotland conducted by Sellers and Carty (2019) identified that their most frequently reported motivations related to cultural heritage. Thirteen per cent of respondents cited being motivated by the view that 'Gaelic is a part of Scotland's culture and heritage', and 12 per cent reported 'help[ing] preserve or revitalise the language' as a learning motivation (Sellers and Carty 2019: 16). Eight per cent of informants expressed motivations related to an interest in Gaelic music, 7 per cent to a general interest in languages and 5 per cent to historic or present familial connection to Gaelic (Sellers and Carty 2019). Notably, instrumental motivations to learn Gaelic to fluency, including employment opportunities and desire to live in Gaelic-speaking areas or to communicate with friends or family in the language, were much less frequently reported (Sellers and Carty 2019).

In Nova Scotia, rather different policy priorities can be observed to operate in relation to Gaelic language planning and revitalisation to those apparent in Scotland. As noted above, the provincial government-supported *Gàidhlig aig Baile* ('Gaelic in community') and *Bun is Bàrr* ('root and branch') programmes both regularly emphasise the importance of ongoing interaction between native Gaelic speakers and learners, for both socialising new Gaelic speakers in the language and developing their identities as Gaels, to a degree rarely observed in contemporary Scotland. Notably, Gaelic educational opportunities in Nova Scotia are limited by comparison with Scotland, where over 6,000 children aged three to eighteen are currently enrolled in GME. However, the establishment in 2021 of Gaelic-immersion education *Taigh Sgoile na Drochaide* ('Mabou/The Bridge Schoolhouse') for nine children in Mabou, Cape Breton, marked a historic juncture for Gaelic development in the province (Taigh Sgoile na Drochaide 2021). The establishment of Gaelic-medium teaching in Nova Scotia at this time joined immersion programmes already available to Indigenous Mi'kmaw children in certain areas, and French-medium schools for Acadian children which had operated since the 1990s (Globe and Mail 2022). Such Francophone and First Nation community schools now often exist in close proximity to formerly predominantly Gaelic-speaking areas in Cape Breton. As discussed in Chapter 1, bilingual Gaelic education, by contrast, was limited until 2021 to a small number of elementary and high schools, evening classes, residential courses and university classes.

Given the small scale and very recent introduction of formal immersion education for (potential) new Gaelic speakers in Nova Scotia, second language teaching in high schools, extracurricular immersion programmes and adult language-acquisition initiatives have formed the basis of revitalisation efforts in recent decades (MacEachen 2008; Dunbar 2008; Watson and Ivey 2016). It will be instructive to follow the growth and development of GME in Nova Scotia in coming years, and the key issues of divergence that are likely to manifest in that context when compared with the experience of immersion schooling in Scotland.

This chapter has sought to review and contextualise key sociolinguistic and anthropological perspectives on the interrelated notions of language and new speakerhood, ethnolinguistic identity, linguistic ideology and language socialisation. These key concepts will form the basis of the analysis presented over the course of the following four chapters in respect of new Gaelic speakers in both contexts. I will return frequently to the relevance of theoretical concerns that this chapter has attempted to summarise as a framework for conceptualising the overarching findings of the book. As an initial point of departure for the analyses, the following chapter introduces the two research sites and seeks to frame a key divergence between the dominant linguistic ideological environments in which new speakers of Gaelic in the two contexts are presently immersed.

THREE

Gaelic Language Ideologies in Scotland and Nova Scotia: An Ethnographic Introduction to the Research Sites

This chapter illustrates key language ideologies that I observed to operate in Scotland and Nova Scotia over the course of my fieldwork in both contexts, and on my own journey towards becoming a new speaker of Gaelic. To depict these sets of ideologies I employ ethnographic vignettes from participant observation in both territories. In particular, field notes compiled over the course of my participation in language learning events and community organisation activities in both field sites form the basis of this chapter's analysis of relevant language ideologies and practices in each site. I initially disclose an autoethnographic biography of my own journey toward learning Gaelic from the age of fifteen into adulthood, my motivations and methods for acquiring the language and my relationship to the current Gaelic community on either side of the Atlantic.

Providing this linguistic background and reflexively unpacking my positionality in the research, as well as my own pathways to language acquisition, can thus be seen as requisite context for interpreting the dataset I outline and analyse in the following chapters. Ethnographic observations in both contexts bring into sharp relief some of the major contrasts between the Gaelic communities of Scotland and Nova Scotia, and the relationship of new speakers to the traditional culture and identities associated with the language. This rich description will conceptualise the two research contexts and set up the analysis of interview and survey data presented over the following three chapters.

The subtitle of this book, 'Heritage, Motivation and Identity' evokes the initial stages of my own journey to becoming a new speaker of Gaelic in the early years of this century. Growing up within a Scottish family in suburban England, I first started working through a softback copy of the well-established *Teach Yourself Gaelic* course book aged fifteen, in 2001. The *TYG* workbook was accompanied by an audio tape of language exercises, which I would faithfully work through with the aid of a battery-operated cassette player, and dutifully listen to on a (near) daily basis until I completed the course. I had developed a keen interest in languages at secondary school, and an awareness from my mother that our own ancestors had spoken the Gaelic language within living memory. My great-great-grandfather, James W. MacKay, was a Gaelic speaker from Sutherland who died at the age of twenty-one, while in the employ of a Highland regiment of the British Army in South Africa in 1901. His daughter, Margaret, whom his new wife had given birth to some months before his death, grew up in Edinburgh without ever learning a word of her father's native Gaelic language. A family anecdote recalled the one occasion that Margaret's grandfather Robert (*Raibeart*, James's own father) visited Edinburgh from Sutherland during her early childhood: he spoke no English and she knew no Gaelic, and any communication across the generations was thus near-impossible. Robert MacKay belonged to the generation of the Highland Clearances, and ended his days in a coastal East Sutherland fishing town many miles from the community in which he had been born and raised (see Dorian 1981). On the marriage certificate of his son James, Robert's occupation is listed as 'Scavenger', reflecting the deep socioeconomic disenfranchisement many of his generation experienced after clearance. Margaret's daughter, my own grandmother, never learned to speak the language as she grew up in Edinburgh, though my own mother later learned a little Gaelic growing up in the same city. She passed on to me what little Gaelic she could, in a small number of phrases and numbers from one to ten, but also, tellingly, a keen awareness of our ethnolinguistic inheritance and the traumatic interruption of Gaelic transmission within our family.

I moved to Edinburgh as a student in 2004, and set myself the task of learning Gaelic in earnest, initially as part of a joint-honours degree programme in languages and linguistics. In our introductory Gaelic language class, the first spoken language exercise required us to ask one another '*Cò às a tha thu?*' ('Where are you from?') and '*A bheil thu pòsta?*' ('Are you married?'). Marital status of our fellow students notwithstanding, the respective places of origin of our fellow students were a considerable source of interest to each of us: Lowland Scots with no immediate or remembered connection to Gaelic, a larger number of North Americans, some Germans, Italians, and three students (myself included) from England. At this stage of my language learning career, I couldn't say with certainty that my motivation to learn Gaelic was determined principally by my heritage in the language, although it was a factor. It occurred to me, however, that I was essentially the only participant in that introductory Gaelic class to be motivated at all by the possession (or at least awareness) of Gaelic heritage.

Between that class and defending a PhD at the same university a decade later, throughout my experience of learning, and relearning Gaelic (having moved away from Edinburgh for postgraduate study) I was constantly mindful that other Gaelic learners in Scotland seemed not generally to be motivated by, or even especially interested in, their own ethnolinguistic heritage. On one occasion, when our university Gaelic teacher had encouraged us all at a conversation class to think of ourselves as Gaels, most students were mystified at the suggestion, lacking any sort of affinity with the islands that was regarded by most as a necessary prerequisite for expressing that identity. Conversely, when some of us made our first visit to the Western Isles during the final year of undergraduate study, our attempts to engage local community members in their vernacular tongue often met with a similar level of mystification. The experience of learning Gaelic in a university setting, and then of attempting to put recently acquired language facilities to use in a community setting, was in itself an education in contemporary linguistic ideologies concerning what it means to be a Gael and a Gaelic speaker in contemporary Scotland.

Nova Scotia Gaelic: experiences of a new speaker in New Scotland

I will now describe several participant observations in Nova Scotia that I feel introduce some of the key distinctions between Gaelic communities in Scotland and Nova Scotia that I observed in my time in the province. I recorded detailed field notes throughout each of these experiences, and have transliterated these notes into narrative explanatory accounts in the following pages. I made three research trips to Nova Scotia over the course of twelve months between autumn 2017 and summer 2018. Over these three field trips, I spent a total of three months in the province: three weeks from September to October 2017, seven weeks from May to June 2018 (during which time I was joined by my partner and infant son) and two weeks on my own in August 2018. When I first arrived in Nova Scotia, in September 2017, the colours of the foliage the province is renowned for were beginning to transform to their striking autumnal tones, and the air was cold and fresh in the early morning. The academic year was just beginning in local universities in the cities of Halifax, Antigonish and Sydney, where I was based for a substantial part of my fieldwork. In the interests of anonymity, I do not specify further the communities in which the following ethnographic observations were made.

The following vignettes and anecdotes illustrate the major, overarching language ideologies I observed to operate in the province, many of which contrasted starkly with the general situation I had observed to predominate among new speakers in Scotland over a longer period (as discussed above). My participant observation in the following four respective speech situations in Nova Scotia assists in the contextualisation of this wider setting, before turning attention to the predominant discourses that emerged through ethnographic interviews in both contexts in the following two chapters. Notably, the language ideologies I observed to operate in Nova Scotia Gaelic speakers' linguistic behaviours and usages piqued my interest in the issue of local heritage from almost the first day of my arrival in the province.

Latha na Fèill Mhìcheil / Michaelmas in Gaelic Nova Scotia

On 29 September 2017 I had an opportunity to take part in marking the feast of Michaelmas (*Latha na Fèill Mhìcheil* in Gaelic) with a group of Gaelic learners at a Nova Scotian university. This event took place as part of a university Gaelic class which was delivered by a new Gaelic speaker employed as teaching assistant in the department. The local university Gaelic class was joined for this day's celebration by ten visiting high school students from Scotland (all aged between fifteen and sixteen) along with the two teachers from the Gaelic-medium class they attended in the west of Scotland. The remainder of the class for the Michaelmas celebration consisted of twelve first- and second-year Gaelic students from the university, each of whom was aged between seventeen and nineteen. Also in attendance were two faculty staff and me, having introduced myself as a researcher from Edinburgh.

During the session, the ten GME students from Scotland sat on the top of a long bench table at the back of the room, mostly looking rather uncomfortable and disinterested. By comparison, the twelve Canadian students sat on chairs at tables toward the front of the teaching room and were all highly engaged in the session. The Gaelic instructor had baked a *bannoch-struthain*, a special loaf traditionally made from barley, oat and rye flour, to mark the harvest for all participants in the class to enjoy. She then explained in detail a number of unique Gaelic Michaelmas traditions in Scotland, before distributing pieces of the *struthan* for everyone in attendance to enjoy. Then all class participants were invited to introduce themselves and say a little bit about themselves in Gaelic. The contrast between the Scottish and Nova Scotian students' self introductions immediately caught my attention: the Scottish students all employed the same grammatically imprecise, set phrase, '*Is mise* [name], *tha mi* [number] *aois*' ('I am [name], I am [number] age'), without going into further detail. The Nova Scotian and other Canadian students attempted to explain where they originated from, and several expanded on their familial ties to the language and specific rationales for learning Gaelic. Several Canadian students deployed the phrase, '*Tha gaol agam air*' ('I love it'), in explaining their motivations and feelings toward Gaelic.

In part, these distinctions may reflect different age cohorts in the two groups of students; although it is important to bear in mind that all present in the class were aged under twenty, high school students of the language and first-year university students clearly represent divergent profiles in terms of age, maturity and motivation. More tellingly, perhaps, the Scottish students had all undergone Gaelic-medium education at primary school, a decision that had principally been made by their parents rather than themselves. Nevertheless, the choice to continue studying the language in high school was clearly indicative of an attachment to Gaelic, albeit one not necessarily stemming from an ideological or identity-related stance as regards the language and its speaker community. The Canadian university students' introductions, by contrast, tended to indicate motivations generally pertaining quite clearly to their own cultural and heritage identities. I return to this matter and its prevalence among new speakers in greater detail throughout subsequent chapters of this book.

The Scottish GME students were then invited to give short, prepared presentations on the theme of 'Life in Scotland', either individually or in small groups of two to three; three of these presentations were delivered in Gaelic. Some students had prepared PowerPoint presentations for this task, while others spoke from notes. Most students appeared somewhat reticent in undertaking the task, and many were clearly indifferent to it. Again, this may be more reflective of the younger age profile of the Scottish group than indicative of other sociocultural factors, but the disparity compared to their Canadian counterparts was clear. The Scottish students each described the town in western Scotland where they lived in relatively superficial terms; most recounted that the town had 'recently got a Subway' sandwich shop, and also benefited from having 'four chippies'. Supposedly nearby places of interest were then depicted with photographs of Edinburgh, Loch Lomond, Loch Ness and the Hebrides. There was no apparent awareness among students of deep, abiding and historic links to Gaelic and Gaels in the particular part of western Scotland the students came from. English versions of placenames rather than Gaelic forms were given for describing each of the (rather more distant) locations that students discussed in their presentations.

In the second of the student presentations, a student described the perceived benefits of GME in terms of the funded trips and excursions which they had enjoyed as Gaelic-medium pupils, including the current trip to Nova Scotia, from which students would be returning via Florida and its theme parks. No mention was made of other perceived beneficial aspects of GME or acquiring Gaelic in Scotland generally. Neither was the significance of Gaelic to the students' specific region of origin discussed, nor the fundamental importance of that area to the history of Gaelic in Scotland. On the other hand, the importance of the local Highland Games to the area was mentioned by a student in the third presentation.

At the end of these student presentations, the class teacher from Scotland asked students from Canada in greater detail about their motivations for learning Gaelic. Many described connections to culture, interest in music and heritage, and Scottish Gaelic ancestry. Questions were then invited from the Canadian students, who attempted to ask Scottish students if they possessed any family connections to the language. The Scottish students each answered 'no', but the class teacher mentioned that one of the pupils' fathers could speak Irish. To the clear surprise of the Canadian students, for whom heritage, culture and ancestry were clearly foregrounded in their own engagement with Gaelic, the teacher explained with a degree of embarrassment that, 'Gaelic is not seen as cool in Scotland.' Some of the Scottish pupils murmured their approval at this observation, while others simply looked on impassively.

In this connection, the teacher suggested that Gaelic development in Nova Scotia appeared to be going much better than in Scotland, both in terms of the language being viewed positively, and of the 'intergenerational transmission' of the language in the province. When she asked the class why this might be the case, the Gaelic instructor asked her Canadian class if they felt it was because Gaelic had been more important to their families, and if it remained precious to them being so far from Scotland. Several Canadian students responded that this was indeed the case for them. An informal discussion about some of the other notable differences between the two contexts continued until the end of the class, with minimal (if any) input from the Scottish GME pupils. To a certain degree, observations from my participation in the Michaelmas Gaelic class concord with conclusions generated in previous research on long-term outcomes of GME in Scotland (see Dunmore 2017, 2019). These studies demonstrate the limited degree to which most former GME pupils make use of Gaelic years after completing their immersion schooling, and the lack of any close association or identification with the language among a large majority. Nevertheless, the lack of engagement in issues of Gaelic language and culture among present GME secondary pupils, on a nominally Gaelic-oriented cultural exchange to Nova Scotia, was both surprising and disheartening from a language policy perspective.

Gàidhlig aig Baile class with education students

A few weeks further into my first research visit to Nova Scotia in autumn 2017, I was invited to take part in a Gaelic language class at a local university. The instructor for this class employed the *Gàidhlig aig Baile* ('Gaelic in the community') methodology, in turn modelled on the Scottish activist Fionnlagh MacLeòid's 'Total Immersion Plus' (TIP) mode of instruction. The underlying principle of *Gàidhlig aig Baile* sessions is to teach vocabulary, idiom and Gaelic cultural identity through day-to-day tasks in domestic contexts. In the case of this particular university class, for instance, the main part of the lesson followed the instructor preparing breakfast, naming items of vocabulary that would be required for the meal itself (bacon, eggs, black pudding and so on) and the types of kitchen apparatus, cutlery and crockery that would be used. In the classroom setting, the actual task of making breakfast was obviously impossible, so a degree of imagination was required, although in many cases *Gàidhlig aig Baile* sessions do indeed take place in such domestic physical settings as the instructor's kitchen or living room. The university students participating in the class were, for the most part, postgraduate students of education training to be teachers, whose previous study of Gaelic was rather limited, but who would all potentially qualify after graduating to teach 'core' Gaelic in Nova Scotian schools. Core Gaelic introduces a few hours of Gaelic teaching through the school week to students who choose it over another modern language, such as French. As such, it is the main means by which most students who ever encounter Gaelic in the Nova Scotia school system do so, although it is generally only available in eastern counties of the mainland and in Cape Breton. The student teachers participating in the class therefore potentially constituted an important future demographic for Gaelic teaching and instruction in the province.

Before starting the language class in earnest, the instructor humorously pretended to address a noisy group of non-Gaelic students who were congregating on the lawn outside the window of the classroom. Leaning over his shoulder and cupping a hand to his jaw he jokingly shouted: '*Oi, a chlanna nan Gall, bithibh sàmhach!*' ('Oi, children of foreigners, be quiet!') to the noisy students, grimacing for humorous effect. In the Scottish context, the word *Gall* typically refers to non-Gaelic speaking, Lowland-dwelling Scots, and is sometimes translated as 'Lowlander'. In the Nova Scotia context, this latter translation was clearly not the intended meaning, however, and the historic use of the phrase to reference (particularly Germanic language speaking) foreigners, as opposed to Gaelic-speaking Gaels (*Gàidheil*), was implicitly understood in the room. The specific phrase *clanna nan Gall* ('children of foreigners') is used in the respected lexicographer Edward Dwelly's (1994 [1901]: 474) dictionary entry for *Gall*, within the phrase '*Buaidh air clannaibh nan Gall*', which he glosses as 'A victory over foreigners'. Whilst such militaristic undertones were clearly not intended aggressively in the class instructor's mock address to the gaggle of noisy students, it served the purpose of delineating the outside world as the realm of an imagined, non-Gaelic 'them', and the classroom community of Gaelic learners as the domain of 'us'.

Contextualising the aims of the lesson further, the instructor reflected on his view that children acquiring Gaelic through core Gaelic and immersion programmes, and new speakers in Nova Scotia generally, often tended to refer to themselves as *Gàidheil* (Gaels) when speaking in Gaelic, but to translate that as 'Scottish' when speaking English. This observed tendency among Gaelic learners in the province to self-identify as ethnically Scottish rather than as Gaels appeared to irk the instructor, rankling with his personal view of Gaelic culture and identity. In particular, he stated that Gaelic identity in his view clashed with more generally held Canadian conceptions of 'Scottish' culture, which imagined such artefacts as bagpipes, haggis, Highland Games, tartans and Lowland accents 'like they come from Glasgow', as genuinely indexical of Scottish culture and identity. The instructor's clear view was that such indexicalities in no way reflected the authentic cultural identity that he was attempting to engender among his students. The shortcomings of the education system more generally to inculcate an enduring usage of and relationship with languages of study was then discussed within the class, and conversation turned to a discussion of French immersion outcomes in Nova Scotia. One student in the language class, who had been educated through that system, claimed he could think of only two former classmates who now worked in and used the French language, to say nothing of their cultural identification or association with Francophone Canadian society.

The main part of the language lesson was then begun by the instructor, who proceeded to explicate the Gaelic words for each of the objects he had brought to prepare the mock breakfast in class, as well as for verbs required to undertake the task, and other idiomatic terms and expressions that occurred to him as he completed the lesson.

Later, over a coffee with one of the participants in the class who had arrived some eighteen months previously from Scotland, I asked about points of commonality and distinction between that context and Nova Scotia. The student observed that the Gaelic community in Nova Scotia sometimes felt more natural ('*nas nàdarra*') to her than in Scotland, but that that feeling might be due to her coming from an urban Lowland background, without Gaelic or Highland ancestral connections. Because of the Nova Scotian community of learners' substantially smaller size, the student sensed a greater degree of connectedness and closeness of Gaelic speakers to one another in the province. She also observed, however, that whilst a focus among teachers and activists in Gaelic Nova Scotia on heritage and ancestry is a source of great energy and enthusiasm for many, she often felt acutely aware of her own lack of such a connection. This affective stance in relation to her ownership of Gaelic had impacted on her perception of the kind of Gaelic she wished to use, and although she employed a number of distinctively Nova Scotian features in her spoken Gaelic, she claimed to be constantly mindful of a lack of cultural authenticity in such linguistic practices.

Throughout our conversation, the student hinted repeatedly at a profound sense of sadness in not having the ancestral or heritage connection to the Gaelic community that we had discussed in class earlier, a feeling that had never previously occurred to her in Scotland. As she questioned aloud what sort of dialect should be her target variety in training to teach Gaelic, I suggested it was possible she would either become sufficiently informed over next year of university study to decide, or would attain such a command of the spoken language that it wouldn't matter to her. Interestingly, she responded that she was already arriving at the latter feeling. I return to ideologies of authenticity, identity and acquisition in greater detail in the following two chapters.

Traditional dance display in Cape Breton

The following month, in October 2017, I was travelling through Cape Breton with friends who were undertaking postgraduate study in mainland Nova

Scotia. One of these companions was particularly keen to conduct a research interview with a person he had identified as a 'local native speaker' of Gaelic, about her childhood experiences in Nova Scotia. Having arranged to meet at a traditional step dance display that was taking place as part of Cape Breton's annual 'Celtic Colours' festival, he later introduced me to the woman in question. Wearing her clan tartan bonnet, complete with a bobble and matching waistcoat, she marched into the room where I was awaiting the start of the event, thrust out a hand and said to me: '*Ciamar a tha thu?*' ('How are you?'), to which I replied: '*Tha mi gu dòigheil, ciamar a tha sibhse?*' ('I'm very well, how are you [polite pronominal form]?'). To my surprise, she then codeswitched immediately to English, exclaiming: 'Your Gaelic is different, I speak Lochaber Gaelic!', wagging a finger in my direction and turning away. The valorisation of 'Lochaber Gaelic', imagined by some Gaelic learners and speakers in Nova Scotia as the direct dialectal continuation of the west Highland variety spoken by their ancestors in the eighteenth and nineteenth centuries, was not a linguistic ideology I had yet encountered, but I soon became familiar with it. She continued: 'And you weren't born with Gaelic, I can tell!'

Such brusque directness was altogether alien to me based on my previous acquaintance with Gaels, and stood in stark contradistinction to my experiences interacting with almost all the L1 Gaelic speakers I had previously met. Tellingly, however, my interlocutor's initial question in the above dialogue was the only conversational Gaelic I heard her employ throughout that day. Throughout the duration of the step dance display, which also featured performers from other Celtic and Acadian cultures, she loudly declaimed and decried the performances to all in the audience. When an Irish performer gave a demonstration, she stated loudly that the style of dance was 'just gimmicks', and a New Brunswick dancer's performance was dismissed as 'just Riverdance'. Eventually our new acquaintance became so irate that she stormed out of the event, but first turned to me and exclaimed: 'You can speak to me outside after this, but I'm leaving. This is an insult to our heritage. It's why Gaelic is gone from here, and from Scotland!'

Later that afternoon, she joined my researcher friends and me for lunch. It became clear that in spite of her reputed 'native speaker' background in rural Cape Breton, her Gaelic ability had by now attrited to the point that she would be unable to substantially assist my friend in his Gaelic-based study. Nevertheless, she explained at length her attitude to Gaelic revival attempts and cultural events that, in her view, were not sufficiently or authentically grounded in local Gaelic heritage and culture. When discussing my previous research on GME leavers' language use in Scotland, she asked of such past students: 'But do they know their ancestry?' She clearly viewed a lack of such awareness among the majority of Gaelic-medium educated students in my previous study as the root cause of their general disuse of the language. Some of our new acquaintance's folk theories regarding Gaelic were more erroneous than others, though the linguistic ideologies they reflected were of clear relevance to this book's general objectives. She stated of the wider Celtic language family, with some confidence: 'It's "Seltic" not "Celtic" because we don't have the "K" in Gaelic,' and that 'the Caledonian race came from Asia Minor.'

While our speaker's ideas concerning Gaelic history and identity were clearly mistaken in certain respects, I sensed that her earlier pugnacious display at the step dance event was more of an affectation for my benefit than an example of her typical day-to-day behaviour. She later commented of my own surname, 'That's from Argyll, that's why we get along!'

Whilst our new acquaintance would speak phrases in Gaelic to exemplify her knowledge of the language, as previously noted, I didn't hear her converse in the language except in the case of her initial question, '*Ciamar a tha thu?*' I expect that substantial attrition of Gaelic as her heritage language underlay her lack of actual usage, and I felt a degree of sympathy for her position. Essentially, she came across as a rather frustrated would-be elder in the local Gaelic community, who clearly regarded her role as that of a gatekeeper and arbiter of authentic Gaelic culture. Yet her apparent lack of facility in Gaelic meant her views were largely either unheard or ignored by community members and policymakers engaged in the actual work of revitalising the language.

Gaelic community meeting in Cape Breton

I returned to Nova Scotia for a longer period of fieldwork in the spring of 2018. In May I had the opportunity to attend an important Gaelic community meeting in the town hall of a small town in western Cape Breton. The meeting was organised and hosted by a third-sector advocacy body, and attended by local Gaelic speakers and advocates, as well as professionals and policymakers from mainland Nova Scotia. The business of the meeting was conducted chiefly through English, though Gaelic was used for introductions and informally in conversation. Over the course of the day, a total of around sixty delegates participated in the various sessions of the day-long summit. Five participants were Scots who had lived in the province for many years. While most of the participants were based in Cape Breton, a substantial number had driven from Halifax and Antigonish County in mainland Nova Scotia to take part in the event.

In small groups of five to six, gathered around tables in the town hall, attendees were initially asked to outline their individual impressions of Gaelic in contemporary Nova Scotia and their aspirations for the future of the language throughout the province. Participants were then invited to come together in their small groups to plan strategic, 'SMART' goals to achieve these aims and aspirations in the short to medium term. (The 'SMART' acronym was explained to denote 'specific', 'measurable', 'achievable, 'relevant' and 'time-bound' steps that could feasibly and practically be undertaken by the community to enact progress for Gaelic in the province.) Discussions arising from this exercise were generally dominated by issues of raising the public profile and awareness of Gaelic, mobilising the Gaelic community more effectively, establishing Gaelic immersion education, bridging perceived gaps between Gaelic speakers and the heritage and culture sector, and expanding 'core' Gaelic language provision in Nova Scotian schools.

With regard to the first of these themes, participants in the forum discussed the perceived importance of raising awareness of the persistence of Gaelic language and identity in Nova Scotia among the estimated one-third of Nova Scotians possessing Gaelic heritage. One speaker described this objective as 'waking the community'. This potentially substantial Gaelic diaspora in the province was thus generally perceived as a key demographic to unlock in revitalising the language, and forum participants employed the phrases 'legitimation', 'mobilisation' and 'politicising the community' to reflect their desired aims for accessing this wider group. The example of the Halifax Lebanese community was offered by several individuals as one of a united community that had successfully maintained its language and identity by lobbying policymakers at the provincial level.

Other 'SMART' goal strategies were discussed for meeting the objectives of establishing a Gaelic immersion class, either inside or outwith the formal provincial education system, with up to three such classes envisaged in Mabou, Halifax and Antigonish. At this stage (May 2018), a Gaelic immersion preschool had already been established in Cape Breton, and the third-sector community group that organised the meeting had been established specifically to campaign and lobby for the sorts of goals discussed. Reflecting the success of this and other grass-roots organisations in meeting their objectives, the establishment in September 2021 of North America's first Gaelic immersion school, *Taigh Sgoile na Drochaide* ('Mabou/The Bridge Schoolhouse') in Mabou, Cape Breton, marked an historic achievement for language policy in the province. Reflecting the 'SMART' discussions I observed in May 2018, the school was established as an independent initiative, outside of the formal provincial education system and reliant on contributions from the community. At the same time, substantial investment of public funds was provided via the provincial government's Office of Gaelic Affairs to renovate and redevelop the *Beinn Mhabou* campus on which the school is located. Resources and investment were also supplied by Bòrd na Gàidhlig, Education Scotland and a number of other public bodies in Scotland to support the school. This hybrid model of private and public support for Gaelic immersion education is essentially unprecedented in Gaelic development, but reflects parents' and Gaels summit participants' views of the preferred method by which to establish such a system.

Participants in the May 2018 community meeting regarded increasing political engagement with Gaelic, both within the Nova Scotia community and among policymakers, as key to sustaining momentum in revitalising the language. The significant achievement that the 2021 establishment of *Taigh Sgoile na Drochaide* reflects can be seen as one outcome of the community's 'bottom-up' campaign strategy, as well as greater 'top-down' support for the language since the start of this century. The next major step envisioned by forum delegates was institutionalising the revitalisation of Gaelic through the goal of establishing municipal Gaelic officers to promote Gaelic in local government throughout Nova Scotia. Speakers at the event regarded this objective as vital to bridging perceived gaps between involvement in Gaelic culture through music and dance, and increased uptake and use of the language itself. Whilst this goal remains unrealised in 2024, the ambitious objectives set out in the 2018 meeting reflect the substantial appetite of predominantly new speakers for developing Gaelic in Nova Scotia. There is now a dynamic and committed core of young new speakers dedicated to campaigning and lobbying policymakers for Gaelic revitalisation, several of whom are raising their own young families principally in Gaelic. I return to these matters in following chapters, but for now it is clearly demonstrated that the language ideologies and desired objectives for Gaelic that new and budding new speakers in the province possess have had a major influence on the character and appearance of the contemporary Gaelic community in Nova Scotia.

This chapter has drawn attention to several of the contrasting language ideologies that I first noticed to distinguish networks of new speakers of Gaelic in Scotland and Nova Scotia after my first visit to the province in 2017. With a view to reflexively establishing my own positionality as a researcher and new speaker of Gaelic, I have demonstrated how my journey toward new speakerhood was similar in different ways to that taken by learners and new speakers in both research contexts. In particular, my interest in my own Gaelic heritage and the importance that I attached to this in my initial decision to learn the language marked me as a somewhat unusual case in the Scottish context, whilst conversely being comparable to the experiences of many new Gaelic speakers in Nova Scotia. I draw attention in greater detail to key distinctions between communities of new speakers in the two research contexts over the following chapters. I first address the reported acquisition pathways and usage patterns of research participants in the two contexts (Chapter 4), before turning to matters of contrasting linguistic ideology (Chapter 5) and then linguistic practice and attitude from a quantitative perspective (Chapter 6).

FOUR

New Gaelic Speakers' Language Acquisition and Use

Throughout this, the first of two in-depth, qualitative analytic chapters focusing on results from detailed interviews in Scotland and Nova Scotia, I critically discuss the key themes that emerged from my analysis in respect of Scottish and Nova Scotian new speakers' Gaelic language use. In particular, I examine research participants' experiences of acquisition and socialisation in the language, day-to-day use of Gaelic, and the relationship between these factors as demonstrated by qualitative analysis.

I first assess the extent to which interviewees and focus group participants report having acquired Gaelic at various stages of their life cycles, employing qualitative techniques drawing on the ethnography of speaking framework (Hymes 1974) to closely and critically examine participants' language use within the interview setting. This method also allows us to distinguish various different kinds of new Gaelic users, whether having learned in school, at university or as a recent, adult learner. This first portion of the chapter also discusses interviewees' reported linguistic practices and use of Gaelic, including their language learning trajectories in terms of the Catalan concept of the 'muda', or key stage in the life cycle at which a decision to fundamentally change one's linguistic behaviour is made. Relevant mudes in both research contexts include childhood exposure to Gaelic in community and school, extracurricular adolescent and adult immersion opportunities, and formal adult education, including study at Scotland's Gaelic college Sabhal Mòr Ostaig.

The next portion of this chapter analyses relevant data in respect of choice in participants' Gaelic use, including the decision of certain Nova Scotian and Scottish participants to focus effort on learning and perfecting a particular regional variety of the language. This choice is discussed in respect of the Gaelic concept of *blas* ('taste', or 'accent') and research participants' perspectives on accent aim in acquiring Gaelic. Speakers' orientations to particular dialects of Gaelic were notably different in Nova Scotia compared to Scotland.

The final parts of the chapter extend this discussion to consider the ideological opposition of discourses drawing on choice and opportunity in language use.

The notion of the sociolinguistic 'muda' (plural 'mudes') is derived from a Catalan term referring to life-changing moments in language users' social and linguistic performances, such as the adoption of a minority language in one's day-to-day language practices, whether in home, school or community (Pujolar and Gonzàlez 2012; Pujolar and Puigdevall 2015; O'Rourke and Walsh 2020). The various mudes that have proved significant in new Gaelic speakers' socialisation and social practice of Gaelic in Nova Scotia and Scotland inform our understanding of their language learning trajectories and social identities. In this first section I explore the various sociolinguistic mudes that emerged in research participants' narrated experiences as being critical in determining their future engagement with the Gaelic language and its community. Interview extracts are examined, providing narratives of childhood Gaelic language learning and socialisation in Nova Scotia and Scotland respectively, experiences of extracurricular Gaelic acquisition and mudes of formal adult language learning activities, both within and outside higher education settings. Significant distinctions and disparities are apparent between Nova Scotian and Scottish participants' experiences in relation to each of the sociolinguistic mudes and biographical life stages discussed by interviewees.

Early family, school and community mudes

At the start of interviews in each research site, interviewees were invited to describe their Gaelic language learning trajectories. Whilst intergenerational transmission of Gaelic from parents was not an experience reported by any of the Nova Scotian interviewees, certain family members were described in accounts to have been instrumental in encouraging and inspiring new speakers to learn the language during childhood. This dimension of sociolinguistic experience, by and large, was absent in Scottish new speakers' accounts, and is thus analytically noteworthy as another specifically Nova Scotian feature of Gaelic acquisition mudes. The role of grandparents, first, is described by speakers in the following two excerpts:

ANTM1	'S e mo sheanair fhèin a thug brosnachadh dhòmhsa
	It was my grandfather who encouraged me
SD	Glè mhath [...] 's dè an aois a bha thu an uair sin?
	Very good [...] what age were you then?
ANTM1	Mm hmm oh bha mi mu- mu deich- 's math dh'fhaoidte mu deich [[bliadhna a dh'aois]
	Mm hmm oh I was about- about ten- perhaps about ten [[years old]

SD	[[Timcheall air sin?]]
	[[About that?]]
ANTM1	No dusan bliadhna leithid sin no 's math dh'fhaoidte [...] chanainnsa gur e fèin-oideachas cha mhòr a bh' ann [...] thug sin seachad dhomh fhìn gu ìre- uill (1.4) uill gu ìre fileantais
	Or twelve around that perhaps [...] I'd say it was mostly self-learning [...] that brought me to a level- well (1.4) to a certain level of fluency
CBIF1	My grandmother on my father's side in <u>particular</u> was a native speaker from [[xxx ((Cape Breton Island))]]
SD	[[Right mm hmm]]
CBIF1	And xxx when she grew up was (.) pro:bably (.) as **Gàidhealtachd** as you could get [...] and as I went through school like elementary school there were just people that I'd say were more <u>cultural</u> people in my life [...] but at <u>that</u> time I still had no exposure to it in school

Grandparents who were L1 Gaelic speakers and continued to speak the language to at least some degree were thus described to have had an important influence on various Nova Scotian new speakers' decisions to learn Gaelic at a later age. In the case of a very few interviewees, parents were regarded as having inspired an interest in learning Gaelic among speakers. Again, however, such inspiration was clearly not reflective of the same level of language socialisation as full intergenerational transmission would involve:

ANTM3	I didn't (.) like <u>actually</u> (.) learn how to ^speak very much of it growing up [...but] I always thought it was really cool when my mom would teach me phrases
SD	Mm hmm
ANTM3	I was like 'Ah! I'm learning Gaelic!'
SD	Yeah?
ANTM3	'Gaelic's such a cool language!'

Parents having taught specific phrases in the home-community sphere was an important first introduction to Gaelic for a small but important subsection of Nova Scotian interviewees. Tellingly, the above interviewee's emphasis on the word 'actually', and rising intonation on 'speak' indicate the limited degree to which actual transmission occurred from his mother. More generally in the Nova Scotia context, familial connections to Gaelic socialisation were rather distant, as described by the following participant:

CBIF2	Bha mo cho-ogha an sàs san aon chlas [Gàidhlig aig Baile] 's ann [...] rachadh sinne a chèilidh air mo shinn sheanmhair xxx [...] nuair a bha

mi aig an taigh aice a' cur cèilidh oirre gu ^math tric nuair a- nuair a bha
còmhradh eadar mi fhìn 's i fhèin ^o:: an uiread triopan a chuala mise
^^'dè tha thu cantainn? Dè tha thu a' cantainn?!' [...] 's i ag iarraidh orm
(1.1) na rudan a chantail anns an dòigh <u>siud</u> gus an robh iad agam mar a
bha ise ag iarraidh [...] 'S e gaol a bha siud
> My cousin was in the same [Gàidhlig aig Baile] class [...] we would go to visit my great-grandmother xxx [...] when I was at her house visiting ^quite often when- when were were chatting ^o:: the number of times I heard ^^'What are you saying? What are you saying?!' [...] because she wanted me (1.1) to say things in <u>that</u> particular way until I had them just as she wanted [...] That was love [that motivated her]

Whilst thus having learned Gaelic in adulthood through community classes in Cape Breton, this speaker in fact attended classes with her cousin, and had many opportunities to visit her great-grandmother, who had encouraged the two learners to speak in the variety and idiom that was native to her. This particular experience – of being able to converse with a great-grandparent – was unique in the dataset, but does reflect a wider tendency among Nova Scotian participants to orientate towards older community members as the best models for their Gaelic acquisition. For the following speaker, it was a great-uncle who first encouraged him to take an interest in learning Gaelic:

HALM2   'S e an t-uncail aige [.i. athair] a rinn an gnothach [...] latha a bha seo is thuirt mi 'Hm nam bruidhneadh tu rium mm math dh'fhaoidte gun- gun togainn an cànan' [...] agus 's ann mar sin a thòisich mise [...] nuair a dh'eug bràthair mo sheanmhair xxx chuir mi romham a bhith bruidhinn ri m' athair a h-uile triop- a h-uile cothrom
> It was his [i.e., father's] uncle who made the difference [...] one day I said 'Hm if you spoke to me [in Gaelic] maybe I- I would pick up the language' [...] and that's how I started [...] when my grandmother's brother died xxx I decided to speak to my father [in Gaelic] every time- at every opportunity

SD   Sgoinneil [...] is dè an aois a bha thu nuair a chuir thu toiseach air [ionn-sachadh]?
> Great [...] and how old were you when you started [learning]?

HALM2   Um math dh'fhaoidte mar sia- sia bliadhna deug
> Um I was maybe six- sixteen

Again, therefore, an unusual form of intergenerational transmission, through conversation in adolescence with elderly family members, was a key sociolinguistic muda that certain Nova Scotian speakers credited as having inspired them to learn Gaelic. In the case of this particular interviewee, having learned Gaelic as a young adult through formal study, a shift in family Gaelic language use with his own native speaker father was inspired by this unique socialisation experience with his great-uncle. Whilst such experiences are unusual in Nova Scotia, they formed a particularly noteworthy subsection of Gaelic mudes in the province, particularly among speakers with close connections to Cape Breton. In Scotland, by contrast, no single interviewee reported childhood interaction with Gaelic-speaking family as having motivated their later acquisition of Gaelic through formal learning. Conversely, the context of school forms a crucial muda that subgroups of interviewees from both contexts described when reporting their first exposures to the Gaelic language.

Formal schooling comprises a notable context for initial socialisation in Gaelic language and culture for subsections of new speakers in both polities under consideration. In Nova Scotia, the growth of provision for Gaelic instruction in state schools – particularly under the rubric of 'core' language teaching, with weekly exposure to the language amounting to a few hours – has been gradually increasing in recent decades, particularly in Cape Breton. In Scotland, the infrastructure of Gaelic education is relatively more developed, with the language as either a subject or teaching medium currently available to around 10 per cent of Scottish pupils (McLeod 2020). The following accounts trace key distinctions between the schooling experiences of Nova Scotian and Scottish interviewees.

As noted above, 'core' Gaelic teaching, in Cape Breton in particular, has become more widespread only relatively recently. As the following interviewee explains, Gaelic instruction at school for her generation was rather limited and ad hoc:

CBIF1	At <u>that</u> time I still had no exposure to it in school
SD	No [[of course]
CBIF1	[[There] was nowhere to take it when I was growing up- I'm thirty-seven now so twenty- you know ((laughs)) […] then I got to high school and I had a teacher called xxx
SD	Hmm
CBIF1	And he had- would say phrases, smatterings like and he probably took a few Gaelic classes over the years himself […] and so that was like my first [realisation] 'Okay!' […] 'Now:: what does that mean? **Rudeigin** [*something*] – okay!'

'Phrases' and 'smatterings' of Gaelic that this speaker describes having learned in high school in the 1980s and '90s contrast relatively clearly with the experiences of interviewees in eastern Nova Scotia who learned Gaelic in a more structured fashion in more recent years, as the following two speakers observe:

SD	Did you hear much Gaelic growing up?
ANTM3	Um (0.6) well we had it in schools

SD	Okay
ANTM3	We took it from grade f:our up until grade nine and then we had the option of Gaelic and French for those years and then we could take it if we wanted to but we didn't have to [...] I didn't (.) like <u>actually</u> (.) learn how to ^speak very much of it growing up
SD	An do rinn thu Gàidhlig san sgoil?
	Did you do Gaelic in school?
CBIF7	<u>Rinn</u> uh huh bha uh xxx ((tidsear)) ann
	<u>Yes</u> uh huh we had uh xxx ((name of teacher))
SD	Glè mhath
	Great
CBIF7	A' teagasg Gàidhlig ann an xxx ((Cape Breton Island)) aig an àm sin agus um (1.1) chuir ise clas air dòigh is aig an àm sin (.) um (1.2) 's e: pàirt den churraicealam a bh' <u>ann</u> ach [...] cha robh i agam **so** bha mi airson (1.3) [[ga togail]
	Teaching Gaelic in xxx ((Cape Breton)) at that time and um (1.1) she held a class at that time (.) um (1.2) it: <u>was</u> a part of the curriculum but [...] I couldn't speak it so I wanted (1.3) [[to learn it]
SD	[[Dìreach] agus gu dè mar a dh'ionnsaich thu a' Ghàidhlig gu ceart ma-tha? An ann anns an sgoil?=
	[[Exactly] and how did you learn Gaelic properly then? In school?=
CBIF7	=^Uill ^thòisich mi san sgoil ach [...] **yeah** ((laughs)) cha do thog mi i!
	*=^Well I ^started in school but [...] **yeah** ((laughs)) I didn't learn it!*

For speakers having attended primary and secondary education since the 1990s, such as the above two interviewees, therefore, early exposure to Gaelic in school, whilst not leading to fluency in childhood, clearly formed a significant juncture, with vital implications for their future acquisition of and socialisation in the language. This dimension is elaborated on by the following interviewee, whose first exposure to Gaelic in extracurricular language classes led to her pursuing a university degree involving Gaelic, before starting a family:

CBIF10	Ann an ^<u>àrd</u>-sgoil (thug) mi Gàidhlig mar chùrsa ach cha robh sin (.) anns an <u>latha</u> sgoile a bha sin- ach às <u>dèidh</u> [...] an uair sin rinn mi: um: (1.8) **Celtic Studies** aig xxx ((oilthigh))
	*In ^high school I (took) Gaelic as a course but that wasn't (.) during the school <u>day</u> but <u>after</u> ((school)) [...] then I: did um: (1.8) **Celtic Studies** at xxx ((university))*
SD	An do rinn? Sheadh
	Did you? Yeah

CBIF10	A:gus:: (.) **so** aig an àm sin cha robh- cha robh mi fileanta <u>idir</u> agus uh thòisich mi uh (1.1) <u>teaghlach</u>! ((laughs)) [...] Cha do rinn mi mòran leis (.) a' Ghàidhlig aig an àm sin
	A:n::d (.) *so at that time I wasn't- I wasn't fluent <u>at all</u> and uh I started uh (1.1) a <u>family</u>! ((laughs)) [...] I didn't do much with (.) Gaelic at that time*

In Nova Scotia, therefore, interviewees who had received some exposure to Gaelic teaching in formal schooling or university in the province tended not to credit such learning experiences as having directly inspired substantial use of the Gaelic, or fluency in the language. Yet it was clear that for younger speakers who had acquired some Gaelic in school in recent decades, this context formed an important muda in their language learning trajectories.

In Scotland, both GME and Gaelic learner education (GLE) have been well established since the 1980s, albeit only for relatively small minorities of Scottish pupils (see Dunmore 2019). The vast majority of pupils in Scotland have no access to Gaelic learning opportunities at present (McLeod 2020: 297). Amongst several subsections of new speakers sampled in the present research, however, both forms of Gaelic education had been important mudes for early exposure to Gaelic. There is a notable qualitative contrast, however, between the language learning experiences of the relatively few participants who studied Gaelic as a subject (GLE) and the five interviewees who received immersion in Gaelic (GME) from an early age.

GLAM6	Anns na sgoiltean cha robh Gàidhlig ann mar chuspair
	In the schools Gaelic wasn't taught as a subject
SD	Mm hmm
GLAM6	A::ch (1.2) um:: (0.9) fhuair mi eòlas air Gàidhlig um:: nuair a bha mi can còig deug no sia deug bliadhna a dh'aois [...] bha (.) um: (0.8) uh fear ionadail- um: luchd-ionnsachaidh [sic] cuideachd uh a bha- a bha air Gàidhlig ionnsachadh- ruith esan leasanan ann an xxx ((Galltachd an iar)) do ^dh'inbhich [...] chanainnsa nach- nach- nach robh mi buileach fileanta an uair sin
	Bu::t (1.2) um:: (0.9) I came to know Gaelic um:: when I was say fifteen or sixteen years old [...] there (.) um: (.) uh a local man- um: a learner who- who'd learned Gaelic as well- he ran lessons in xxx ((west Lowlands)) for adults [...] I'd say that- that I wasn't- I wasn't completely fluent at the time
SD	**Oh right**
GLAM6	Uh:: nach robh mi ach aig em aig ìr- ìre eadar-mheadhanach [...] dìreach gu robh class ^<u>ann</u> agus um (1.8) bha foghlam mar sin ri fhaotainn
	Uh:: that I was only at em at a- an intermediate level [...] it's just that there ^<u>was</u> a class and um (1.8) education like that was available

GLAM2   Bha mi anns a' chòigeamh bliadhna anns an àrd-sgoil [...] cha robh Gàidhlig ann mar chuspair ach bha tidsear ann a b' àbhaist a bhith teagasg Gàidhlig anns a- anns an sgoil ud (0.7) ach eh:: anns an latha sin bha e teagasg eachdraidh (.) thuirt e rium (1.1) nam bithinn ag <u>iarraidh</u> dh'fhaotgum faotadh e (1.2) **like** (.) bha **Standard Grade** ann no rudeigin mar sin [...] **so** rud a rinn mi air a' chòigeamh- 's e deugaire rud beag annasach a bh' annam 's dòcha [...] Aig an sgoil sin san t-siathamh bliadhna agus Gàidhlig a dhèanamh leis an- leis an tidsear sin

I was in fifth year in high school [...] Gaelic wasn't available as a subject but there was a teacher who used to teach Gaelic in the- in that school (0.7) but eh:: in those days he taught history (.) he said to me (1.1) if I <u>wanted</u> he could- that he could (1.2) **like** *(.) teach* **Standard Grade** *or similar [...] so what I did in fifth year- perhaps I was quite a strange teenager! [...] In sixth year at that school I took Gaelic with that teacher*

In both above accounts, therefore, the opportunity to take Gaelic on a one-to-one basis through GLE came via relatively fortuitous acquaintances with Gaelic teachers in mainstream Scottish schools. It is particularly noteworthy that none of the thirty new speakers interviewed in Scotland undertook study of Gaelic as a school subject within classes at primary or secondary school. By contrast, five interviewees had been enrolled in GME during childhood, an experience which formed a crucial juncture of their acquisition and socialisation trajectory (cf. Dunmore 2019). For speakers such as the following two interviewees, first exposure to Gaelic through GME occurred so early that they could not remember starting the language learning process:

GMEF1   Chanainn (.) gu- thòisich mi cho òg bha mi dìreach trì bliadhna a dh'aois (.) em (.) bha fios agam gu robh Gàidhlig ann (.) ach: [...] bha mi òg, òg (.) agus em: cha robh- ach chan eil cuimhne agam air beatha às aonais Gàidhlig [...] bha mi dìreach ag ràdh an-diugh gur e an rud as fheàrr a rinn mo phàrantan dhomh

I would say (.) that- I started so young I was only three (.) em (.) I knew that Gaelic existed but [...] I was so young (.) and em: I didn't- but I don't remember life without Gaelic [...] I was just saying today that it was the best thing my parents ever did for me

SD   An robh Gàidhlig agad mus do thòisich thu ann am foghlam tro mheadhan na Gàidhlig?
Could you speak Gaelic before you started in GME?

GMEM2   Eh bho thùs? Chan eil cuimhn' agam feumaidh mi aideachadh oir bha mi cho beag ach: [...] cha bhithinn fileanta mura deach mi dhan (bhun-sgoil)

[...]	mar eisimpleir [...] aidh is cinnteach nach biodh Gàidhlig agam eh tha fhios'am
	Eh from the start? I don't remember I must admit because I was so young bu:t [...] I wouldn't be fluent if I hadn't gone to (primary GME) for example [...] yeah I know I certainly wouldn't have been able to speak Gaelic [without GME]
SD	An do chòrd e riut a bhith ann am- nuair a bha thu ann am foghlam tro mheadhan na Gàidhlig?
	Did you enjoy being in- when you were in GME?
GMEM2	Air an aon làmh tha e duilich a ràdh- eh fhios agad 's e an sgoil a bh' ann! ((laughs)) [...] Tha mi smaointinn gu robh- mar àrainneachd- na clasaichean Gàidhlig a' còrdadh rium nas motha [...] fios agad cha robh cothroman agamsa san taigh agus bha e dìreach a' fàs mearachdach 's mearachdach- eil fhios agad bha e dìreach **rusty**
	*On one hand it's hard to say- eh you know it was school! ((laughs))[...] I think that- as an environment- I enjoyed the Gaelic classes more [than the English...] you know I didn't have opportunities at home [my Gaelic] was just becoming more and more inaccurate- you know it was just **rusty** [after GME]*

On one hand, therefore, speakers such as the two above Gaelic-medium educated interviewees could rarely recall the specific process of learning Gaelic in GME since they were so young when they started in the system (generally at the age of four – or earlier, in Gaelic-medium preschools). On the other hand, a lack of opportunity to use Gaelic with family members or wider social networks outside the school led in the majority of cases to a loss of linguistic abilities after leaving school (cf. Dunmore 2017, 2019). Lack of language use after completing GME had led to a marked decline in Gaelic skills for most of the five new speakers who had gone through the system, as described in the following account:

SD	Dè a' bhuaidh a bh' aig foglam Gàidhlig ortsa, an canadh tu?
	What effect did GME have on you would you say?
GMEF2	Em (.) uill sa chiad dol-a-mach cha robh buaidh cho mòr ann chanainn em (.) nuair a dh'fhàg mi an àrd-sgoil cha do chleachd mi a' Ghàidhlig airson 's dòcha ochd bliadhna is chaill mi a' mhòr-chuid dheth
	Em (.) well initially it didn't have much of an effect I would say em (.) when I left high school I didn't use Gaelic for perhaps eight years and I lost most of it

As I have discussed elsewhere (Dunmore 2017, 2018a, 2018b, 2018c, 2019) a clear majority of former GME pupils who attended GME during the first years of its availability did not maintain the high levels of Gaelic oracy they had attained in immersion education, due to lack of opportunities to use the language outside the school setting. Language ideologies that interviewees conveyed in these wider studies of GME outcomes also tended to rationalise the limited degree to which past students reported using the language. As speaker GMEF2 describes in the above excerpt, she essentially 'lost' most of her Gaelic after school due to not using it for eight years in early adulthood. The choice to then reacquire Gaelic abilities can be seen as reflective of a distinct muda related to specific motivations at that time of life. Yet for the five Gaelic-medium educated new speakers discussed here, the experience of GME itself was a crucial muda on the complex journey towards acquiring fluency in the language and using it in daily life. Immersion in the language from a young age appears, from participants' accounts, almost to bridge (or blur) the conceptual divergence between L1 and L2. This sense is conveyed clearly in the following extract:

GMEM3   'S e dìreach **immersion** a bh'ann
         It was just **immersion**
SD   'S e aidh
         Yes
GMEM3   Riamh cha do dh'ionnsaich mi cànan dìreach ri bhith leughadh leabhair neo coimhead air structar gràmair no **sentence structure** [...] mura b' e (.) foghlam tro mheadhan na Gàidhlig cha bhiodh na sgilean agamsa **you know** na sgilean cànain airson an obair seo a dhèanamh [...] Cha b' e taghadh a rinn mi (.) ach leis gu robh Gàidhlig agam nochd an uimhir de chothroman
         I never learned a language just by reading a book or looking at structure or grammar or **sentence structure** *[...] if (.) it hadn't been for GME my skills wouldn't be* **you know** *the language skills [I need] to do this job [...] It wasn't my choice [to do GME] (.) but because I could speak Gaelic so many opportunities presented themselves*

GME is thus regarded to represent a unique muda in the Gaelic acquisition and socialisation experience of a notable subsection of new Gaelic speakers in Scotland. Yet the relative scarcity of GME graduates among the thirty new speakers interviewed in this context (five individuals, or 17 per cent of the sample) reflects the substantial scale of the challenge facing policymakers in respect of creating new generations of Gaelic speakers through this system (see also Dunmore 2019). The benefits of immersion education for developing (Gaelic) language skills in early childhood, and for providing subsequent opportunities for employment, however, are clearly apparent in the above speaker's account, as was the case among the other four former GME students in the sample.

For this subgroup, the experience of GME was thus a critical muda in their Gaelic language learning and socialisation.

(Post-)adolescent immersion in Gaelic

As has been highlighted in respect of GME in Scotland, immersion language learning opportunities are frequently presented as an ideal acquisition opportunity for learners in varied contexts. In both Nova Scotia and Scotland, diverse and divergent experiences of Gaelic linguistic and cultural immersion were described by certain interviewees as forming an influential and impactful stage of their Gaelic acquisition journey.

In Nova Scotia, in particular, immersion activities directed at adult language learners emerged as a key theme in interviewees' narrated accounts of their learning experiences. This reflects Nova Scotian policymakers' investment in the *Gàidhlig aig Baile* and *Bun is Bàrr* language programmes in the province, as becomes clear in the following two accounts:

CBIF3	I- I realised that my ^ancestors spoke Gaelic like I grew up knowing they were Scottish […] a **h-uile sgàth sheadh rinn mi Bun is Bàrr ach** (.) [*everything yeah I did Bun is Bàrr but (.)*] ^mostly community classes […] I:: took advantage of a lot of opportunities like I didn't have just one teacher I ^never did any formal uh (.) study […] *Gàidhlig aig Baile* for sure […] it <u>has</u> helped people come on a <u>lot</u>
CBIF1	I wasn't comfortable speaking it [after university classes] then I started community classes like the **Gàidhlig aig Baile** (.) style [[classes]
SD	[[Sure] yeah yeah
CBIF1	^Yeah and (.) different (.) things like that- and I <u>still</u> do that
SD	Yeah is that- do you find that quite helpful- **Gàidhlig aig Baile**?
CBIF1	<u>Ab</u>solutely! ((laughs))
SD	Yeah?
CBIF1	Yeah! It was a <u>big</u> change (.) it took a ^long time though to get over the <u>guilt</u> […] I call it my- the Gaelic guilt […] I always felt coming out of university I should have been further than what I ^was […] you might think that you have a <u>bowl</u> full of Gaelic just now but what you actually have is a teaspoon

Other participants contrasted their (relatively limited) experiences of learning Gaelic in secondary school with their more intensive exposure to and acquisition of the language through immersion programmes targeted at adolescents and adults outside of the formal education system, as the following two interviewees (siblings whom I interviewed together) explain:

ANTF4	We start core Gaelic from Grade 4 at school so
SD	Oh yeah [...] so was it mostly through high school that you guys got conversational in Gaelic?
ANTF4	Um I would say for me it was kind of in the junio- middle school because I did **Na Gaisgich Òga** [*The Young Heroes*]
SD	**Na Gaisgich Òga** [[seadh] *yeah*
ANTF4	[[And xxx did too] yeah
ANTM5	[[It was the same for me]
SD	So is that kind of over weekends and in the evenings?
ANTF4	It's a- it was- once a month you meet with <u>everyone</u> and you stay for like a weekend and it's immersion (0.9) and then you also get like a Gaelic mentor so for me when I was like in Grade 8 I think and Grade 9 I would meet with xxx [mentor name] I'd meet with her every Tuesday after school and we would just do whatever!

Na Gaisgich Òga ('The Young Heroes') is a particular variation of the *Bun is Bàrr* master-apprentice scheme funded by the Office of Gaelic Affairs that aims to pair up native or fluent speakers with adolescent learners, in addition to *Gàidhlig aig Baile* residential weekend immersion programmes. This particular scheme is relatively new, but I was fortunate to interview several other recent graduates of *Na Gaisgich Òga*. Although both siblings in the above extract had studied some Gaelic in middle and high school, both identified undertaking this scheme as the crucial muda that led to their speaking the language. In the following two accounts, my interviewees explain how school teaching of Gaelic had not taught them the language, but that their fluency in the language had instead developed through the *Bun is Bàrr* and *Gàidhlig aig Baile* schemes. Specifically, my interviewees report utilising pedagogic techniques such as Total Immersion Plus (TIP) and Total Physical Response (TPR), adapted from other contexts, after completing formal education:

CBIF7	Uill ^thòisich mi san sgoil ach
	Well I ^started in school but
SD	Thòisich
	Yes
CBIF7	Bha e- **yeah** ((laughs)) cha do thog mi i! [...] Fhuair mi gu <u>robh</u> clasaichean a' dol air adhart [...] chaidh mi ann agus: (.) uh ^thàinig a h-uile sìon a dh'ionnsaich mi anns an sgoil air <u>ais</u> [...] Agus an uair sin fhuair mi àite ann am Bun is Bàrr (.) am pròpgram sin is [...] dh'ionnsaich mi a' <u>mhòr</u>-chuid de- dhan Ghàidhlig (1.2) roimhe sin uh anns a' chla- anns na clasaichean uh (.) Gàidhlig aig Baile- **Total Immersion Plus**
	It was- **yeah** *((laughs)) I didn't learn it! [...] I later learned there <u>were</u> classes happening [...and] I went and: (.) uh everything ^came <u>back</u> that*

SD	*I'd picked up in school [...] And then I got a place on* Bun is Bàrr *(.) that programme and [...] I learned <u>most</u> of my Gaelic (1.2) before now uh in the cla- in the* Gàidhlig aig Baile *classes-* **Total Immersion Plus** Yeah
CBIF7	**T-P-R Total Physical Response** [...] bidh e ag <u>obair</u> airson (.) <u>pàirt</u> dhiubh! [...] *it <u>works</u> for (.) some!*

CBIF2	Chaidh mi dhan Fhraing [aois naoi deug] is bha mi ann fad dà mhìos [...] is bha mi ag àdhainn- bha mi ag innse rium fhìn 'oh **wow** tha <u>cultar</u> aca- tha <u>cànan</u> aca' (.) **you know** [...] thòisich mi sa chlas seo ann an xxx ((Urban Cape Breton)) [...] bha an clas a' dol fad an latha Disathairne dìreach triop san t-seachdain Gàidhlig aig Baile no **TIP** mar a dh'abras iad [...] agus chaidh mi gu clas- gu cùrsa aig a' Cholaiste- Colaiste na Gàidhlig a mhair ^sia seachdainean [...] 's e- sin an <u>aon</u> chùrsa bogaidh a bh' ann riamh a mhair sia seachdainean *I went to France [at the age of nineteen] and I was there for two months[...] and I was tell- I was saying- I told myself 'oh **wow** they have a <u>culture</u>- they have a <u>language</u>' (.) **you know** [...] I started in this class in xxx ((Urban Cape Breton)) [...] the class ran all day Saturday just once a week* Gàidhlig aig Baile *or* **TIP** *as they call it [...] and I went to a class- to a course at the Gaelic College that lasted ^six weeks [...] that's the <u>only</u> immersion course they ever ran that lasted six weeks*

The key muda that interviewee CBIF2 identifies in inspiring her desire to become fluent in Gaelic was upon attaining adulthood and experiencing the culture and language of another society. In addition to the *Gàidhlig aig Baile* TIP mode of language learning, this interviewee also undertook immersion instruction at the Gaelic College in St Ann's, Cape Breton, a key site for the language learning of many other interviewees in Nova Scotia as well. Intriguingly, in the following account, participant ANTF2, who studied Gaelic in Scotland before undertaking further training in Nova Scotia, mentions some of the unintended consequences of this particular teaching methodology:

ANTF2	Rud eile an-seo tha (1.6) air sgàth 's gu bheil <u>glè</u> bheag de dhaoine ann a tha (.) a tha ag ionnsachadh no a' teagasg a' chànain- gu h-<u>àraidh</u> a' teagasg (.) 's e na beachdan <u>aca</u> agus dh'fhaoidte gur e beachdan (1.8) <u>pearsanta</u> a th' aca ach (0.9) air sgàth 's nach eil <u>mòran</u> dhiubh ann tha na beachdan pearsanta sin (1.2) um tha iad air an sgaoileadh mar- mar (shìol) [...] **so** 's toil leam am prionnsabal ((laughs)) a th' aig cridh' Gàidhlig aig Baile is toil leam pròrgramman (leithid) Bun is Bàrr ach dh'fhaotadh buaidh car neònach a bhith aca uaireannan

> *Another thing here is (1.6) because there are <u>very</u> few people who (.) who are learning or teaching the language- <u>especially</u> teaching (.) it's <u>their</u> opinions and it might just be their (1.8) <u>personal</u> opinions but (0.9) because there aren't <u>many</u> of them here those personal opinions (1.2) um they can be spread like- like (seed) [...] so I like the principle ((laughs)) that is at the heart of* Gàidhlig aig Baile *and I like programmes (like)* Bun is Bàrr *but they can have some slightly strange effects sometimes*

The spreading like 'seed' (*sìol*) of the relatively few Nova Scotia Gaelic instructors' 'personal opinions' (*beachdan pearsanta*) among learners in the province is identified by my interviewee here as one of the 'slightly strange' effects that the *Gàidhlig aig Baile* teaching model can have. The nature of some of these rather idiosyncratic attitudes is discussed in further detail below.

Whilst formalised opportunities for adult Gaelic immersion are somewhat limited in contemporary Scotland, the importance of such contexts for bringing new speakers to fluency was one particularly notable finding of my analysis. These contexts of linguistic and cultural immersion, whilst unfortunately becoming increasingly scarce in contemporary Scotland, may still be accessed even in Scotland's cities, as interviewees explain in the following two accounts. The first interviewee recalls his experiences learning Gaelic in pubs whilst a student in Edinburgh:

EDIM5   'S e an t-eadar-dhealachadh a bh' ann a <u>riamh</u> [nam oileanach] 's e gu robh mise cur (1.2) um: <u>tòrr</u> a bharrachd (1.1) ùine seachad anns na taighean seinnse ach bha mi **bruidhinn** ri Gàidheil
       The difference with me was that [as a student] I <u>always</u> spent (1.2) um: <u>loads</u> more (1.1) time in the pubs but I was <u>speaking</u> with Gaels

SD   Bha
       Yes

EDIM5   Um:: agus tha mi smaoineach' gun do rinn <u>sin</u> diofar agus dìreach a bhith (1.6) 'g èisteachd ri daoine a's- anns an taigh-seinnse no mun cuairt is rudan mar sin (.) um:: (1.1) tha thu ag ionnsachadh agus chan e: dìreach ionnsachadh às an leabhair mar gum biodh [...] uh: dìreach **prac-** dèanamh **practise** an uiread sa ghabhadh le- dìreach le bodaich 's: caillich [...] feumaidh tu a bhith (.) bruidhinn ri Gàidheil tha mi smaointinn
       Um:: and I think <u>that</u> made a difference and just (1.6) listening to people in the- in the pub or out and about and things like that (.) um:: (1.1) you're learning and it's not just book learning as it were [...] uh: just **prac- practising** *as much as was possible with- just with older people [...] you have to (.) speak to Gaels I think*

EDIM6   Bha mi ag obair ann am Fìobha [...] um agus um: an-sin smaoinich mi 'Uill 's dòcha gum bi mi ag ionnsachadh (.) Gàidhlig' [...] chunna' mi ann am pàipear Feasgair Dhùn Èideann [...] bha sanas ann mu dheidhinn um (.) buidheann (.) uh: a chruinneachadh gach feasgar- gach um- gach Diardaoin tha mi smaoineachadh
    I was working in Fife [...] um and um: then I thought 'Well perhaps I'll learn Gaelic' [...] I saw in the Edinburgh Evening News [...] there was a notice about um (.) a group (.) uh: that met every- every Thursday I think
SD   Uh huh
EDIM6   Uh agus uh 's e- 's e uh cearcall ^còmhraidh agus cha do stad mi bhon a sin!
    Uh and uh it- it was a ^conversation circle and I never looked back!

For both speakers above, immersing themselves in Gaelic conversation in Edinburgh formed the basis for their attainment of fluency in the language. When I spoke to interviewee EDIM5, he was in his mid-twenties, recalling recent memories of university, whilst EDIM6 was in his late eighties, describing events fifty years previously. Scotland's capital, and its resident population of native Gaels who have been drawn to the city for centuries, have provided an important platform for the instruction and creation of new speakers. For others, growing up in the Lowlands with a close family connection to the language allowed for substantial Gaelic language socialisation and immersion, albeit in ways rather different to learning on a parent's knee in early childhood. The following participant explains how she and her mother, a native Gaelic speaker who lacked confidence to speak it to her in childhood, attended Gaelic classes together to (re)learn the language when she was a teenager:

GLAF4   Bha cailleach ann [...] 's bha ise dèanamh um clasaichean Gàidhlig ((sa choimhearsnachd)) [...] chaidh **Mum** dhan fheadhainn- dìreach son an cothrom a bhith bruidhinn- sin a bha i ag iarraidh le daoine aig an robh Gàidhlig is chaidh mise dhan fheadhainn airson (1.1) daoine- luchd-ionnsachaidh so bha sinn dol ann=
    *There was an old lady [...] and she did um Gaelic classes ((in the community)) [...] **Mum** went to some- just to get the chance to speak- that's what she wanted with people who could speak Gaelic and I went to some for (1.1) people- for learners so we went=*
SD   =Sheadh=
    =Yeah=
GLAF4   =Ach às dèidh greis (1.2) ((sighs)) bha mi ann le daoine aig nach robh facal [...] chaidh mi dhan chlas aig **Mum** 's bha sinn dol ann ^còmhla 's bha e cho:: snog! Aig a' cheann thall bha sinn dìreach a' dol dhan taigh aice 's: (0.9) gabhail dramaichean is ceipearan 's ga bruidhinn [...] 's an uair sin chaidh mi- thàinig mi gu Oilthigh xxx ((Galltachd)) 's bha cothrom agam air Gàidhlig

=*But after a while (1.2) ((sighs)) I was in with people who couldn't speak a word [...] I went to* **Mum***'s class instead and we went ^together and it was so:: nice! In the end we would just go to her house and (0.9) have drams and sandwiches and speak [...] and then I went- I came to xxx University ((in the Lowlands)) and I had the opportunity [to speak] Gaelic*

Whilst, in contrast to Nova Scotia, immersion opportunities that explicitly connect learners to native speakers for purposes of Gaelic acquisition are not generally funded formally by Scottish policymakers at present, seeking out such opportunities voluntarily was described by many new speakers in that context as having been vital to their learning Gaelic. Encouraging the development of similar programmes in Scotland will be an important policy objective for increasing speaker numbers in coming years.

University and adult study muda

A second crucial muda that interviewees in both research contexts described as having been instructive to their Gaelic acquisition was that of university or private study in early adulthood, without full immersion in the language. I draw attention in this section to discourses Nova Scotian and Scottish speakers produced in respect of this muda in determining their future linguistic practices. As Nova Scotian interviewees describe in the following two extracts, formal study of Gaelic at university constituted a crucial moment in their becoming new speakers of Gaelic, opening doors to their future use of the language in various different settings:

ANTM2   Cha robh (0.8) clasaichean aige [Ollamh] airson na Gàidhlig ach bha clasaichean aige son (.) òrain Ghàidhlig [...] agus uh (1.2) uh (.) thòisich mi air a' Ghàidhlig an uair sin agus leis gu robh mi a' dol air adhart bhithinn na b' fheàrr 's na b' fheàrr [...] agus rachainn dhachaigh (.) aig deireadh na seachdain (x) agus thighinn a-mach às an eaglais mar a bhios iad ag ràdhainn sa Bheurla **'they- they were coming out of the woodwork'** gam ionnsaigh agus a' bruidhinn na Gàidhlig rium

> *[The professor] didn't (0.8) run Gaelic classes at the time but he ran classes in (.) Gaelic songs [...] and uh (1.2) uh (.) I started Gaelic then and as I was going forward with it I got better and better [...] and I'd go home (.) at the weekends (x) and I'd come out of the church and as they say in English* **'they- they were coming out of the woodwork'** *to speak Gaelic to me*

ANTM7   Aig Colaiste na Gàidhlig dh'ionnsaich mi (1.4) a' phìob agus bha- bha clas Gàidhlig ann [...] cha do dh'ionnsaich mi mòran ach dh'ionnsaich mi

	facal no dhà [...] agus nuair a cheumnaich mi às an àrd-sgoil thàinig mi gu xxx ((oilthigh ann an Alba Nuadh))

> At the Gaelic College I learned (1.4) the bagpipes and there- there was a Gaelic class [...] I didn't learn much but I learned a word or two [...] and when I graduated from high school I came to xxx ((Nova Scotian university))

SD Agus an e Ceiltis a rinn thu?
> And you did Celtic Studies?

ANTM7 'S e [...] agus an uair sin chaidh mi gu xxx ((oilthigh eile)) son MA is PhD ann an Ceiltis an-sin
> Yes [...] and then I went to xxx ((another university)) for an MA and PhD in Celtic Studies

While formal college or university study within the province was less frequently mentioned by Nova Scotian participants than those based in Scotland (see below), it clearly formed an important social and linguistic muda for those who had undertaken different levels of higher education relation to Gaelic.

In Scotland, by contrast, formal study in a university or other adult education setting was frequently referred to by research participants as a key moment in their linguistic trajectories toward Gaelic acquisition. As interviewees explain in the following two extracts, the decision to take tentative first steps on the journey to learning Gaelic often began with the choice to undertake self-led or distance study of the language:

SD Cuin a thòisich thu Gàidhlig ionnsaschadh?
> When did you start learning Gaelic

EDIF4 Um (.) tha mi a' smaointinn gur ann ann an (1.1) **1997** no '98 [...] chaidh mi gu clas uh aig (0.9) uh clasaichean fosgailte - clasaichean oidhche um [...] an uair sin rinn mi ^Higher uh le um: **distance learning** [...] Bha mi ag obair sa xxx ((roinn phoblach)) [...] bha xxx fhèin a' cur leasannan air dòigh don luchd-obrach [...] bha mi air tòiseachadh mus d'fhuair mi an obair sin **just as a passing whim- 'why don't I try this?'**
> Um (.) I think it was in (1.1) **1997** or '98 [...] I went to a class uh at (0.9) uh open classes- evening classes um [...] then I did ^Higher uh with um: **distance learning** [...] I was working ((in the public sector)) [... and] xxx were offering classes to staff [...] so I had started before I got that job **just as a passing whim- 'why don't I try this?'**

SD Tha thu air a bhith ag ionnsachadh na Gàidhlig a-nis airson::=
> You've been learning Gaelic now for::=

EDIM3 =Uill uh trì bliadhnaichean
> =Well uh three years

SD	Trì [[bliadhnaichean]
	Three [[years]
EDIM3	[[Seo an ceathramh] bliadhna [...] tha mi a' dèanamh rannsachadh tro mheadhan na Gàidhlig [...] bha ùidh agam uh (.) anns a- anns a' chànan fhèin [...] bha a h-uile caraidean [sic] agam a' dèanamh- dèanamh Gàidhlig [...] rinn mi clasaichean a' chiad bhliadhna agus rinn mi **auditing** am bliadhna às dèidh
	*[[This is the fourth] year [...] I'm doing research through the medium of Gaelic [...] I was interested in uh (.) in the- in the language itself [...] all my friends were doing- doing Gaelic [...] I did classes in first year and did **auditing** [of Gaelic] the year after*

For other interviewees, the decision to initiate Gaelic study in a university setting, or to undertake self-led learning in early adulthood, stemmed from somewhat political interests, albeit not necessarily defined by party political allegiances:

GLAF1	Chunna' mi ((sighs)) sanas airson **PhD** a dhèanamh an-seo [... bha mi] a' smaoineachadh 'oh (1.6) **d'you know** tha Gàidhlig agus Gaeilge- tha iad gu math coltach' [...] agus 's dòcha gu robh **kind of aspect** rud beag (2.7) rud beag **nationalist** [...] gu robh ùidh agam (.) anns an (1.4) ceangal eadar (1.5) an cànan (.) agus cultar na h-Èireann 's dòcha
	*I saw ((sighs)) an advert to do a **PhD** here [... I was] thinking 'oh (1.6) **d'you know** Gaelic and Irish- they're quite similar' [...] and perhaps there was a **kind of aspect** of it being (2.7) a little bit **nationalist** [...] that I was interested (.) in (1.4) the linkage between (1.5) the language (.) and culture of Ireland perhaps*
SD	So thòisich thu air a' Ghàidhlig ann am xxx ((Europe)) fhèin [...] cionnas a rinn thu a' chùis?
	So you started Gaelic in xxx ((Europe)) [...] how did you manage it?
GLAM5	Bha sin dìreach air-loidhne le caraid dhomh [...] siud far a ghabh mi ùidh gu ceart ann a bhith ga h-ionnsachadh (.) fhad 's a bha mi fhathast aig an oilthigh [...] Às dèidh an reifreinn bha mi ann an Èirinn aig àm na bliadhn' ^ùir' le caraidean is uh: (.) bha sinn aig taigh-seinnse [...] is a h-uile duine bruidhinn Gaeilge ann
	That was just online with a friend of mine [...] that was where I properly took and interest in learning it (.) while I was still at university [...] After the ((2014 independence)) referendum I was in Ireland around the new year with friends and uh: (.) we were at the pub [...] and everyone was speaking Irish
SD	Sheadh
	Yeah

GLAM5   Is thug sin orm dìreach- bha mi cho brònach co-dhiù le toradh an reifreinn [...] sin nuair a chuir mi romham (.) a bhith fileanta sa Ghàidhlig- cho luath sa ghabhas! ((laughs))
    And that just inspired me- I was so sad at the result of the referendum anyway [...] that's when I decided (.) to become fluent in Gaelic- as quickly as possible! ((laughs))

'Nationalist' political motivations and varying connections to Ireland are both invoked in the two above extracts. In the first account, speaker GLAF01 refers to an interest, having grown up in the Republic of Ireland, in connections between Irish language and culture, which eventually found expression in her taking up PhD study in Scottish Gaelic, moving to Scotland and learning the language. For speaker GLAM05, by contrast, the motivation to acquire Gaelic was linked explicitly to the result of the 2014 referendum on Scottish independence and, ironically, his experience of being in Ireland and hearing Irish speakers conversing shortly afterwards. In the following account, the *Teach Yourself Gaelic* workbook constituted the initial step toward attaining fluency in the language, as was the case for me (see Chapter 3):

INVM1   Dar a bha mi anns an oilthigh (1.2) um: (.) eh thòisich mi air an ^dàrna bliadhna 's dòcha an ((Oilthigh Gallta)) agus (.) thòisich mi a' dol gu clasaichean [...] chleachd mi an eh: an cothrom sin airson: leasan ann an **Teach Yourself Gaelic** a dhèanamh a h-uile latha
    =When I was in university (1.2) um: (.) eh I started maybe in ^second year at ((Lowland university)) and (.) I started going to classes [...] I used the eh: the opportunity to do a **Teach Yourself Gaelic** *lesson every day*
SD   Mm hmm
INVM1   Agus dol tro na h-eacarsaichean [...] sin (.) a thug dhomh (0.9) sgrìobhadh agus leughadh
    And going through the exercises [...] that's (.) what taught me (0.9) writing and reading ((in Gaelic))

It is interesting to note, therefore, that private study of the language whilst at university was an important element for several Scottish interviewees (others not discussed here also recalled similar learning trajectories in interviews) and was similarly so for a rather smaller group of Nova Scotians. A further crucial subcategory of the university or adult study *muda* discussed in this section was study, by both Nova Scotian and Scottish respondents, at Sabhal Mòr Ostaig.

It is perhaps surprising, given the attention paid frequently in Nova Scotia to the nativeness of Gaelic in discourses around the province's own Gaelic community since the eighteenth century (see Chapter 3, above) that many of the most proficient and committed new speakers I met there had studied in Scotland. In particular, over a third of my interviewees in Nova Scotia described their experiences of adult study at Sabhal Mòr Ostaig, on the Isle of Skye's south-western Sleat peninsula, as having been especially instructive for their Gaelic acquisition and socialisation. As speakers ANTM1 and CBIF5 indicate in the two following accounts, while self-study in Nova Scotia may have opened initial doors in the language learning journey, it was study at Sabhal Mòr Ostaig that formed the first major muda on their roads to fluency in Gaelic:

ANTM1	Chanainnsa gur e fèin-oideachas cha mhòr a bh' ann […] thug sin seachad dhomh-fhìn gu ìre- uill (1.4) uill gu ìre fileantais […] chaidh mi (1.3) a dh'Alba (.) dhan Eilean Sgitheanach
	I would say it was mostly self study […] that brought me to a level of- well (1.4) well a level of fluency […] I then went (1.3) to Scotland (.) to the Isle of Skye
SD	Dhan [[t-Sabhal Mhòr?]
	To [[Sabhal Mòr?]
ANTM1	[[Dhan (x)] agus ghabh mi nam oileanach san t-Sabhal Mhòr […] ann an '87 agus bha ^ìre mhòr (1.4) ^ìre (1.6) <u>cuimseach</u> math de dh'fhileantas agamsa
	[[To (x)] and I enrolled as a student at Sabhal Mòr […] in '87 and I reached a high ^level (1.4) a ^level (1.6) of <u>reasonable</u> fluency
CBIF5	Chaidh mi dhan t-Sabhal Mhòr (.) nuair a bha mi ochd bliadhna deug
	I went to Sabhal Mòr (.) when I was eighteen
SD	Mm hmm
CBIF5	Agus bha mi a' smaointinn gu- gu robh- gum biodh mo cheann dìreach ga sgobadh
	And I thought that- that- that my head would just burst
SD	((laughs))
CBIF5	Ris an t-<u>uabhas</u> a bha agam ri ionnsachadh ach bha e cho <u>nàdarra</u>- tha mi smaointinn gu robh na stuthan bunaiteach agamsa […] Bha mi ann ceithir bliadhnaichean [… ach] feumaidh mi aideachadh nach robh mi <u>uabh</u>asach fhèin sgoileireil aig an àm!
	With the <u>amount</u> that I had to learn but it was so <u>natural</u>- I think I had the basics […] I was there for four years […but] I must admit I wasn't <u>terribly</u> studious at the time!

For Nova Scotian new speakers of these two individuals' profile – now aged in their 50s – study at Scotland's Gaelic college was generally self-funded. For interviewee ANTM6 in the following account, by contrast, publicly funded exchange and study scholarships, which have been developed in recent years as a consequence of official support, enabled him to take up a place to further develop Gaelic language skills at Sabhal Mòr Ostaig:

> ANTM6   Tha mi air a bhith fuireach ann an Alba fad (1.2) bliadhna- am bliadhna sa chaidh
> *I lived in Scotland for (1.2) a year- this past year*
> SD   O a bheil? Càite robh thu stèidhichte?
> *Oh really? Where were you based?*
> ANTM6   Sabhal Mòr air an **exchange** [...] thòisich mi ann an clas ann an Oilthigh- ((Alba Nuadh)) (0.8) bha mi ann am prògram diofraichte
> *Sabhal Mòr [Ostaig] on the **exchange** [...] I started learning in class at ((a Nova Scotian)) university (0.8) in a different degree program*
> SD   Seadh (.) an do chòrd Sabhal Mòr riut?
> *Okay (.) did you enjoy Sabhal Mòr?*
> ANTM6   Chòrd **yeah** [...] cha robh Gàidhlig (0.6) math [*sic*] agam nuair a thòisich mi
> *Yes **yeah** [...] I didn't have (0.6) good Gaelic when I started there*

Whilst the mudes that most Nova Scotian new speakers reported as their first encounter Gaelic were generally within the province, the significance of Sabhal Mòr Ostaig as a site of language instruction for so many was an unexpected finding. In Scotland itself, by contrast, the college has long formed one of the most important contexts in the whole country for Gaelic learning and socialisation (cf. McLeod 2020: 330).

For over half of the interviewees from Scotland, study at Sabhal Mòr Ostaig – whether on campus or via distance learning – was reported to have formed a crucial muda in their breakthrough to fluency in Gaelic, with major consequences for their future use of Gaelic in their day-to-day lives. It is perhaps also worth noting at this point that in Scotland, new speakers of Gaelic tend to come from diverse national backgrounds and, for many, the decision to learn Gaelic after their arrival in Scotland reflected various factors. As discussed further in Chapter 3, ethnolinguistic or heritage identity in the language was rarely described as a significant motivating factor among Scottish new speakers. For speaker EDIF5, in the following account, studying at Sabhal Mòr Ostaig for a year was a transformative, if sometimes difficult experience:

> EDIF5   Thòisich mi ri Gàidhlig ionnsachadh aig Oilthigh xxx ((Galltachd)) ach bha agam ri tilleadh agus crìoch a chur air mo cheum [...] ann an ^2008 agus thàinig mi (.) um (.) gu Sabhal Mòr Ostaig airson bliadhna
> *I started learning Gaelic at ((Lowland)) University but I had to return and complete my degree programme [...] in 2008 I came (.) um (.) to Sabhal Mòr Ostaig for a year*

[...]
SD   Ciamar a chòrd a' bhliadhna air an Eilean Sgitheanach riut?
            How did you enjoy your year in Skye?
EDIF5   ^Um:: (1.5) ^chòrd e rium ann an grunn dòighean [... ach] anns an ^fharsaingeachd dh'fhàg e (.) blas car searbh um: (.) na mo bheul [...] 's e briseadh-dùil a bh' ann (.) ach dh'<u>ionnsaich</u> mi Gàidhlig
            ^Um:: (1.5) I ^enjoyed it in some ways [... but] in ^general it left a rather bitter taste um: (.) in the mouth [...] it was a disappointment (.) but I <u>learned</u> Gaelic

For the above speaker, a sense of negative affect was betrayed by her high intonation, elongated 'um' and extended pause in response to my question. The interviewee then answered that, while she enjoyed the year in Skye in some ways, the experience of the college was generally disappointing (although she successfully learned Gaelic).

Many participants who spent time at Sabhal Mòr Ostaig had been there for at least a full year; for the following interviewee, a summer spent immersed in successive levels of the college's week-long summer courses after leaving school formed the platform for his further study of Gaelic there and at university in the Lowlands:

GLAM2   An àite siathamh bliadhna àrd-sgoile a dhèanamh (.) chaidh mi:: (0.9) eh fhuair mi na **Highers** a bha a dhìth orm anns a' chòigeamh bliadhna fhaighinn a-steach dhan oilthigh (.) chuir mi seachad an sàmhradh aig Sabhal Mòr air na cùrsaichean goirid
            *Instead of doing sixth year in high school (.) I went:: (0.9) eh I got the **Highers** I needed in fifth year to get into university (.) I spent the summer at Sabhal Mòr Ostaig doing the short courses*
SD   Sheadh
            Okay
GLAM2   Agus fhuair mi àite an uair sin air an **HNC** (.) Gàidhlig is sgilean conaltraidh [...] bha mi ann aon bhliadhna 's an uair sin chaidh mi a xxx ((oilthigh)) (.) rinn mi ceum (1.3) eh Gàidhlig agus Eachdraidh
            *And I got a place on the Gaelic and Communication Skills **HNC** [Higher National Certificate] [...] I was there for one year and then I went to xxx ((university)) (.) I did a degree (1.3) in Gaelic and History*

For Scottish-based speakers who have more recently begun courses at Scotland's Gaelic College, greater opportunities for distance learning and part-time study allows for participation in Gaelic courses whilst also working elsewhere in Scotland. Interviewee GLAM3 describes such an experience below:

SD	Tha thu nad oileanach aig astar an-dràsta aig [[Sabhal Mòr Ostaig]
	Just now you're a distance student at [[Sabhal Mòr Ostaig]
GLAM4	[[Aig Sabhal Mòr] Ostaig- **okay so** uill ((sighs)) thèid mi air ais **so** 's e xxx ((obair chruthachail)) a th' annam [...] agus sinne a' tadhal air na h-eileanan air saor-làithean <u>gach</u> bliadhna (.) bha sinn eòlach air (1.8) daoine a bha an sàs ann an Gàidhlig [...] tha ùidh tòrr nas motha agam air (3.3) cor a' chànain [...] is mi nam neach na Beurla aona- chànanach- <u>cho</u>:: **entitled**!
	*[[At Sabhal Mòr] Ostaig- **okay so** well ((sighs)) I'll go back a bit **so** I'm a ((creative professional)) [...] we would visit the isles on holiday <u>every</u> year (.) and came to know (1.8) people involved in Gaelic [...] I became much more interested in (3.3) the state of the language [...] as a monoglot English speaker I felt so:: **entitled**!*

As a response to his becoming more aware of Gaelic and its decline through yearly holidays to the islands, and to his sense of discomfort as an 'entitled' monolingual English speaker, this participant enrolled on a distance course at Sabhal Mòr Ostaig. Varied experiences of the college are reported by Scottish new speakers in my sample, but all are unanimous in reporting the importance of their study there in acquiring Gaelic to fluency. It is very telling that a third of Nova Scotians and half of Scots in my interview corpus reported Sabhal Mòr as such an important site for their instruction and socialisation in Gaelic, within the wider 'adult study' muda outlined above. In many ways, the adult study muda discussed in this section constituted the first opportunity many new speakers had to engage with the wider community, and in that sense was not restricted to the formal education sphere. For others, however, especially in the Nova Scotian context, exposure to Gaelic in the home and community formed the earliest stage of their Gaelic acquisition.

Diverse and distinctive experiences of new Gaelic speakers in both research contexts are thus recounted by interviewees. The sociolinguistic mudes and life stages to have had major and beneficial consequences for new speakers' Gaelic language learning in both contexts range from certain amounts of community and family socialisation (in Nova Scotia) to immersion education (in Scotland). These two contexts of language socialisation form a key distinction between Nova Scotian and Scottish research participants. Conversely, extra-curricular immersion experiences in the language and enrolment on courses at Sabhal Mòr Ostaig each formed sociolinguistic experiences that were common to learners and new speakers in both contexts. The significance of Sabhal Mòr, in particular, for informing new speakers' learning and socialisation experiences, is a relatively understudied area of Gaelic language policy and planning. In general, it is noteworthy that sociolinguistic mudes in adolescence and adulthood were recounted by majorities of participants in both Nova Scotia and Scotland as being particularly formative, notwithstanding the rather few individuals to have acquired some Gaelic in childhood through community and education.

'Blas', accent aim and dialectal diversity in Nova Scotia and Scotland

One concept discussed previously in respect of new Gaelic speakers in Scotland is that of *blas*, or accent in Gaelic, which, it has been suggested, is often regarded by learners and new speakers as a guiding motivation in language learning aspirations (McLeod, O'Rourke and Dunmore 2014; Nance et al. 2015). To have a good *blas* in Gaelic refers not only to targeting nativelike Gaelic phonology and pronunciation, but to perceptions of 'naturalness', flow and fluency in the language. A large part of the concept's mobilisation in new speaker discourses nevertheless relates explicitly to producing Gaelic with an accent that reflects traditional dialects of particular areas where Gaelic use may have been relatively common until recently, in both Nova Scotia and Scotland. As will be demonstrated, contrasting evaluations of *blas* and what the notion signifies are apparent in the two contexts under investigation. We may first consider how the notion of *blas* is deployed by Nova Scotian new speakers in their discussion of local dialects (*dualchainntean*) and accents of Gaelic. For the following speaker, local attention to such considerations at first appeared rather quaint:

ANTF2 Bidh iad a-mach air dualchainnt uill (.) tha mi air cluinntinn gu bheil (daoine) a' smaoineachadh air dualchainnt Ceap Breatainn a-nis [...] 'Oh ann an Ceap Breatainn bidh sinn ag ràdh blah blah' ach chan ann ann an Ceap Breatainn uill (1.2) 'ann an Ceap Breatainn'- tha sin a' ciallachadh dè? [...] Ach tha mi air mothachadh gu bheil iad uh (3.2) sean-fhasanta ((laughs)) ann an dòigh [...] Chan eil fhios'am dè (2.9) dè an seòrsa (1.0) dè an t-amas [blas-chainnt] a bu chòir a bhith againn

  They do go on about the dialect well (.) I've heard *what people* think *is Cape Breton dialect now [...] 'Oh in Cape Breton we say this blah blah blah' but it's not in Cape Breton and well (1.2) 'in Cape Breton'- that means what exactly? [...] But I've noticed that they are uh [...] old fashioned ((laughs)) in a way [...] I don't personally know what (2.9) what sort of (1.0) what [accent] aim we should have*

The attention that local speakers appear to pay to dialectal and traditional features in local spoken Gaelic is thus regarded by the above speaker as rather old-fashioned (*'sean-fhasanta'*), though she admits to not personally having a clear idea of what kind of Gaelic to emulate in her own pronunciation, having recently arrived from Scotland. By contrast, the following speaker has a clearer impression of both the importance of local dialects for new speakers generally and for his own accent aim:

ANTM2	'S e rud a rinn- (.) tha sinne gu mòr air na dualchainntean a chumail suas an-seo
	The thing we've done- (.) we've really maintained the dialects here
SD	Gu deimhinne
	Certainly
ANTM2	Agus (.) cha chreid mi gu bheil sin cho cudromach (.) thall san t-seann dùthaich agus (0.8) tha mise (mothachail) air cho cudromach 's a tha e dar a bhios (.) luchd-labhairt dùthchasach againn son sin
	And (.) I don't think that's so important (.) over in the old country [i.e., Scotland] and (0.8) I'm (mindful) of just how important it is when we have (.) traditional native speakers for that
SD	Hmm
ANTM2	**Like** bha e duilich dhomh dar a bha mi a' toiseachadh (1.2) air sàilleabh 's gun abrainn (.) abair rud Leòdhasach
	***Like** it was difficult when I started (1.2) because I'd say (.) something say in a Lewis way*
SD	Sheadh
	Yes
ANTM2	No rud Sgitheanach agus bha e duilich gu leòr oir cha robh iadsan cleachte ri luchd-ionnsachaidh na Gàidhlig […] nì mi seo mar eisempleir ((stilted, robotic voice)): 'You can un-der-stand every-thing I'm say-ing <u>now</u> but you would-n't want me to talk like this all-day'
	Or a Skye way and it was pretty difficult because they weren't used to hearing Gaelic learners […] I'll show you an example ((robotic voice)): 'You can un-der-stand every-thing I'm say-ing <u>now</u> but you would-n't want me to talk like this all-day'

The phrase *'an t-seann dùthaich'* ('the old country') is commonly used in Nova Scotia Gaelic to describe Scotland. The above speaker describes perceived dialectal divergences between varieties of Gaelic that are still relatively commonly used (and thus taught) in Scotland, such as Lewis and Skye Gaelic, and the traditional dialects that were maintained through community use in Nova Scotia. Although not described as incomprehensible to traditional L1 speakers locally, the variety of Gaelic he had acquired (largely through study and travel in Scotland) is likened to a rather stilted, robotic or computer-assisted accent, in the example English sentence he produces. In the oppositional dynamic envisaged in this example, L1 traditional speakers' dialects are constructed, by implication, as natural and organic, rather than stilted or mechanical as in the robot-voiced utterance at the end of the excerpt. In the following extract, upon asking an adolescent new speaker about their future plans to visit the Scotland for Gaelic learning opportunities, the issue of dialectal divergences is again foregrounded:

SD	Could you imagine travelling to the old country- **dhan t-seann dhùthaich? Airson beagan Gàidhlig ionnsachadh no a chleachdadh?**
	...to the old country? To learn or to use some more Gaelic?
ANTM3	Uh yeah I have thought about it
SD	Hmm
ANTM3	My only problem is that- is just like the different dialect of Gaelic
SD	Yeah
ANTM3	So I'd have to translate it to my dialect [...] It's like- it's <u>really</u> similar but it's not quite the same so it's just kind of (necessary) to me [to translate]

Unfamiliarity with alternative varieties to those most commonly spoken and learned in Nova Scotia (such as in and around Mabou, in western Cape Breton) was described by several Nova Scotian participants as a source of anxiety when attempting conversation with Gaelic speakers from Scotland. A handful of features in the spoken Gaelic of L1 and L2 speakers in Nova Scotia do indeed mark out local varieties of Gaelic as distinctive, since historically these features were widespread in Gaelic dialects which are now highly obsolescent in Scotland. One particular feature, which has acquired the status as something of a shibboleth, distinguishing Gaelic as spoken in Nova Scotia from its counterpart varieties in Scotland, is the pronunciation of broad, 'dark' [L] as /w/ in local speech forms. Historically, this feature of dark l-vocalisation was widespread in Gaelic varieties in and around Lochaber and the 'Small Isles' of Eigg, Rum and Canna.

SD	An e sin an seòrs' Ghàidhlig a bha thu airson togail? Fhios'ad blas-chainnt Ceap Breatainn?
	Was that the kind of Gaelic you wanted to learn? You know the Cape Breton accent?
HALF3	Lochabar ann an dòigh? Um:: ^uill (.) bidh mise ga cleachdadh [...] Dh'ionnsaich mi /L/ agus tha mi feuchainn ri /w/ a chleachdadh [...] agus 'às deoghaidh' an àite 'às dèidh' is stuth mar sin
	Lochaber in a way? Um [...] ^well (.) I do use that accent [...] I learned /L/ and I try to use /w/ [...] and 'a:fter' instead of 'after' and things like that

The importance of learning to use features of this kind as part of local accent aim, and thereby maintaining local aspects of linguistic diversity and distinctiveness, was frequently described by Nova Scotian new speakers in relation to their wider Gaelic acquisition activity. As will be seen below, such accent aims pertaining to traditional varieties were rarely expressed in Scotland. A perceived proliferation in opportunities for learning Gaelic, including via internet apps and smart phones, was described by several Nova Scotian new speakers, albeit the forms of Gaelic available for study using such methods were not generally felt to accommodate Nova Scotian dialects:

CBIF1	There's <u>so</u> much available online and there's <u>so</u> many apps now
SD	Yeah
CBIF1	It's not always the <u>dialect</u> (.) of here [...] That's not a big (.) deal but that comes from being more fluent too ((laughs)) right? [...] Like I think that a stumbling block for people here is the dialect that should be used for certain areas [...] it doesn't <u>need</u> to be a stumbling block [...] I never heard my grandmother speak well so when I'm trying to- to choose a di- ((laughs)) <u>choose</u> a [[dialect]
SD	[[Choose] a dialect yeah ((laughs))
CBIF1	Right? I'm kind of between Glendale- **Bràigh na h-Aibneadh**

The above speaker highlights the importance locally of 'choosing' an appropriate dialectal variety to learn in Nova Scotia, which, she observed, can become a 'stumbling block' for learners who lack an immediate familial connection or memory of the kind of Gaelic which elderly relatives may have spoken in their youth. For other Nova Scotian interviewees, however, any potential obstacles to learning Gaelic presented by issues of dialectal diversity were sidestepped fairly easily. By choosing not to aim for any particular local variety or accent of Gaelic, such speakers tended to aim for a generalised Nova Scotia Gaelic accent. As the following two participants exemplify, individuals whose main conversational opportunities derived from networks of other L2 users tended not to claim to speak with a particularly traditional, Cape Breton–influenced accent:

CBIF4	Bha sinn a' coinneachadh gach seachdain dìreach airson Gàidhlig a bhruidhinn ach bha e doirbh gu leòr airson dìreach ga chumail sa Ghàidhlig [...] **so** sin an sgeul **so** sin as coireach nach eil dualchainnt (1.3) gu math (.) Ceap Breatannach agamsa 's e seòrsa dualchainnt luchd-ionnsachaidh a th' agam! ((laughs))
	We would meet every week just to speak Gaelic but it was quite hard to just keep it in Gaelic [...] so that's the story so that's why I don't have (1.3) much (.) of a Cape Breton accent it's sort of a learner dialect that I speak! ((laughs))
SD	Fhad 's a bha thu a' feuchainn ri Gàidhlig a thogail 's ionnsachadh an robh thu ag amas air dualchainnt (.) shònraichte? An e dualchainnt Cheap Breatainn a bh' ann?
	While you were trying to learn Gaelic did you aim for any particular (.) dialect? Was it a Cape Breton dialect?
ANTM1	'S e rud (èibhinn) (.) gus an fhìrinn innse cha robh mi uh (1.1) a' toirt (urram) gu dualchainnt sònraichte (.) dìreach an dual- an dualchainnt a

bha cumanta am me- am measg nan daoine ris a bha mi bruidhinn [...] B' e dualchainnt air <u>leth</u> fhèin neònach a's na: (1.1) a's:: (1.2) a's na sgìrean sin às an tàinig Gàidheil Cheap Breatainn- leithid Moideart far nach eil Gàidhlig ga bruidhinn <u>idir</u> an latha an-diugh

> It's a funny thing (.) to tell the truth I wasn't uh (1.1) interested in a particular dialect (.) just the dial- dialect that was common amo- amongst the people I was speaking to [...] It was a <u>very</u> strange dialect in the: (1.1) in the:: (1.2) in those areas where the Cape Breton Gaels came from- like Moideart where Gaelic isn't spoken <u>at all</u> these days

A lack of any specific target traditional variety in new speakers' accent aim was only reported by a relative minority of Nova Scotian interviewees, however. Whilst a reported tendency instead to have acquired a generalised Nova Scotia Gaelic accent – or even a 'learners' dialect', as the first of the above participants indicated – was professed by some speakers, the majority in Nova Scotia attempted to acquire features of specific local speech forms through interactions with the remaining L1 speakers or fluent L2 users. As will be demonstrated below, we may contrast this general pattern with the Scottish context, in which the reverse of these patterns was identified.

Among Scotland-based new speakers, discourses pertaining to concrete attempts to acquire specific dialects or accents of Gaelic were notable by their general scarcity in interviews. The two following extracts exemplify the interest that a small minority of speakers expressed in learning to use forms of language associated with particular dialects. Whilst demonstrating the interest they (previously) had in learning dialectal varieties, both interviewees problematised an emphasis on the importance of such varieties at the expense of wider comprehension:

INVM1	'S e Gàidhlig Bhaideanach a bha mi cuimseachadh air [...] ach chan urrainn dhomh is cha b' urrainn dhomh aig an àm a ràdh gun robh mi ag ionnsachadh dualchainnt ud
	It was Badenoch Gaelic that I was aiming for [...] but I can't now and couldn't at the time say that I was really learning that dialect
SD	An robh thu ag amas air sin?
	Were you aiming for that?
INVM1	Oh aidh (.) ach bhiodh e do-dhèanta is bha mi mothachail air sin ach bha e cudromach dhomh [...] <u>tha</u> e cudromach dhomh gu bheil corra (.) comharra na mo chainnt
	Oh aye (.) but it would have been impossible and I was mindful of that but it was important to me [...] it <u>is</u> important to me that there are a few (.) signs [of that dialect] in my speech
SD	Hmm

INVM1	((laughing)) Dhòmhsa co-dhiù ged nach eil e buileach follaiseach do dhaoine eile is ged nach eil e fìor ach ((laughing)) dhòmhsa tha iad nan comharra! Dhan fheadhainn sin a tha air Gàidhlig Chomhghall ionnsachadh [...] 's e faoineas a th' ann gu ìre
	((laughing))) To me anyway even though it's not entirely obvious to other people and it's not true but ((laughing)) to me they are signs! [Also] for those people that have learned Cowal Gaelic [...] it's silliness in a way
GLAF3	Bhon (.) **like** (2.3) fiù 's eh leis gun do dh'ionnsaich mi Gàidhlig Earra-Ghàidheal
	*Since (.) **like** (2.3) even eh though I learned Argyll Gaelic*
SD	Hmm
GLAF3	Bha daoine mar 'carson a tha- chan eil- cha bhi daoine a' ^<u>bruidhinn</u> Gàidhlig Earra-Ghàidheal!' Agus uill bidh [[**actually**]
	People were like 'why are you- there aren't- people don't ^<u>speak</u> Argyll Gaelic!' And well they do [[actually]
SD	[[Bidh] **yeah**
	*[[Yes] **yeah***
GLAF3	Chan eil mòran ach bidh aig- fiù 's ann an Lios Mòr ann an (0.8) Ìle [...] ach chan eil e cho làidir agam 's a bha e air sgàth 's gu bheil mi air a bhith ag obair le (1.1) Gàidheil às àiteachan eadar-[[dhealaichte]
	Not many but they do- even in Lismore and (0.8) Islay [...] but I can't speak that way as much as I could because I have been working with (1.1) Gaels from other [[places]
SD	[[Sin agad e]
	That's it
GLAF3	Agus dar a tha thu ag obair le òigridh cuideachd (.) chan eil iad gad thuigsinn
	And when you're working with young people too (.) they don't understand you

The first of the above two participants describes having at first tried to learn a rather obsolescent Gaelic dialect (that of Badenoch), but realising that the possibility of his successfully achieving that objective was limited. Whilst he claims that it remains important for him personally to use aspects of that variety as a symbolic marker or 'sign' (*comharra*) of its significance to him, he states that seeking fully to acquire obsolescent dialects such as that of Badenoch or Cowal (in Argyll) is ultimately just 'silliness'. The second interviewee observes that whilst she had at first learned a relatively little-used Argyll dialect, she had subsequently lost most of that variety's distinguishing features since other Gaelic speakers she worked with (including young people) found them too hard to understand. Overwhelmingly in the dataset, new speakers in Scotland reported never having attempted to learn a particular dialect, largely for this very reason. The following speaker elaborates on potential obstacles that she felt having particular accent aims in her language learning would present to ensuring clear communication in her use of Gaelic:

EDIF1	Cha robh mi riamh ag amas air dualchainnt sònraichte [...] chan e gu bheil (2.6) dhèanainn fhathast e nan robh (.) ceangal agam le (sgìre)
	I was never aiming at a particular dialect [...] it's not that (2.6) I would still do it if I had (.) a connection to an (area)
SD	Hmm
EDIF1	Ach chan eil e ann an dòigh (ciallach) a bhith a' taghadh dualchainnt (x) b' urrainn dhomh a dhèanadh agus rannsachadh a dhèanadh [...] bhiodh ùidh agam barrachd (fhaighinn) air an dualchainnt Diùrach ach (.) a-rithist tha fhios nach eil mòran luchd-labhairt ann
	But in a way it's not (sensible) to choose a dialect (x) I could do it and do research [...] I'd be interested in finding out more about the Jura dialect but (.) again I know that there aren't many speakers left
SD	Seadh
	Yes
EDIF1	(Cha bhiodh) sin feumail airson conaltradh
	(It wouldn't) be useful for communicating

The idea expressed in this excerpt – that whilst dialectal diversity in Gaelic is interesting in and of itself, focusing too closely on any one specific speech form is undesirable for new Gaelic speakers (as it is likely to impede communication) – was conveyed frequently among participants in Scotland. As the following two speakers observe, learning specific Gaelic dialects or accents is regarded as unimportant, in sharp contrast with the dominant view expressed in Nova Scotia:

EDIF4	Bidh blasan: cainnt (.) a' tighinn (.) air do chainnt ann an cànan sam <u>bith</u>
	Accents: (.) come (.) into your speech in <u>any</u> language
SD	Hmm
EDIF4	A rèir cò tha thu a' ^bruidhinn [...] ach ma- nan- nan robh mi ag ràdh uill 'You know I won't feel like a proper Gaelic speaker until I have mastered the dialect of North Lochs'
	Depending on who you're ^speaking [to] but if- if- I I said well **'You know I won't feel like a proper Gaelic speaker until I have mastered the dialect of North Lochs'**
SD	((laughs))
EDIF4	Chan eil- **you know** chan eil siud cudromach dhomh idir
	That's not- **you know** *that's not important to me at all*

EDIF5   Chan fheum- cha chreid mi gu bheil e: <u>cho</u> deatamach gu bheil blas sònraichte agam (1.1) à eilean air choreigin anns nach robh mi a' fuireach a-riamh [...] tha gun teagamh (1.1) seòrsa **cache**- seòrsa luach ann am: (.) blas (1.2) às na h-eileanan [...] am feum pàistean ann an Glaschu a bhith bruidhinn ri (.) <u>blas</u> ^Barraigh? [...] Cha robh mi <u>ann</u> am Barraigh riamh- tha- bha mi ^riamh a' faireachdainn gu robh e rudeigin ^**inauthentic** mu dheidhinn a bhith- nam <u>bithinn</u> ag ionnsachadh (dualchainnt)

It's not necessary- I don't think it's: <u>so</u> necessary that I have a particular accent (1.1) from some island or other that I've never lived in [...] there's certainly (1.1) a sort of **cache**- *a kind of value in an: (.) accent (1.2) from the islands [...] do children in Glasgow need to learn to speak with a (.) ^Barra <u>accent</u>? [...] I've never <u>been</u> to Barra- I think- I ^always felt that it was a bit ^**inauthentic** to be- if <u>I had</u> learned (an accent)*

Where speaker EDIF4 observes that the task of perfecting a traditional dialect (such as that of North Lochs in Lewis) is not at all important to her, interviewee EDIF5 states in the second extract that learning to speak Gaelic with the accent of an island she has never been to (such as Barra) would be 'inauthentic'. Discourses of authenticity and 'naturalness' tended to predominate in Scotland-based new speakers' discussions of their lack of specific accent aim or dialectal language learning effort in Gaelic. As the following two extracts exemplify, interviewees frequently regarded it as more important to sound natural and authentic in their spoken Gaelic than to try to employ an accent or dialect of Gaelic that they had not acquired 'naturally' as an L1:

EDIM2   Chan eil Gàidhlig Àrainn ann fhathast agus chan eil mi airson a bhith ag ionnsachadh bho na clàraidhean [...] Chanainnsa (2.2) gum biodh ionnsachadh Gàidhlig Àrainn na (1.6) um seòrsa (.) ideòlas [...] tha mi an dòchas gum bi dualchainnt- gum bi cainnt nàdarra [agam] anns an àm ri teachd

Arran Gaelic isn't spoken any more and I don't want to learn from the recordings [...] I would say (2.2) that learning Arran Gaelic would be (1.6) um a sort of (.) ideology [...] I hope that my dialect- that my speech will be natural in the future

GLAM5   Chan eil mi a' feuchainn a bhith cumail a-mach gur ann às na h-<u>eileanan</u> a tha mi **so** (.) ann an dòigh tha mi faireachdainn gum bu chòir dhomh dìreach Gàidhlig a bhruidhinn gu nàdarra le blas gu math Glaschu 's dìreach a ràdh 'Carson- carson nach biodh?'

I don't try to make out that I'm from the <u>islands</u> **so** *(.) in a way I feel I should just speak Gaelic naturally with quite a Glaswegian accent and say 'Why- why wouldn't I?'*

SD	Seadh- gun teagamh
	Yes- indeed
GLAM5	Ach aig an aon àm (.) ((laughing)) b' fheàrr leam gum biodh daoine toilichte bruidhinn riumsa!
	But at the same time (.) ((laughing)) I would rather people were happy to speak to me!

The sense of 'naturalness' that both above speakers describe striving for in their spoken Gaelic, and rejection of particular accent aims in their language learning aspirations, is representative of the wider Scottish dataset. Related to this notion is a sense of honesty or 'full disclosure' in not seeking to conceal one's own positionality by pretending to be from islands and employing an accent associated with particular communities there. This sense of conveying 'full disclosure' of one's status as having learned Gaelic (cf. McLeod, O'Rourke and Dunmore 2014) is emphasised in the following account:

GLAM2	Chan eil nàire sam bith ormsa mun a sin [...] bha uair ann 's dòcha nuair a thigeadh cuideigin a bha air Gàidhlig ionnsachadh nuair a thigeadh iad gu fileantachd (.) bha iad rud beag diùid a bhith ag aideachadh gur e ionnsachadh a rinn iad ach chan eil mise [[mar sin]
	I'm not at all ashamed about that [...] there was a time perhaps when someone who'd learned Gaelic and had come to fluency (.) they would then be quite shy to admit that they had learned but I'm not [[like that]
SD	[[Chan ann] mar sin a tha thusa a' faireachdainn
	[[You don't] feel that way
GLAM2	Tha mi smaoineachadh gu bheil e cudromach gun- gun <u>inns</u> mi sin do dhaoine [...] chan e <u>aon</u> dualchainnt làidir Ghàidhlig a th' agam [...] a' Ghàidhlig a th' agam sin a' Ghàidhlig a th' agam- chan eil mi dèan-amh oidhirp sam bith a bhith bruidhinn ann an dòigh Uibhisteach no Hearach no Sgitheanach 's e dìreach tha a' Ghàidhlig a th' agam mar a tha i! ((laughs))
	I think it's important that- that I <u>tell</u> people that [I learned Gaelic...] I don't speak <u>any</u> type of strongly dialectal Gaelic [...] the Gaelic I have is the Gaelic I have, I don't make any attempt to speak in a Uist way or a Harris or Skye way it's just- my Gaelic is the way it is! ((laughs))
SD	Blas-chainnt na Gàidhlig san fharsaingeachd- an e nach eil sin 's dòcha buileach cho cudromach dhutsa?=
	[Concerning] accent in Gaelic- is that not so important to you?=
GLAF1	=Chan eil e: cho cudromach dhomh [...] <u>uair</u>eannan **though** tha mi **kind of** (1.1) 'oh it would be so much better if I spoke it properly' tha mi faireachdainn nach eil mi ga bruidhinn <u>ceart</u> (.) leis nach eil blas nas fheàrr

dhomh ach **actually I don't really care** [...] nan robh mi dol a dh'ionnsa-ich (.) dualchainnt shònraichte (.) 's e dualchainnt Uibhist a bhiodh ann ach chan eil mi dol a- agus feumaidh tu obair gu cruaidh air sin agus chan eil ui- chan eil ùine gu leòr agam son airson obair air sin

=*It's not so: important to me [...]* sometimes *though I'm kind of (1.1) 'oh it would be so much better if I spoke it properly' I feel that I don't speak it* correctly *(.) since I don't have a better accent but* **actually I don't really care** *[...] if I was going to learn (.) a particular dialect (.) it would be Uist dialect but I'm not going to- you need to work hard on that but I don't- I don't have enough time to work on that*

Both speakers in the above extracts emphasise a sense of relative ease with their spoken accent in Gaelic, with both explicitly rejecting the idea of aiming for a particular dialect variety in their orientation to the spoken language generally. As has been demonstrated in various accounts, this finding overwhelmingly reflects the experience of most Scotland-based new speakers in the dataset, contrasting clearly with the reported accent aims and high value placed on dialect features by informants based in Nova Scotia. In terms of the phonological acquisition of regional and dialectal forms of Gaelic (or notably, in Scotland, lack thereof), a key distinction is again evident between the datasets collected between in the two contexts.

Among Nova Scotian participants, the importance of acquiring distinctive accent and dialect features based on the spoken Gaelic of the last L1 speakers in the province was a theme emphasised in many interviews. In Scotland, by contrast, a large majority of interviewees dismissed the suggestion of learning a particular dialect or accent as impractical or otherwise undesirable. The importance and interest that new speakers in Scotland attached to Gaelic dialects, on one hand, tended not to be matched with any sense of commitment to acquiring dialectal forms of the language, as to do so was generally seen to be inauthentic or unnatural. This contrasts quite clearly with new speaker orientations towards spoken L1 dialects in Nova Scotia. Such clear distinctions are also apparent in relation to speakers' attitudes to the degree that opportunities for using Gaelic exist subsequent to having acquired an initial competence in the language.

Opportunity and use: linguistic practice in Nova Scotia and Scotland

I now highlight the discourses that Nova Scotian participants produced in their discussion of opportunity and choice in their language use. In particular, one such discourse advanced frequently by Nova Scotian informants holds that the creation of opportunities to use Gaelic is often the responsibility of individuals, rather than wider communities or policymakers. Whilst some speakers questioned the availability of sufficient opportunity in Nova Scotia to speak the language, most appeared to emphasise the agency of individuals to find and create their own opportunities to use Gaelic. I then discuss how discourses produced by Scottish new speakers tend, by contrast, to downplay the existence of opportunities to use Gaelic in Scottish society, before exploring potential reasons for this disparity between the two research contexts.

Generally among Nova Scotian interviewees, whether based in Halifax, Antigonish County or Cape Breton, many opportunities for using Gaelic in daily interactions were felt to exist within their social networks. It is perhaps in this sense, as closely networked communities of practice (after Wenger 1998), that Nova Scotian Gaelic speakers access opportunities to use the Gaelic that they have acquired through active effort in adolescence or adulthood. In the first extract below, a participant who has spent time within Gaelic communities in both Lowland Scotland and mainland Nova Scotia describes the wealth of opportunity for communicating in Gaelic that she feels to exist in the province:

ANTF2   Tha e ^còrdadh rium dìreach a bhith cleachdadh mo chuid Ghàidhlig gach latha- seo an aon- dh'fhaoidte gur e seo an aon àite san t-saoghal 's:: (.) far am faod tu dol agus (.) Gàidhlig a bhruidhinn sa- sa cho- theacs tha seo ((bùth cofaidh)) (.) taobh a-muigh na h-Alba [...] tha mi faireachdainn car (.) feumail an-seo
    I ^enjoy just being able to use my Gaelic every day- perhaps this is the only place in the world that:: (.) where you can go and (.) speak Gaelic in this context ((i.e., in a coffee shop in town)) (.) outside of Scotland [...] I feel (.) useful here

Describing the context of our Gaelic interaction in a coffee shop on the main street of a small town in eastern Nova Scotia, the above interviewee thus states that Nova Scotia is the only place in the world (*'an aon àite san t-saoghal'*) where a Gaelic speaker could communicate in Gaelic on a daily basis outwith Scotland. Significantly, and perhaps in implicit contrast to her previous experiences using Gaelic in Scotland, the speaker observes that she feels useful (*'feumail'*) in Nova Scotia. As an increasingly socially networked (rather than geographically concentrated) language, Gaelic usage in Nova Scotia appears to rely on speakers' efforts to actively pursue opportunities to use the linguistic abilities they have acquired, whilst numbers of L1 traditional speakers continue to abate. Perhaps it is in this sense that speaker ANTF1, above, regards herself to be more useful in the Nova Scotian context than in Scotland. The following two accounts exemplify the perceived need among Nova Scotian Gaelic speakers to create opportunities for their use of Gaelic:

HALF2	I'm actually having a cèilidh tonight with um some of my friends from class
SD	Awesome
HALF2	Cause our classes got pushed ahead a week so we were like 'we don't wanna give up on (2.1) the time we set aside to learn' so we're gonna meet up and learn together
SD	That's great
HALF2	So (.) a very Gaelic day for me! [...] I feel like the once a week- if you're just going once a week ((to class)) but don't know anybody else who speaks it you're not using it

ANTM1	Uill gus mo chuid Gàidhlig a chumail <u>beò</u> bhithinn ri cleas- tha mi gabhail gur e rud cumanta a th' anns a sin (0.9) a' bruidhinn rium fhìnmar amadan ((laughing)) a' bruidhinn rium fhèin fad an t-siubhail sa Ghàidhlig!
	Well to keep my Gaelic <u>alive</u> I had a trick- I understand that this is quite a common thing (0.9) speaking to myself- like a fool ((laughing)) speaking to myself all the time in Gaelic!
SD	((laughs))
ANTM1	Nuair a gheibhinn cothrom air sin- dìreach a bhith ga cumail beò [...] ach (3.9) 's e mo bhàrdachd a thug putadh dhomh 's a thug brosnachadh dhomh gus an cànan a chumail beò
	When I would have the opportunity for it- just to keep it alive [...] but (3.9) it was my poetry that encouraged me to keep the language alive
SD	Seadh
	Sure
ANTM1	B' e- b' e: (.) deagh adhbhar a bh' ann (0.6) deagh <u>leisgeul</u> a bh' ann
	It was- it was: (.) a good reason (0.6) a good <u>excuse</u> to do that

For both speakers above, therefore, using Gaelic – whether by speaking it to oneself or meeting up regularly to practise the language – is regarded as a priority that needs to be pursued, in order for Nova Scotian new speakers to amass sufficient opportunity to speak it. This sense was seldom expressed to the same degree in Cape Breton, where many interviewees felt that opportunities for speaking Gaelic were relatively plentiful:

CBIF7	Tha dìreach paidhle Ghàidhlig mun cuairt [...] tha sinne airson a bhith <u>bruidhinn</u> na Gàidhlig agus gabhail òrain agus (0.9) uh ag innse ^sgeulachdan 's seanchas [...] Tha càirdean agam aig a bheil a' Ghàidhlig
	There is just so much Gaelic around [...] we want to <u>speak</u> Gaelic and sing songs and (0.9) tell stories and chat [...] I have family who speak Gaelic
SD	Dìreach- tha e mun cuairt
	Exactly- so it's around

CBIF7	Tha piuthar agam a-nis is tha i gus a bhith fileanta cuideachd so tha (.) Gàidhlig sa h-uile àite [[nam bheatha]]!
I have a young sister now and she's almost fluent so (.) Gaelic is everywhere [[in my life!]]
SD	[[Tha]]
[[Yes]]
CBIF7	Agus tha e nas cuideachaile dhòmhsa ann an Ceap Breatainn na bhith a' bruidhinn cànan sam bith eile
And it's more useful to me in Cape Breton than any other language

Working predominantly through Gaelic in her job in Cape Breton and having family members who have learned the language to a high level, the above interviewee therefore regards her life as currently providing plenty of opportunity to use Gaelic. Whilst such professional backgrounds were rare across the Nova Scotia dataset, the importance of family, and particularly of pursuing opportunities to use Gaelic with children, was a theme that was frequently conveyed by Nova Scotian participants. As noted above, the importance placed by many Nova Scotian new speakers on creating one's own opportunities to use Gaelic in the province often extended to speaking the language with children. For the following speaker, a teenager whose mother sometimes spoke Gaelic to him in order to create opportunities to use Gaelic, but who did not raise him speaking Gaelic from an early age, being the beneficiary of such intergenerational language practices is regarded in positive terms:

SD	So do you use it much these days or how do you find it these days?
ANTM3	Um I ^don't use it much I only use it uh (.) around certain people like sometimes (.) my mom and I will speak Gaelic to each other
SD	That's good
ANTM3	Like it's <u>not</u> all that common sometimes she'll just switch to Gaelic from English […] I'm still not fluent so she has to teach me some of the things she's saying but yeah […] I don't think I have very much to go until I'm fluent (and) it helps that there are people in the community who are fluent and they'll speak to me and I'll kind of gain confidence

Whilst his mother's use of Gaelic with him might not thus be considered full language transmission or socialisation as viewed from a monolingual perspective, ANTM3 clearly does regard the greater opportunity for speaking Gaelic that this linguistic practice provided as having helped bring his abilities in the language close to fluency. Conversely, the challenges that parents face in attempting to raise children in Gaelic, along with the greater opportunity for Gaelic use that results from these attempts, are outlined in the following two excerpts:

ANTM4   Bidh mi bruidhinn ris uh- ris mo mhac sa Ghàidhlig
I speak to my uh- to my son in Gaelic
SD   Seadh
Yes
ANTM4   Agus uh tha- tha e- tha e ^tighinn air adhart math gu leòr […] tha sin dèanamh feum <u>mhòr</u> dhòmhsa cuideachd […] chaidh mi-fhìn 's mo mhac a chèilidh air uh seann bhoireannach a tha fuireach ann an ((CBI)) agus bha mise bruidhinn <u>rithe</u> anns a' Ghàidhlig […] nuair a dh'fhalbh sinn thuirt e (.) 'I wanna speak more Gaelic- more (.) I wanna have more words!'
And uh he- he- he's ^coming on all right […] it's <u>really</u> useful for me too […] my son and I went to visit uh an old lady who lives in ((Cape Breton)) and I was speaking to <u>her</u> in Gaelic […] when we left he said (.) 'I wanna speak more Gaelic- more (.) I wanna have more words!'

HALM2   Bha mise airson 's gum biodh iad ((.i. mic)) a' tuigsinn gur e (.) dìreach <u>cànan</u> coltach ris a h-<u>uile</u> cànan eile
I wanted them ((i.e., two sons)) to understand that it ((i.e., Gaelic)) is (.) just a <u>language</u> like <u>every</u> other language
SD   Hmm
HALM2   Agus (.) cha bhi: bah (0.7) fhios agad (0.7) faodaidh sinn bruidhinn air gach cuspair tron chànan a tha seo agus um (2.6) 's mar sin uh (1.5) bidh mi ris a sin a h-uile latha 's uh (0.6) 's tha iad- tha iad ^fi:leanta tha iad- chan eil iad cho <u>deònach</u> a bhith bruidhinn rium a bhith freagairt- bidh- bidh mi- bidh mi: (.) toirt orra (.) a bhith gam fhreagairt […] agus a' feuchainn ri- chan eil fhios'am- seòrs' de (.) lèirsinn (.) chultarail cuideachd a thoirt dhaibh
And (.) it's not: bah (0.7) you know (0.7) we can talk about any subject through this language and um (2.6) so (1.5) I do this every day and uh (0.6) and they- they are ^flu:ent they- they aren't so <u>willing</u> to speak in answer to me- I- I- I: (.) make them (.) answer me […] and try to give them- I don't know- a sort of (.) cultural ((Gaelic)) vision (.) as well

The inherent difficulties many parents face in attempting to raise children to speak Gaelic (rather than simply to understand it) – as well as the benefits that Gaelic-speaking parents encounter in doing so – are clearly conveyed by speakers in the two above extracts. Firstly, interviewee ANTM4 states somewhat hesitantly, 'tha e tighinn air adhart math gu leòr' ('he's coming on all right'), but notes that greater exposure to language use in the community encourages his son in the learning process. In the second extract, HALM2 notes of his sons (with raised intonation and elongation of 'fluent' indicating a degree of uncertainty), *'tha iad- tha iad ^fi:leanta'* ('they- they're ^flu:ent'), but that they often require encouragement to respond in Gaelic. The perceived importance – but frequently encountered difficulties – of parents raising children with Gaelic in Nova Scotia is likewise conveyed in the following extract:

CBIF11   On a bha mi òg thuirt mi 'Dar a <u>bhios</u> clann agam tha mi dol a bhruidh- tha mi dol a theagasg Gàidhlig dhaibh' ach cha ro:bh (1.2) chan eil ^fhi- os'am cha do ghabh mi mòran beachd air dìreach [...] tha <u>còmhraidhean</u> mar sin air a bhith agam- againn- mi-fhìn 's xxx (.) gu bheil buaidh na Beurla cho làidir agus ma bhios sinn a' bruidhinn na Gàidhlig <u>feumaidh</u> sinn a' Ghàidhlig a bhruidhinn so chan eil Gàidhlig san taigh- fhios agad chan eil Gàidhlig aig an duine agam, chan eil Gàidhlig aig mo phàran- tan so <u>feumaidh</u> sinn cothroman a chur air dòigh [...] tha sinn air<u>son</u> a bhith brudhinn na Gàidhlig so:: tha mi faighinn beagan de foghlam an-dràst' bidh mise a' bruidhinn na Gàidhlig 's tha esan gam fhreagairt sa Bheurla

Since I was young I said 'When I <u>have</u> children I'm going to spea- I'm going to teach them Gaelic' but I di:dn't (1.2) I don't ^know I didn't think much about it just [...] I- we have had <u>conversations</u> like that- myself and xxx ((husband)) (.) that there is such a strong influence of English and if we're speaking Gaelic we <u>have</u> to speak Gaelic so we don't speak Gaelic at home- you know my husband can't speak Gaelic, my parents can't speak Gaelic so we <u>have</u> to create opportunities [...] we <u>want</u> to speak Gaelic so:: I'm learning a bit about it at the moment I speak Gaelic and he ((son)) answers me in English

Widespread appreciation of the perceived need both for Gaelic-speaking parents to use their Gaelic with children in order to transmit the language, and for the creation of opportunities to speak Gaelic, was apparent throughout the Nova Scotia dataset. Difficulties in attempting to socialise and raise children in a richly Gaelic environment in contemporary Nova Scotia – and particularly in encouraging children to acquire active speaking ability in the language – were nevertheless often reported by parents of young children. Furthermore, whilst most new speakers in the Nova Scotian context were mindful of a perceived need for speakers to create their own opportunities for Gaelic use, a minority of interviewees stated that opportunity to speak the language remained limited in their lives.

For a small but noteworthy minority of interviewees in Nova Scotia, who perhaps lacked extensive networks of other Gaelic speakers in their social lives, the decline of the traditional L1 community in the province was viewed as undermining opportunities to use the language generally.

HALF1	An cothrom ionnsachaidh as fheàrr a th' agam an-diugh gu bheil mi ri cèilidh um (0.7) cho tric sa ghabhas [ach ...] tha na cothroman gann (.) tha sinn uile sgàipte bho chèile
	The best learning opportunity I have today is that I visit people um (0.7) as often as I can [but...] there are not many opportunities (.) we're all so scattered
SD	Tha
	Yes
HALF1	Agus um (.) a h-uile duine **busy** a' feuchainn ri beòthachd a chumail san t-saoghal Beurla [...] mura bi cothrom a-mach às na clasaichean (.) carson a tha sinn ga togail co-dhiù?
	*And um (.) everyone is so **busy** trying to make a living in the world of English [...] unless there is an opportunity ((to speak Gaelic)) outside of classes (.) why are we learning it anyway?*
SD	Hmm
HALF1	Feumaidh cothroman sòisealta a bhith ann [...] far a bheil cothrom agad càirdeas a thogail [...] feumaidh tu a bhith a-measg Ghàidheil
	There have to be social opportunities [...] where there is a chance to make friendships [...] you have to be among Gaels

The need to be able to use Gaelic outside of the formal learning context – and to be 'among Gaels' ('*am measg Ghàidheil*') in order to access social opportunities ('*cothroman sòisealta*') to speak Gaelic regularly is clearly expressed by HALF1 in the above extract. I return to the issue of Gaelic identities – and who should be considered Gaels – in the following chapter. For present purposes, however, the speaker's emphasis on lack of opportunity for social interaction in Gaelic, contrasting with most Nova Scotian participants, is clear from this excerpt. This sense of lack of opportunity for Gaelic use is similarly conveyed by interviewees in the following two accounts:

SD	Do you find there are many opportunities to use Gaelic?
CBIF3	Um ((sighs)) n::ot ((laughs)) (x) opportunity- what opportunity? Yeah
SD	Yeah
CBIF3	Um: (1.7) um (.) <u>no</u>- and- I've talked to many of my ((service users)) about it and I'd say that maybe a third (0.7) to a half – and I might be ^underestimating – would have- their grandparents lived in one of the rural Gaelic communities
ANTF5	In a nutshell- I've been kinda at it off and on [...] but what I've <u>found</u> is that my comprehension (.) stays (.) quite ^good
SD	I see yeah [[yeah I understand that]

ANTF5 [[But uh in terms] of my fluency and speaking I uh I get very uncomfortable very quickly [...] the obstacles are not different- it comes down to time and opportunity you know? [...] I'll always go back to it- Gaelic I mean- the whole experience that's around that (.) um (0.6) I don't think I'll <u>ever</u>- I don't think it will ever not be part of (.) who I am

It is noteworthy that both speakers CBIF3 and ANTF5 opted to conduct interviews principally in English, due in large part to their lack of confidence in the language stemming from reported lack of opportunity to speak it. Such accounts differ starkly from the majority of Nova Scotian interviewees' insistence that it was vital in the province to actively seek out opportunities to use Gaelic within their social networks – or, if they did not currently exist, to create those opportunities. The rapid decline of Gaelic in rural Cape Breton is described in the first of the two above accounts as a contributory factor in the apparent shortage of opportunity to use the language at present. Participant ANTF5 states that in spite of such a lack of opportunity, Gaelic 'will never not be part' of she is.

I return in greater detail to relevant issues of identity in the following chapter. The general pattern that emerges from my analysis in Nova Scotia in respect of usage and opportunity is that of a widespread sentiment that sufficient opportunity does exist in the province to make use of linguistic skills that new speakers have acquired. As illustrated above, this sense was questioned by a small but noteworthy minority of interviewees, whose accounts tended to parallel those of new speakers in Scotland, to whom I now turn attention.

As I have discussed elsewhere (Dunmore 2018b, 2019), Gaelic speakers in Scotland who have acquired high levels of speaking ability in the language tend frequently to describe a lack of opportunity to use Gaelic in the course of their daily lives. In contrast to the emphasis placed by Nova Scotian new speakers on the importance of actively creating such opportunities, the lack of sociolinguistic spaces in which the language can be utilised is identified by many Scottish informants as a fundamental problem in their lived, sociolinguistic realities. The issue is clearly problematised in the following two accounts:

EDIF4 Tha mi- tha mi an-<u>còmhnaidh</u> a' coinneachadh ri <u>tòrr</u> luchd-ionnsachaidh is mi smaoineachadh gu bheil (1.3) gu <u>leòr</u> aca- tha iad ag ionnsachadh gu <u>ìre</u> (.) 's an <u>uair</u> sin- 's tha iad ^comasach
    I- I <u>always</u> meet <u>loads</u> of learners and I think (1.3) <u>many</u> of them- they learn to a certain <u>level</u> (.) and then- they're ^able to communicate
SD Hmm

EDIF4	Ach chan- an <u>uair</u> sin chan eil àrainneachd (1.1) far an- far an <u>gabh</u> (0.7) uh an cànan a chleachdadh (.) agus siud as adhbhar nach eil iad a' dol nas fhaide agus tha iad- tha iad a' <u>tighinn</u> gu ìre is cha tèid iad nas fhaide na sin
	But there's no- <u>subsequently</u> there is no environment (1.1) where- where the- (0.7) uh language can be used (.) and that's why they don't progress any further and they- they <u>come</u> to a certain level [of aptitude] and don't progress further than that
[...]	
SD	A bheil thu creidsinn gu bheil cothroman gu leòr sa cho-theacs a tha seo- sa bhaile- Gàidhlig a bhruidhinn?
	Do you think there are enough opportunities in this context- this city- to speak Gaelic?
EDIF4	Uill chan eil mi dol a-mach gan sireadh! ((laughs)) [...] Ma tha mi ag ràidh ((whiney voice)) 'Oh: no: there's ^just no opportunities' air **you know** [...] 's dòcha gu bheil iad ann ach tha mise air a bhith aig an taigh feuchainn ris an leabhar sgriosail agam a sgrìobhadh! Mar a chanas iad sa Bheurla **life intervenes**
	Well I don't go out looking for them! ((laughs)) [...] If I say ((in a whiney voice)) 'Oh: no: there's ^just no opportunities' for it **you know** *[...] maybe they do exist but I've just been at home trying to write my terrible book! [...] As they say in English* **life intervenes**
EDIM4	An trioblaid as motha agam chan urrainn dhomh còmhraidhean a lorg fad na h-ùine [...] bha e gu math doirbh còmhraidhean a lorg ann an Inbhir Nis [...] ach (1.9) ((sighs)) chuir mi romham an àite sin (.) gu bhith a' leughadh agus ag èisteachd ris a' chànan nuair nach b' urrainn dhomh a bruidhinn
	My biggest problem [is] I can never find opportunities for conversation it was even quite hard to find conversations [when I lived] in Inverness [...] but (1.9) ((sighs)) I decided instead of that (.) to read and listen to the language since I couldn't speak it
SD	Sin agad e agus mar sin tha thu cumail na sgilean [cànan] agad a' dol mar gum biodh
	That's it and then you keep the [language] skills going so to speak
EDIM4	Chùm sin na structaran (.) agus am briathrachas (1.4) nam cheann
	That kept the structures (.) and the vocabulary (1.4) in my head

In the first interview extract above, speaker EDIF4 observes in general terms that new speakers encounter difficulties, once they have reached a degree of fluency in Gaelic, in accessing opportunities to use and improve their spoken language. When I asked later in the interview if sufficient opportunities to speak Gaelic existed in the city where she was currently based, EDIF4 responded candidly that she didn't actively seek them out (*'chan eil mi dol a-mach gan sireadh'*), explaining in English that 'life intervenes'. This sense of having priorities over seeking out opportunity to speak Gaelic was also a common finding in my (2018b, 2019) analysis of ideologies of opportunity and choice among former Gaelic-medium students. In the second account above, EDIM4 notes that, lacking opportunity for frequent conversation in Gaelic, his only recourse has been to focus on maintaining his reading and listening skills in the language. A shortage of conversational opportunities is likewise described by the interviewee in the following excerpt, who also draws on the trope discussed by GLAF4, above, that 'life intervenes', preventing more frequent use of Gaelic:

GLAM6 Bha mi mothachail aig an àm nach robh cothroman ann sa choimhearsnachd Gàidhlig a bhruidhinn agus <u>siud</u> as coireach gun deach mi dhan t-Sabhal Mhòr [...] an dèidh ^sin is mi tòiseachadh san oilthigh cha robh mi <u>tòrr</u> an sàs anns a' Gàidhlig bha (.) bha agam ri ceum a dhèanamh [...] chaidh mi um a dh'Uibhist a ^Deas [...] nam shaor-thoileach an ^uair sin (.) tha mi an-dràsta fuireach ann an xxx ((Galltachd)) agus um (.) chan eil tòrr cothrothoman ri bhith::- chan eil (.) tòrr cothroman <u>còmhraidh</u> ann

   I was aware at that time that there weren't opportunities in my community to speak Gaelic so <u>that's</u> why I went to Sabhal Mòr [Ostaig] [...] after ^that when I started at university I wasn't much involved in Gaelic I (.) I had to do a degree [...then] I went to ^South Uist [...] as a volunteer and ^then (.) I currently live in xxx ((Lowlands)) and um (.) there aren't many opportunities to be::- there aren't (.) many <u>conversation</u> opportunities

A lack of opportunity to speak Gaelic was widely observed by many Scottish new speakers as an obstacle to making more extensive use of Gaelic in their day-to-day lives. Other competing priorities were observed often to militate against frequent usage of the language, such as having to do a professional degree through the medium of English (*'bha agam ri ceum a dhèanamh'*). At the same time, whilst seeking out opportunity for Gaelic use was described as having been an important priority for some interviewees (for example by enrolling at Sabhal Mòr or moving to South Uist, as speaker GLAM6 recounts above), others tended to downplay the importance of using their Gaelic, particularly for social functions. This tendency is exemplified in the following two accounts, in which interviewees describe their Gaelic communities being largely confined to the workplace:

GMEF3 Tha mi a' teagasg ann an clas a h-aon an-dràsta agus 's e em **Gaelic immersion** a th' ann **so** cha bhi thu a' bruidhinn riutha ann am Beurla idir em ge- ma gheibh- ma tha duilgheadas mòr aca ('s ann) bidh mi a' bruidhinn riutha ann am Beurla ach 's e **immersion** a th'ann

	I teach in class one just now and it's em **Gaelic immersion** *so you don't speak English to them at all altho- if there- if they have major difficulty [understanding] (then) I will speak English to them but it's* **immersion**
[...]	
SD	A-mach às an sgoil am bi thu a' buntainn ri buidhnean Gàidhlig idir?
	Outside school do you belong to any Gaelic groups at all?
GMEF3	^Chan eil
	^*No*
SD	Chan eil
	No
GMEF3	No
SD	Agus: a-rithist taobh a-muigh na sgoile am bi thu a' cleachdadh Gàidhlig tric anns a' choimhearsnachd?
	An:d again outside of school do you often use Gaelic in the community?
GMEF3	Cha bhi
	No
SD	Am bi thu a' cleachdadh tòrr Gàidhlig an lùib do bheatha làitheil?
	Do you use much Gaelic in your daily life?
GLAF1	Eh (0.8) **no**
	Eh (0.8) **no**
SD	Dìreach san àite obrach an e?
	Is it just at work?
GLAF1	Dìreach anns an àite obra- obrach **I mean** tha caraidean agam [...] aig a bheil Gàidhlig agus cha bhi mi a' cleachdadh Gàidhlig còmhla riutha em: (1.9) no chan eil [...] Chan eil (.) coimhearsnachd Gàidhlig agam taobh (a-muigh) (.) an àite-obrach [...] chan eil ùidh agam ann an **kind of** cultar traidiseanta **so** tha sin (.) a' cur (.) **barrier** orm tha mi a' smaoineachadh gus a cleachdadh nas trice
	Just at wo- work **I mean** *have friends who* can *speak Gaelic and I don't use Gaelic with them em: (1.9)* no *I don't [...] I don't have a Gaelic community outside (.) the workplace [...] I don't have any interest in* **kind of** *traditional culture so that (.) places (.) a* **barrier** *between me and my using it more frequently I think*

The lack of interest or engagement with traditional Gaelic cultural and musical activity that GLAF1 describes above was also reported by many other Scottish-based interviewees as a factor that reinforced their lack of opportunity to speak Gaelic more frequently. This rather prevalent attitude among Scottish new speakers stands in stark contrast to that reported by the majority of Nova Scotian participants (as discussed in the following chapter). Whilst relatively few Scottish participants reported that their Gaelic community was limited to the workplace (as GLAF1 observes above), for others, the contemporary Gaelic community was regarded to be largely 'hidden in plain sight' within speakers' social networks:

GLAM4   I mean (.) feumaidh tu a bhith (1.7) an sàs ann an saoghal na Gàidhlig mar a tha e is an uair sin (.) chì thu e [...] so tha mi faighinn cothrom- ach feumaidh tu a bhith (0.8) a-staigh an lìonradh [...] ach tha e **hidden in plain sight** chanainn
  I mean (.) you have to be (1.7) involved in the Gaelic world as it is and then (.) you will see it [...] so do I get opportunity- but you have to be (0.8) inside the network [...] but it's **hidden in plain sight** *I'd say*

The view that greater opportunity to use Gaelic socially is simultaneously widely available and partially concealed from new and potential speakers of the language is articulately voiced in the above excerpt. Whilst a great many Scottish-based new speakers discussed their current linguistic practices in terms of limited opportunity for Gaelic use, in contrast to most Nova Scotian speakers, an area of commonality that emerged across the two contexts was the greater opportunity for Gaelic use that starting a family could provide. As several Nova Scotian participants similarly recounted, some Scottish interviewees who had recently become parents referred to this important life stage as impacting positively on their use of Gaelic in the home domain:

GLAF4   Nuair a cheumnaich mi bha: Gàidhlig (0.6) gu math lapach agam [...] feumaidh mi a ràdh gu robh mi leisg- cha do uh (.) bha mi- bha mi **really** leisg mun a' Ghàidhlig [...] cha robh mise airson sin a dhèanadh
  When I graduated my: Gaelic (0.6) was pretty rusty [...] I have to say I was lazy- I didn't uh (.) I was- I was **really** *lazy about Gaelic [...] I just didn't want to do it*
SD   Cha robh thu cho (.) co-cheangailte mar gum biodh
  You weren't so (.) connected so to speak
GLAF4   Em agus:: uill bha- ((hushed)) uill 's e saoghal beag a th' ann agus (.) bha mi ag iarraidh faighinn às [...] tha mi a' glacadh a h-uile cothrom a-nis Gàidhlig a ùisneachadh [...] airson xxx is xxx ((mac agus nighean)) (1.2) em (.) tha mi a' feuchainn (1.2) em (1.1) gum bi iad a' smaointinn uill tha iad a' smaointinn gur e cànan a tha- a dh'fhaotadh a bhith aig a h-uile duine [...] is ann à Uibhist a tha an duine agam so tha Gàidhlig (.) gu leòr aige **of course**
  Em an::d well it was- ((hushed voice)) well it's quite a small world and (.) I wanted to escape [...] now I seize every opportunity to use Gaelic [...] for xxx and xxx ((son and daughter)) (1.2) em (.) I try (1.2) em (1.1) to get them to think- well they do think it's a language that- that everyone could speak [...] my husband is from Uist so he can speak (.) plenty of Gaelic **of course**

For parents like the above interviewee, the experience of starting a family, and of using Gaelic with her children, is clearly contrasted with her use of Gaelic immediately after completing formal study of the language at university. The conscious decision to raise children as Gaelic speakers is similarly foregrounded in the following extract:

> SD A bheil àrainneachd Ghàidhlig agaibh a-staigh- aig an taigh cuideachd?=
> > *Do you have a Gaelic environment in- at home as well [as at work]?=*
>
> INVM1 =Tha [...] **yeah** àrainneachd a tha ag obrachadh gu ì:re (.) tha triùir againn [...] 's e còmhradh (2.4) eatarra a tha sa Ghàidhlig ach an tè anns a' mheadhan [...] Tha: an dachaigh air a bhith anns a' Ghàidhlig (1.7) mus do phòs sinn [...] ged a bha sinn air (2.2) eh (1.7) **bonded** anns a' Bheurla (.) gabhaidh sin atharrachadh ach (.) chan eil e furasta
> > *=Yes [...] **yeah** it's an environment that works to some degree (.) we have three kids [...] conversation (2.4) between them is in Gaelic except for the one in the middle [...] Our home has: been in Gaelic since we got married [...] although we were (2.2) eh (1.7) **bonded** in English (.) that can be changed but (.) it's not easy*

The maintenance of a Gaelic-dominant home environment is a linguistic situation that the above interviewee describes as working to some degree (*'gu ìre'*, with particular stress on the second word). Nevertheless, he highlights challenges with regard to the middle child's language use with siblings, and shifting to Gaelic use with his spouse, having been 'bonded' in English. The following account illustrates this particular challenge:

> SD A bheil Gàidhlig aig do bhean?
> > *Can your wife speak Gaelic?*
>
> GMEM3 Tha **yeah** tha
> > *Yes **yeah** yes*
>
> SD Uh huh 's am bi sibh cleachdadh na Gàidhlig aig an taigh mar sin?
> > *Uh huh and do you use Gaelic at home then?*
>
> GMEM3 Cha bhi (.) 's e seo- **no** seo fìor (.) airson adhbhar air choireigin cha bhi sinn a' bruidhinn Gàidhlig ro thric [...] 's e [gainnead] misneachd a th' ann tha e glè cheart (.) neo seòrsa **whatever it's called linguistic relationship** le diofar dhaoine
> > *No (.) this is- no that's true (.) for some reason we don't speak Gaelic too often [...] but I don't know why [...] it's [a lack of] confidence it is very true (.) or a sort of **whatever it's called linguistic relationship** with different people*

The above interviewee thus notes that although his wife could also speak Gaelic, the couple rarely used the language with one another, referring to both a lack of confidence, and the 'linguistic' relationship that had already been established between the pair (in English). Therefore, while several participants described the establishment of family life as having positively impacted on their greater Gaelic use (as in Nova Scotia), this was not always true.

Once again, key contrasts have been highlighted in understandings of opportunities for Gaelic use in the two research contexts, with Nova Scotian participants frequently highlighting the importance of their own agency in creating such opportunities within their social networks. In Scotland, new speakers often expressed awareness of their agency in this way, but observed more frequently that other aspects of their lives (whether within the domains of work or home) had led them to deprioritise using Gaelic. Possible exceptions to this general pattern were exemplified in accounts of home life after starting a family, though such descriptions featured less prominently than in the Nova Scotia data.

Overall, this chapter has highlighted distinctions and commonalities in the two research sites in relation to new speakers' acquisition and use of Gaelic. In terms of the key sociolinguistic mudes to have impacted on participants' use of Gaelic over the course of their respective life trajectories, diverse and distinctive experiences were recounted by interviewees in this section. The mudes and life stages to have had major and beneficial consequences for new speakers' Gaelic use in both contexts range from community and family socialisation (in Nova Scotia) to immersion education (in Scotland). These two contexts of language socialisation form a key distinction between Nova Scotian and Scottish research participants. Extracurricular immersion experiences in the language, formal adult study and, crucially, enrolment on courses at Sabhal Mòr Ostaig each formed sociolinguistic experiences that were common to substantial subgroups of new speakers in both contexts. The significance of Sabhal Mòr Ostaig for informing new speakers' learning and socialisation experiences is a relatively understudied area of Gaelic language policy and planning. In general, it is noteworthy that sociolinguistic mudes in adolescence and adulthood were recounted by majorities of participants in both Nova Scotia and Scotland as being particularly formative, notwithstanding the few individuals to have acquired some Gaelic in childhood through community and education.

Among Nova Scotian participants, the importance of acquiring distinctive accent and dialect features based on the spoken Gaelic of the last L1 speakers in the province was a theme emphasised in many interviews. In Scotland, by contrast, the suggestion of learning a particular dialect or accent associated with an island or region was dismissed by a large majority of interviewees as impractical. Such distinctions were similarly apparent in relation to speakers' attitudes to the degree that opportunities for using Gaelic exist subsequent to having acquired an initial competence in the language. In particular, Nova Scotian accounts of the need for new speakers to proactively create opportunities to speak Gaelic tended to contrast with Scottish speakers' discussion of choice in Gaelic use. The following chapter turns to some of the key contrasts in language ideology and cultural identity that may help to explain and contextualise the distinctions that this chapter has illustrated.

FIVE

Contrasting Gaelic Identities: Heritage, Language Ideologies and Motivation

Interviewees' ideologies, particularly in relation to their ethnocultural and heritage identities, can be particularly revealing for understanding the role that their motivations may play in determining their current language practices. The chapter focuses on the identity constructions of interview participants in the two research contexts. I firstly consider the relationship between Gaelic and Gaels in the words of research participants themselves, discussing the role of heritage and identity in Gaelic language learning motivations in Nova Scotia and Scotland. Whilst the term 'Gael' was enthusiastically embraced by the majority of Nova Scotian participants, reasons for rejection of or indifference toward this label among a minority are noteworthy. Crucially, such reasons are notably different from those expressed by Scottish new speakers for disassociating with the term. The next parts of the chapter analyse speakers' perceptions of cultural and community change in Gaelic-speaking communities, considering perceived distinctions between native and new Gaelic speakers in Nova Scotia and Scotland as well as discourses concerning the growth and rejuvenation of Nova Scotia's Gaelic communities. In contrast, Scottish participants' discourses often sought to address opposition to such policies of growth in the Highlands and Lowlands of Scotland, as I discuss before considering interviewee narratives concerning family socialisation and Gaelic heritage. Lastly, some concluding thoughts will be presented concerning Nova Scotian and Scottish speakers' identity constructions, language ideologies and language socialisation as conveyed in interviews.

Gaelic identities – new speakers as Gaels?

The relationship between Gaelic and new speakers' identity as Gaels is best revealed in interviewees' own words, as they seek to address the respective roles attributed to heritage and identity in accounts of Gaelic language learning motivations in Nova Scotia and Scotland. As I demonstrate, whilst the term

'Gael' is enthusiastically embraced by the majority of Nova Scotian participants, the reasons for a rejection of or indifference toward this label among most Scottish-based interviewees are multiple and complex. I draw attention to contemporary meanings and conceptions of Gael(ic) identity among new speakers in both research sites. One particularly striking distinguishing feature of discourses concerning Gaelic identity in Nova Scotia is the confidence that many new speakers conveyed when discussing their self-identification as Gaels. In the following account, the interviewee responds without a moment's hesitation to my question as to whether she is a Gael:

SD	An e Gàidheal a th' annadsa?=
	Are you a Gael?=
ANTF1	='S e
	=Yes
SD	'S e=
	Yeah=
ANTF1	='S e
	=Yeah
SD	An ann air sgàth a' chànain fhèin a tha sin air no air sàilleabh chultair agus òrain 's a h-uile càil mar sin?
	Is that because of the language itself or more due to the culture and songs and everything like that?
ANTF1	(1.1) Ah uill (2.4) 's e um (.) cànan (1.9) mo shinn- mo shinnsearan a bh' ann [...] Bidh mi a' cleachdadh Beurla air sàilleabh 's gu bheil (2.2) feum agam air a bhith (.) a' bruidhinn còmhla ri (1.9) daoine ach
	(1.1) Ah well (2.4) it's um (.) the language (1.9) of my anc- of my ancestors [...] I use English because (2.2) I have to speak it (.) with (1.9) people but
SD	Hmm
ANTF1	Is fheàrr leam Gàidhlig
	I prefer Gaelic
SD	Carson a tha sin nad bheachd?
	Why do you think that is?
ANTF1	^Chan eil mi cinnteach um
	^I'm not sure um
SD	Hmm
ANTF1	'S e um (.) cànan (1.1) mo shinnsearan a th' ann an [[Gàidhlig]
	Gaelic um (.) is the language (1.1) of my [[ancestors]
SD	[['S e]
	[[Yes]
ANTF1	Um (.) 's e cànan (5.1) chan <u>e</u> cànan mo shinnsearan ((laughs)) a th' ann am Beurla!
	Um (.) it is (5.1) English is <u>not</u> ((laughs)) the language of my ancestors!

This interviewee's metapragmatic reflections on her language use, as a new speaker of Gaelic and first language speaker of English, are particularly interesting. Whilst she answers without a moment's hesitation at the start of the extract that she is a Gael, she is much more circumspect when responding to my later question as to why this might be the case, producing lengthy pauses (several of over two seconds' duration) whilst considering an answer. Toward the end of the extract, the interviewee again pauses for lengthy periods before stating that Gaelic is the language of her ancestors and English is not. Some of the possible reasons for this ethnolinguistic ideology are considered by another interviewee in the next extract.

ANTF2	Ann an Alba Nuaidh [...] tha mi smaoineach' gu bheil (0.8) gu bheil cultar (1.8) agus (0.8) dualchas gu math cudromach dha na daoine an-seo san fharsaingeachd
	In Nova Scotia [...] I think that (0.8) culture (1.8) and (0.8) heritage are quite important to the people here generally
SD	Hmm tha sin gu math follaiseach=
	Hmm that's quite clear=
ANTF2	=Ge- ged a tha [...] ann an Ceap Breatainn tha mi smaoineachadh gu bheil (1.2) fios aca air cò às a tha iad air- seòrsa tha beachd (.) uh beagan nas soilleire air a' chultar aca 's air an eachdraidh aca 's tha e <u>anabarrach</u> fhèin cudromach dhan- son- dhan fheadhainn [...] ann an dòigh 's e seòrsa an cultar agus am fèin-aithne an rud as cudromaich' agus tha Gàidhlig xxx air cùlaibh sin uh [...] ann an Alba chan eil an dà rud co-cheangailte dh'fhaoidte- fèin aithne agus an cànan
	=Altho- although [...] in Cape Breton I think that they (1.2) know where they come from- they have a sort of clearer idea of their culture and history and it's incredibly important to- for- to those people [...] in a way it's like culture and identity are the most important thing and Gaelic is xxx behind that [...] in Scotland the two things aren't so connected perhaps- identity and the language

This speaker's sense, as a recent emigrant to Nova Scotia, that a connection between language, culture and identity is both more widely felt and more acutely appreciated in the province than in Scotland is thus clearly conveyed. As the following two speakers indicate, a more widespread identification with the ethnolinguistic category 'Gael' is viewed as being a key part of this interconnection in Nova Scotia:

SD	Do you feel kind of a strong connection to the language and community generally? [...] Or are you kind of working your way in?
ANTF3	(1.2) U::m (1.1) like I feel connected to it because like I know that it was in my <u>family</u> [...] I feel yeah definitely like more connected to like my great grandparents and- and like their way of life

SD	Yeah (x)
ANTF3	If that makes sense ((laughs))
SD	Yeah absolutely (.) so in that way would you see yourself as a Gael? Does that word have much meaning for you?
ANTF3	^Yeah
SD	Yeah?
ANTF3	^Yeah (.) I'd say like- I know a lot of people don't even know like (0.8) their geneology at <u>all</u>- which is like really- it's like <u>strange</u> to me like I feel <u>strongly</u> like- like 'who am I?' Like I wouldn't say I was really even Canadian I would say I'm Scottish
ANTF5	Antigonish County (1.1) um (.) lost its language earlier than Cape Breton
SD	Yeah
ANTF5	But the thing is (1.6) is that we're the same people really [...] <u>culturally</u> (.) um (1.8) I f:: I- I felt a lot of it growing up
SD	Hmm [...] do you think now that you have a certain amount of Gaelic and that you've studied in Scotland that you have an identity as a Gael?
ANTF5	I- I- I think I <u>do</u> [...] and (.) for ^myself (.) um (2.2) I don't think it's hokey to say it's there

Both interviewees in the above extracts report a sense of connectedness to Gaelic culture, community and identity through their upbringing in eastern Nova Scotia. Although neither of the speakers had ever met with Gaelic-speaking family members, who died generations before they were born, both report feeling closely connected to the Gaelic language, and identifying as Gaels due to the cultural distinctiveness of the eastern Nova Scotian communities in which they were raised. Expounding on this element of Gaelic culture and identity, the following interviewee refers explicitly to the strong connection between language and identity in western Cape Breton communities in particular:

SD	An canadh tu gur e Gàidheal a th' annad sa chiad àite?=
	Would you say that you're a Gael principally?=
ANTM1	=Chanainnsa gur e chanainnsa gur e
	=I'd say so I'd say so
SD	(Da-rìribh)
	(Really)
ANTM1	Agus an rud [...] tha sinn caran <u>diùid</u> ann an- an-seo ann an Alba Nuaidh a thaobh sin is a' sealltainn (2.9) air- air a' bhràthair mhòr mar gum biodh ann an- air a' Ghàidhealtachd <u>fhèin</u> agus dh'fhaoidte a' smaointinn nach- nach eil dad <u>againne</u> ri thoirt seachad a tha <u>luachmhor</u> [...] ach chanainnsa gu <u>bheil</u> oir 's e (grunn rud) a bh' ann san sgìre seo- an <u>dàimh</u> a th' ann eadar- (.) eadar dualchas nan Gàidheal- <u>dualchas</u> na Gàidhlig (.) agus an cànan

	And the thing is [...] we're rather <u>shy</u> in- here in Nova Scotia about that and tend to look (2.9) to- to the big brother so to speak in- in the ((Scottish)) <u>Highlands</u> and perhaps think that- that <u>we</u> don't have anything to contribute that's <u>valuable</u> [...] but I'd say that we <u>do</u> since we had (lots of things) in this area- the <u>connection</u> that exits between (.) between the Gaels' heritage- Gaelic heritage (.) and the language
SD	Sin e
	That's it
ANTM1	Bha sin ann daonnan (.) bha sin <u>làidir</u> daonnan [...] tha an cultar 's an dualchas ann fhathast- tha e daonnan mun cuairt orra is ma thèid thu dha na dannsaichean ann am **Brook Village, West Mabou, Glencoe- the holy grail!- Glencoe Mills-** (chì thu) sin
	That was always there (.) that was always <u>strong</u> [...] the culture and heritage is still there- it's always around and if you go to the dances in **Brook Village, West Mabou, Glencoe- the holy grail!- Glencoe Mills-** *(you can see) that*

Once again, we see in the above account how extralinguistic and cultural elements of Gaelic heritage are viewed in Nova Scotia as important components of local Gaelic identity, with the ongoing popularity of community dances in western Cape Breton cited as a specific example of the ongoing strength of Gaelic culture in eastern Nova Scotia. As demonstrated in previous extracts, interviewees in Nova Scotia frequently emphasised such artistic and cultural practices in the discussion of Gaelic. Similarly, in the following account, my interviewee describes how he would identify as a Gael irrespective of his having learned Gaelic to fluency as an L2:

SD	A thaobh togail na Gàidhlig dhutsa an [...] robh thu coimhead ort fhèin mar Ghàidheal?=
	In terms of your learning Gaelic [...] did you see yourself then as a Gael?=
ANTM2	=O gu deimhinne
	=Oh for sure
SD	An robh?
	Did you?
ANTM2	Bha ach bha mi coimhead orm fhìn mar sin mun d'fhuair mi a' Ghàidhlig [...] Chaidh mo thogail le (1.5) naidheachdan (x) (2.6) sgilean cho làidir sa ghabhas [...] cho math sa bha iad gu sabaid- rudan a bhiodh uabhasach Gàidhealach (.) 's e sluagh (.) mileanta a th' annainn [...] Nam biodh duine sam bith an-seo a' tighinn thugam-sa agus a bhith ag ràdhainn (.) 'O! (1.4) Dè tha thu dèanadh an-seo leis a leithid seo?' no rud mar sin uill- rud a tha Gàidhealach 's e a ràdhainn 'Bu chòir dhut stad de sin' [...] cha bhithinnsa fada gan cur a-mach às an doras dìreach le (x)

> Yes but I viewed myself that way before I learned Gaelic [...] I was raised with (1.5) storytelling (x) (2.6) skills that were as strong as could be [...] how good they were at fighting- things [like that] that were extremely Gaelic (.) We [Gaels] are a militant people [...] If anyone came up to me here and starting saying to us (.) 'Oh! (1.4) What do you think you're doing here with all this [speaking in Gaelic]?' or something like that well- the Gaelic thing to do is to explain 'You need to stop that behaviour' [...] I wouldn't be long putting them out the door (x)

SD   Hmm [...] an e sin an fhèin-aithne Ghàidhealach mar gum biodh?
> Hmm [...] is that the Gaelic identity so to speak?

ANTM2   Uill bha sinn riamh mar sin
> Well we were always like that

Again, therefore, we see in this extract the pre-eminence attributed to non-linguistic, ethnocultural traits and practices in the definition of Gaelic identity; the speaker's possession of a strong sense of identity as a Gael is viewed as stemming principally from his upbringing, community members' storytelling skills and their quickness to defend (by force, if necessary) their own customs and culture. Yet whilst the possession of a sense of identity as Gaels was frequently traced by Nova Scotian participants as reflective of their extralinguistic cultural traits, certain interviewees reported becoming aware of these distinctive traits and behaviours – and the importance of language to the identity they index – only after learning Gaelic. This sense is clearly conveyed by the two following speakers:

CBIM1   Tha cànan agus cultar (.) a' dol còmhla [...] ach dar a bha mi (.) òg cha ro:bh (.) cha robh mi a' tuigsinn dè cho- dè cho cudromach 's a bha ^sin [...] cha do thuig mi (1.5) um: gu buileach (.) dè cho cudromach 's a tha an cànan fhèin
> Language and culture (.) go together [...] but when I was (.) young I: didn't (.) I didn't understand how- how important that ^was [...] I didn't understand (1.5) um: entirely (.) how important the language itself is

SD   Hmm

CBIM1   Uh [...] 's e pàirt- 's e- 's e Gàidheal a th' annam
> It's a part- I- I am a Gael

SD   'S e mm hmm
> Yeah mm hmm

CBIM1   Uh huh thug mi an aire (.) air a sin no bha mi a' tuigsinn [...] 's a bha mi ag ionnsachadh agus (.) dar a bha mi- dar a bha mi car cuimseach fileanta um: (1.5) bhuail e orm an uair sin [...] tha **identity** gu math cudromach dhan a h-uile duine
> Uh huh I noticed (.) that or I understood that [...] whilst I was learning and (.) when I was- when I was reasonably fluent um: (1.5) it occurred to me then [...] **identity** is important to everyone

HALF1	Dar a thòisich mi air a' Ghàidhlig [...] bha iad a' bruidhinn air um (.) sloinneaidhean agus dìreach bha ^bing 'O! Siud as coireach gu robh iad ag èigheadh Sarah Archie Angus ris an t-seann tè a bha sin dar a bha mi òg!' Cha b' urrainn dhomh tuigsinn riamh carson a thug iad Archie air boireannach!
	When I started (learning) Gaelic [...] they were talking about um (.) patronymics and it was just like ^<u>bing</u> 'Oh so that's why they called that old lady Sarah Archie Angus when I was young!' I couldn't understand why they called a woman Archie!
SD	Hmm
HALF1	Agus rudan eile mar sin agus aig ceann na seachdain thuirt mi '^<u>oh my God</u> I think I'm Gaelic!' ((laughs)) [...] mura biodh ceangal ann le Gàidhlig air bith (x) cha- cha b' <u>urrainn</u> dhomh cumail orm ann an Alba Nuaidh [...] tha mi a' smaoineach' (.) feumaidh (.) Gàidhlig a bhith nad chridh'
	And other things and at the end of the week I said '<u>oh my God</u> I think I'm Gaelic!' ((laughs)) [...] if I'd had no connection with Gaelic (x) I couldn't- I <u>couldn't</u> have continued ((learning Gaelic)) in Nova Scotia [...] I think (.) Gaelic (.) has to be in your heart
SD	Hmm
HALF1	Air neo (0.8) feumaidh tu ceangal a- a dhèanadh (.) um:: do fèin aithne aig duine
	Or (0.8) you have to- to make a connection (.) um:: to someone's identity
SD	Mm hmm mm hmm
HALF1	Um an dòigh air choreigin (.) uh ach chan eil mi bruidhinn air **DNA**
	Um in some way or another (.) uh but I'm not talking about **DNA**

In this extract, the sudden dawning awareness of the participant's Gaelic identity is likened to the ring of a bell: a dramatic realisation at the start of her journey toward Gaelic acquisition. In the previous account, CBIM1 notes that an awareness of his identity as a Gael and of the importance of the language to his cultural identity developed only after he had become somewhat fluent in the language. These kinds of narrative, locating acquisition of Gaelic as a pre-eminent condition for the dawning awareness of identity, were more unusual in Nova Scotia. As shown above, Gaelic identity tended here to be viewed as deriving from extralinguistic factors, although learners' possession of a Gaelic identity through cultural attachment often inspired the later acquisition of fluency. As the following interviewee notes, it is a matter of conscious effort for teachers and activists to develop learners' understanding of what it means to be a Gael, as a precondition to revitalising the Gaelic language:

HALM2	Tha sinn a' cur (.) um (.) prìomhachais air ciamar as urrainn dhuinn – fhios agad – seòrsa de (2.6) lèirsinn ciamar a bhith nad Ghàidheal a chruthachadh
	We (.) um (.) prioritise how we can – you know – kind of (2.6) create a vision of how to be a Gael
SD	Tha sin inntinneach
	That's interesting
HALM2	Agus um (.) tha sinn- tha sinn a' creidsinn gur e (2.2) an dòigh gun do chaill sinn sin […] sin far a bheil sinn air fhaicinn (2.0) fhaclan ùra a' tighinn a-staigh fhios agad um (3.9) san fharsaingeachd '**Scottish**' […] '**Highland Scottish**' no '**Scotch**'
	*And um (.) we- we believe that (2.2) in a way that we lost that (vision) […] that's where we see (2.0) new words coming in you know um (3.9) generally speaking '**Scottish**' […] '**Highland Scottish**' or '**Scotch**'*
SD	((laughs)) **Scotch**=
HALM2	=No fiù 's '**Celtic**' [[(x) na faclan sin uile]
	*=Or even '**Celtic**' [[(x) all those words]*
SD	[[An àite Gàidhealach]
	[[Instead of Gaelic]
HALM2	Seadh […] chaill daoine (2.2) an: dearbh aithne aca fhèin ann an dòigh
	Yeah […] people lost (2.2) their own identity in a way

The sense conveyed here of a deliberate effort to reclaim and revive in people a sense of identity as Gaels, as a means of rectifying an historic loss of identity that accompanied the loss of Gaelic in Nova Scotia, is one that is encountered frequently in discourses of Gaelic language and identity in the province. As I show in the following pages, the significance attached to this identity category by new speakers in Nova Scotia far outstrips that which may occasionally be encountered in Scotland at present.

First, however, it is worth noting the relatively few examples of Nova Scotian new speakers of Gaelic who were somewhat more circumspect in describing their identities as Gaels, or who rejected the term. The interviewee in the previous extract highlights the multiplicity of terms historically employed by Nova Scotians to index their identities as Scottish (Gaels) in the province, which the interviewee in fact suggests indicates a loss of historic Gaelic identity. The following speaker reflects on the historic use of similar terminology ('Scottish', 'Celtic') and how recent attempts to rehabilitate the term 'Gael' in the province do not always sit comfortably with her:

SD	Bheil thu coimhead ort fhèin mar bhana-Ghàidheal?
	Do you see yourself as a (female) Gael?

CBIF5	Uh huh (.) ^uill [[ann an <u>dòigh</u>]
	^well [[in a <u>way</u>]
SD	[[An canadh tu sin?]
	[[Would you say that?]
CBIF5	Ann an dòigh ach tha cuimhne agam nuair a bha mi aig an t-Sabhal Mhòr bhiomaid <u>daonnan</u> a-mach air a' chuspair seo
	=In a way but I remember when I was at Sabhal Mòr [Ostaig Gaelic college] we were <u>always</u> speaking about that subject
SD	Yeah
CBIF5	Agus <u>uair</u>eannan bhithinn ag ràdh (.) 'carson?' [...] Tha mi coimhead orm fhìn mar bana-Ghàidheal math dh'fhaoidte air sàilleabh 's gu bheil mi ag obair airson cor na Gàidhlig [...] tha e gu ^math cudromach an-seo- tha sinn a' feuchainn a bhith cleachdadh an fhacail siud- Gàidheal
	And sometimes I would say (.) 'why?' [...] I view myself as a Gael perhaps because I work to improve the state of Gaelic [...] it's ^quite important here- we try to use that word- Gael
SD	Hmm
CBIF5	Uh (.) oh tha e air atharrachadh tro na linntean
	Oh it's changed through the years
SD	Sheadh
	Yeah
CBIF5	Bho- **you know**- 'Highlander' [[no 'Scots']
	From- **you know**- 'Highlander' [[or 'Scots']
SD	[[**Highlander yeah**]
CBIF5	'Scottish', 'Celtic' – diofar- diofar rudan ann an um (1.4) ann an:: chan eil fhios'am- **vogue** ach a-nist tha sinn <u>really</u> a' feuchainn a bhith a' cleach- dadh a facail sin- 'na Gàidheil'
	'Scottish', 'Celtic' – different – different things in um (1.4) in I dunno in:: **vogue** but now we're <u>really</u> trying to use that word – the Gaels

My interviewee qualifies her assertion of ethnocultural identity as a Gael with the phrase 'in a <u>way</u>' (*ann an <u>dòigh</u>*), producing rising intonation and heavy emphasis on the last word to convey this qualification clearly. These para- linguistic cues in her speech acts suggest that she views the possession of this identity as potentially problematic. She recounts a sense of disillusionment at how prevalent discussion of the term seemed to her while studying at Sabhal Mòr Ostaig. Nevertheless, she goes on to explain that she habitually does in fact describe herself as a Gael and, indeed, notes that language advocates in Nova Scotia consciously attempt to encourage the use of that term. In the past, she notes that Gaels in the province themselves might have identified to a greater degree as Highlanders, Scots or, rather less precisely, as 'Celtic'.

This multiplicity of terms for cultural identities in Nova Scotia Gaeldom is again apparent in the following extract:

SD	You mentioned your paternal granny was a Gael- she would have regarded herself like that?=
CBIF1	=I don't think <u>she</u> would have regarded herself as that
SD	No? That's not a label she'd have recognised?
CBIF1	Well it's really not a word that's been <u>used</u> much here […] there's kinda been like a ((tuts)) (1.0) a <u>confusion</u> with the labels
SD	Hmm=
CBIF1	=So am I Scottish? Am I:: Celtic? (.) Am I:: Gaelic? […] Even me myself- saying 'I'm a Gael'
SD	Hmm
CBIF1	I don't know <u>why</u>
SD	Hmm
CBIF1	It's just feel like '^am I?' Like 'what does this <u>really</u> mean?'

For the interviewee in the following extract, the use of term 'Gael' locally is problematised due to the extent of linguistic decline in Cape Breton:

SD	Do you kind of feel your<u>self</u> to be a Gael? How do you identify with it?=
CBIF3	=Yeah I ^<u>do</u>:: (0.9) um (1.6) I <u>do</u>- I- yeah I- I don't know what I want to say um (3.9) I mean I ^really appreciated moving into xxx ((rural Cape Breton)) […] like the opportunity to be (1.3) in a place with a strong <u>sense</u> of ^place
SD	Yeah
CBIF3	Um:: […] I mean it's <u>complicated</u> because most people don't speak the language
SD	No
CBIF3	And (1.2) I think- it's a mostly Protestant community- Protestant communities lost it earlier […] like it would have been 100% Gaelic

Again, metapragmatic cues to the speaker's sense of uncertainty over her own identity as a Gael are apparent in the rising intonation and elongation in the phrase 'I do' and frequent long pauses while she thinks of how best to describe her relationship to the local community. It is noteworthy, however, that this speaker reports an association with the term Gael, in spite of lacking any immediate family connection to Gaelic. The importance of the 'place' and of the cultural distinctiveness of rural Cape Breton are described to endure even in spite of the lack of Gaelic linguistic competence among the vast majority of local inhabitants today.

As with the relatively few speakers, above, who appeared rather more circumspect than the majority of Nova Scotian interviewees as regards their identity as Gaels, a small minority of speakers in Nova Scotia rejected that term as a descriptor of themselves. For the following participant, a lack of immediate family heritage connection to Gaelic and an emphasis on having learned the language are emphasised in his reported lack of identity as a Gael:

SD	A bheil fèin-aithne agad mar Ghàidheal no mar neach-labhairt [[na Gàidhlig?]
	Do you have an identity as a Gael or as a [[Gaelic speaker?]
ANTM7	[[Ah] mi-fhìn?
	[[Ah] myself?
SD	Mm hmm
ANTM7	(1.6) Uh: cha- chan ^eil **actually**
	(1.6) Uh: nn- ^no **actually**
SD	Hmm
ANTM7	Cha chanainnsa
	I wouldn't say so
SD	Nach can?
	No?
ANTM7	Cha chan uh <u>dh'ionnsaich</u> mi an cànan ach chanainnsa gu- cha chanainnsa gur e Gàidheal a th' annam […] a chionn 's nach- (.) nach eil <u>ceangal</u> **really** agamsa […] dh'ionnsaich mi an cànan is tha gràdh agam air ach chan eil e agam san teaghlach agam
	*No uh I learned the language but I'd say that- I wouldn't say I'm a Gael […] because (.) I don't **really** have a <u>connection</u> […] I learned the language but I don't have it in my family*

The speaker emphasises his experience of having learned Gaelic as a second language, in the absence of intrinsic motivation deriving from personal heritage, in explaining his lack of association with the term 'Gael'. This extract stands as a relative outlier in the Nova Scotia dataset, in which a majority of participants were in large part motivated to learn Gaelic by their family heritage and already (at least somewhat) well-developed sense of identity as Gaels. As we shall see in the following accounts, this general pattern stands in stark contradistinction to the majority of new speakers I interviewed in Scotland. Subsequently, analysis will demonstrate the apparent reasons attributed to this distinction in discourses of Gaelic revitalisation, heritage and socialisation in the two polities.

Scottish new speakers: rejection of Gael(ic) identity

For a clear majority of interviewees in Scotland, the suggestion that they, as new speakers of the language, would identify as Gaels or associate closely with that term was rejected out of hand. Some of the reasons and explanations that my respondents conveyed discursively for this stark rejection of the appellation 'Gael' will be discussed in the following accounts, before my analysis considers the possible sociolinguistic correlates of these discourses. In the following two extracts, Scottish interviewees' general discomfort with labels of identity, on one hand, and awareness of the cultural distinctiveness of Gaels as a group historically, on the other, are clearly expressed:

SD	An canadh tu gur e Gàidheal a th' annad?
	Would you say that you are a Gael?
EDIF3	Cha chanainn idir
	I wouldn't say so at all
SD	Hmm
EDIF3	((laughs)) Tha mi air <u>tòrr</u> ùine a chur seachad a' smaoineachadh ((laughs)) air na rudan seo!
	((laughs)) I've spent a <u>lot</u> of time thinking ((laughs)) about these things!
SD	A bheil?
	Have you?
EDIF3	**Yeah** (.) is (.) chan eil mi cho measail air **labels** idir mar sin **so**
	Yeah (.) and (.) I'm not very fond of labels like that at all so
SD	Dìreach
	Exactly
EDIF3	Chan eil mi airson a ràdh gur e (1.2) Gàidheal idir a th' annam
	I don't want to say that (1.2) I'm a Gael at all
EDIF1	Cha do dh'ionnsaich mi a' Ghàidhlig gus a bhith nam Ghàidheal
	I didn't learn Gaelic to be a Gael
SD	Hmm
EDIF1	Cha do dh'ionnsaich mi i gu robh mi- air sgàth 's gu robh mi ag iarraidh ri bhith (1.5) um: (1.1) ann an cinneadh (.) eile
	I didn't learn it because I- because I wanted to be (1.5) um: (1.1) in a different (.) ethnic group
SD	Sheadh
	Yeah
EDIF1	Um (.) bha:: (1.7) ach bha mi- bha mi ga fhaicinn mar ^^phàirt den teaghlach agus mar phàirt den dùthaich agam
	Um (.) I:: (1.7) but I- I saw it as a ^^part of my family and as part of my country

The discussion of Gaelic identity and cultural distinctiveness unpacked in both of the above accounts is interspersed with (para)linguistic cues to the speakers' pragmatic meanings. In the first extract, my interviewee distances herself from the identity label 'Gael', switching to English to emphasise this, while in the second account, the interviewee explains that she did not learn Gaelic to become a Gael, although she did regard it as a part of her family and country. Nevertheless, the sharp rising tone used on the word 'part' (*mar ^^phàirt*) may be read here to indicate the rather limited degree to which she viewed Gaelic as part of these aspects of her identity. It is likely that this particular ideology, concerning the relevance of Gaelic to Scots outwith the Highlands, is reflective of more mainstream attitudes to Gaelic in Scotland.

A slightly different perspective is brought to bear on the question of Gaelic identity by new speakers of the language now resident in Scotland, but who were raised in Ireland. Such individuals constitute a substantial and noteworthy element in the new speaker demographic in Scotland, due in part to the (supposed or actual) linguistic similarity of Scottish Gaelic to Irish (cf. McLeod and O'Rourke 2015). Nevertheless, my interviewees tended to concord with Scottish-born new speakers' views of their own identity as Gaels, as is clearly expressed in the following two accounts:

SD	A bheil fèin-aithne agad mar Ghàidheal?
	Do you have an identity as a Gael?
GLAF1	Uh **no absolutely not** [...] is dòcha (1.2) gur e rud eachdraidheil a th' ann- bha na Gàidheil ann an Alba **really** (1.1) **cut-off deliberately** [...] em:: **and** (1.2) bha iad (0.8) **othered** em: agus is dòcha gu bheil (1.1) gur e sin e **like** ann an Èirinn cha chreid mi gu robh (.) na Gaelgeoirí cho **othered** sin [...] ann an Èirinn cha robh mi a' faireachdain **'oh yeah there's the Gaels and then there's us'** ach tha mi faireachdainn sin 's dòcha ann an Alba
	*Uh **no absolutely not** [...] perhaps (1.2) it's a historical thing- the Gaels in Scotland were **really** (1.1) **cut-off deliberately** [...] em:: **and** (1.2) they were (0.8) **othered** em: and perhaps that's (1.1) that's it **like** in Ireland I don't think (.) Irish language speakers were as **othered** as that [...] in Ireland I never felt like **'oh yeah there's the Gaels and then there's us'** but I do perhaps feel that in Scotland*
EDIF2	'S ann à Èirinn a Deas a tha mi ach em 's e:: Pròstanach a tha nam mhàthair [...] bha ceangalan againn le- ri Èirinn a Tuath
	I'm from the south of Ireland but em my mother is a Protestant [...] we had connections to- to Northern Ireland
SD	Bha
	Yes

EDIF2	Agus bhiodh daoine ann an-sin ag ràdh **you know** 'oh 's e **Brits** a th' annaibh' (.) bha mi- bha mi mì-chofhurtail san dùthaich agam fhìn [...] cha robh mi <u>riamh</u> na mo Ghàidheal- cha robh mi a-<u>riamh</u> [...] ann an Èirinn cha chanadh sinne (0.7) cha chanamaid (0.6) 'Gàidheal' 's fheàrr leinne '**Celt**'
	And people there would say **you know** *'oh you're* **Brits**' *(.) I was- I was uncomfortable in my own country [...] I was* <u>never</u> *a Gael- I* <u>never</u> *was [...]in Ireland we didn't say (0.7) we wouldn't say (0.6) 'Gael' we prefer* '**Celt**'
SD	Sheadh uh huh
	Yeah uh huh
EDIF2	So:: chanainnsa gur e **Celt** a th' annam
	So:: I'd say I'm a **Celt**

For rather different reasons, both speakers above reject the term 'Gael' as a descriptor of their identities. Clearly the term carries different nuances of semantics in Ireland, and whilst the first interviewee observes that Scottish Gaels were 'othered' in Scotland in a way that was not the case in Ireland, the second speaker reports never having been a Gael either at home in Ireland (perhaps partly as a consequence of experiencing sectarian insults) or in Scotland, preferring instead to associate with the term 'Celt'.

When Scottish-born interviewees reflected on the meaning of the word '*Gàidheal*', on the other hand, there was often a tendency to question what the term might actually denote in the twenty-first century. As has been observed many times in recent years, uncertainty around the specific meaning of the term has become increasingly conspicuous in Scotland (if not, as seen previously, in Nova Scotia). This uncertainty is exhibited in the following account:

SD	A bheil beachd làidir agad mar sin air cò na Gàidheil?
	Do you have a strong idea of who the Gaels are?
GLAM4	Uill sin e 's e ce::ist (.) a th' ann agus ann an dòigh [...] Eil sinn a-mach air cànan? No=
	Well that's it it's a que::stion (.) and in a way [...] Are we speaking about language? Or=
SD	=No cultar no?
	=Or culture or?
GLAM4	A thaobh ^fala no dè? An e rud dùthchasach a th' ann? [...] Tha mi <u>eòlach</u> air agus tha- tha an deasbad- deasbad ann aig an t-Sabhal Mhòr an-dràsta cuideachd- dè a th' ann an Gàidheal? Dè a th' anns a' ^Ghàidhealtachd an taca ri (1.1) eh: eh seach- no an taca ri **Highlands**? [...] tha e rudeigin gu ma:th (1.2) mì: (.) mì-seasmach no **nebulous you know**? [...] **I mean** gu: (.) **eh intuitively you know** cha chan- cha chanainn Gàidheal a th' annam

	co-dhiù [...] Chanainn Gàidheil ri daoine eile (.) 's e Gàidheal **ethnicity** [[an an dòigh]
	In terms of ^blood or what? Is it a hereditary thing? [...] I <u>know</u> about it and the debate- the debate is ongoing at Sabhal Mòr [Ostaig, Gaelic college] just now as well- what is a Gael? What is the ^Gàidhealtachd compared to (1.1) eh: eh as opposed to the **Highlands**? *[...] it's something that's qui:te (1.2) undefined or nebulous you know? I mean (.) eh intuitively you know I wouldn- I wouldn't call myself a Gael anyway [...] I'd call other people Gaels (.) Gael is an* **ethnicity** *[[in a way]*
SD	[[Uh huh]
GLAM4	Chan e a thaobh fala ach tha mi smaoineachadh air **ethnicity**
	Not in terms of blood I think but of **ethnicity**

Uncertainty and lack of clarity over the exact meaning of the term *Gàidheal/Gael* is emphasised in the above interview excerpt, therefore. Indeed, the interviewee describes the notion of the Gael as 'nebulous', querying whether the word should be defined principally in terms of kinship, descent or blood, before settling on the definition of Gael as a marker of 'ethnicity' which he does not personally profess. Similarly, the term *Gàidhealtachd* is viewed as indexing a degree of common descent and heredity, as opposed to the more neutral English term 'Highlands' for places ideologically associated with Gaelic use, as the language's traditional, notional heartland. Place, viewed in such terms, was frequently emphasised in Scottish new speakers' accounts of their lack of identity as Gaels, along with a clear desire not to appropriate the term in a culturally insensitive manner. This dimension of the issue is evident in the following extract, for example:

SD	A bheil beachd agad air cò na Gàidheil?
	Do you have an opinion as to who the Gaels are?
GLAF5	O::::: cac!
	Oh::::: shit!
SD	((laughs))
GLAF5	(5.5) ((quietly)) Uill 's e ceist inntinneach a th' ann [...] ann an Glaschu
	Well it's an interesting question [...] in Glasgow
SD	Uh huh
GLAF5	Oir tha sinn- **you know** tha sinn ag obair <u>uabhasach</u> cruaidh [...] cumail foghlam tro mheadhan na Gàidhlig (.) fosgailte airson a h-<u>uile</u> duine [...] tha mi a' <u>tuigsinn</u> (0.8) gu bheil ceangal (1.2) <u>làidir</u> eadar an cànan agus um (3.1) **Gaeldom**=
	Because we- you know we work <u>really</u> hard [...] to keep Gaelic-medium education (.) open to <u>every</u>one [...] I <u>understand</u> (0.8) that there is a (1.2) <u>strong</u> linkage between the language and um (3.1) **Gaeldom**=

SD	=Hmm
GLAF5	Airson daoine (2.1) em (.) bho na h-^eileanan […] **so yeah** ((tuts)) ach yeah (.) ((laughing)) chan eil fhios agam! Tha e cudromach dhomh- tha e <u>uabhasach</u> cudromach dhomh […] **I would never want to deprive someone of their (.) Gaeldom if they don't speak Gaelic**
For people (2.1) em (.) from the ^islands […] so yeah ((tuts)) but yeah (.) ((laughing)) I dunno! It's important to me- it is <u>really</u> important to me […] I would never want to deprive someone of their (.) Gaeldom if they don't speak Gaelic
SD	Hmm
GLAF5	And I would <u>never</u> have the confidence to say 'I'm a Gael' because I- just because I speak Gaelic

The above interviewee's references in the extract to 'the islands' (*na h-eileanan*) and, somewhat less precisely, to 'Gaeldom' locate Gaelic as belonging chiefly to a specific geographically and culturally defined group, whether or not that group can be defined by its actual capacity to communicate in Gaelic. Her initial response to my question on who she understands Gaels to be (*'o cac'* – oh shit – with several moments' elongation of the vowel in '*o*') perhaps reflects an implicit understanding of controversy surrounding the identiy of Gaels and who may (and may not) be regarded and accepted as such. The interviewee's reference to Gaelic-medium education in Glasgow in relation to Gaels' identity is particularly pertinent. Amongst the subset of interviewees who had become new speakers via that system in school, discourses around Gael(ic) identity – and the majority of past-GME students' weak association with that identity – are frequently encountered (cf. Dunmore 2019). One example of this discourse is conveyed by the following interviewee:

GMEM3	Tha mi smaoineachadh gu bheil ceangal nas làidire agamsa ris a' cho-imhearsnachd air an eilean (.) air sgàth 's gun d'fhuair mi (.) foghlam tro mheadhan na Gàidhlig […] ged nach eil mise a' smaoineachadh orm mar Ghàidheal airson tha seòrsa **stigma attached** a tha mise faicinn
*I think I have a stronger connection to the community on the island (.) because I received Gaelic-medium education […] although I don't see myself as a Gael because there's a kind of **stigma attached** that I see*
SD:	Tha
Yeah
GMEM3	**Identity** 's chan eil mi airson a bhith a' dol a-staigh dhan a' chòmhradh a tha sin idir [… ach] chan e Gàidheal a th'annam idir idir
*An **identity** and I don't want to get into that discussion at all […but] I'm not a Gael at all*

SD	Nach e hmm
	Aren't you hmm
GMEM3	Chan eil mise ag aont- chan eil **association** agamsa leis a seòrsa **idea** a tha sin (.) chan eil fiù 's fios agam buileach dè a th'ann!
	*I don't agr- I don't have an **association** with that sort of **idea** (.) I don't even really know what it is!*

The sense of 'stigma' that the interviewee describes in relation to Gael(ic) identity is not fully explained by him; he states simply that he is unwilling to elaborate further by going into a deeper discussion of the issue. It is clear from his subsequent statement, however, that uncertainty over what the term signifies is part of his own lack of affiliation with it (*'chan eil fiù 's fios agam buileach dè a th'ann!'*). Yet the sense that the term 'Gael' is loaded with negative affect and stigmatised social meaning was communicated frequently in interviews with Scottish-based new speakers. In the following extract, my interviewee describes this sense in terms of 'baggage':

EDIF4	Chan eil mi faicinn adhbhar sam bith a bhith a ràdh **you know 'I:::** (.) **oh actually I <u>really</u> come from such and such an island'** ((laughs)) **you know?** [...] Nan canadh tu 'Gàidheal'
	*I don't see any reason to make out that **you know 'I:::** (.) **oh actually I <u>really</u> come from such and such an island'** ((laughs)) **you know?***
	[...but] if you say 'Gael'
SD	Hmm
EDIF4	Tha tòrr **baggage** timcheall air- air an fhacal sin
	*There's a lot of **baggage** around- around that word*
SD	Mm hmm
EDIF4	Chan eil **baggage** sam bith timcheall air (1.2) duine a tha (.) bruidhinn na Gàidhlig [...] 's ann aig daoine <u>eile</u> a tha e a bhith cur na **labels** orm
	*There's no **baggage** whatsoever around (1.2) someone who (.) speaks Gaelic [...] it's up to <u>other</u> people to put **labels** on me*
SD	Hmm
EDIF4	Chan eil mise dol a thogail am <u>bratach</u> seo seach bratach eile
	I'm not going to raise this <u>flag</u> in place of any other flag

The 'baggage' surrounding the term 'Gael' – and its association particularly with certain island communities in the present day – is alluded to throughout the interviewee's discussion of the term. She also expresses a reaction against the idea of 'labels' as 'flags' or markers of identity with which she appears uncomfortable in principle. In the following extract, my interviewee explains his own aversion to the cultural signifier 'Gael/s' in rather different terms, reflecting that an emphasis on the separateness of Gaelic culture (compared to the rest of Scotland) is not helpful to the language community:

INVM1	Bha Gàidhlig aig uh:: (.) oh nist (1.1) rudeigin mar mo shinn (4.1) sinn sinn sinn seanair **so** sia ginealaich air ais [...] ach uh (0.7) chan- cha bhi mi a' cleachdadh an fhacail [Gàidheal] ach (.) corra uair [...] 's e bacadh air- air adhbhar na Gàidhlig a bhith a' cantainn (.) 'tha sinne fa leth mar sluagh' *Something like my uh:: (.) oh now (1.1) like my great (4.1) great-great-great-grandfather spoke Gaelic **so** six generations back [...] but uh (0.7) I would only use the word [Gael] (.) very occasionally [...] it's an obstacle to- to the Gaelic cause to say (.) 'we are a separate people'*
SD	Hmm
INVM1	Aon- cha bhiodh a h-uile duine a' gabhail riumsa mar- mar Ghàidheal co-dhiù oir dhaibhsan tha e barrachd mu dheidhinn (.) càite an deach do thogail *One- not everyone would accept me as a- as a Gael anyway because for them it's more about (.) where you were raised*
SD	Hmm
INVM1	Dè an seòrsa àrainneachd anns an deach do thogail em [...] agus cuideachd chan eil e a' leigeil daoine ùra a-staigh um (.) tha an cunnart sin na lùib [...] Mar sin **nah-** cha bhithinn a' cleachdadh 'na Gàidheil' *What sort of environment you were brought up in em [...] and also it doesn't let new people in [to the Gaelic community (.) there is that danger involved [...] So **nah-** I wouldn't use the term 'the Gaels'*

Here the interviewee describes what he sees as the inherent 'danger' of emphasising the discreteness of Gaels and Gaelic speakers as a separate (ethnic) group, arising chiefly from the necessary boundary keeping that use of the term entails, which is seen to prevent much-needed new cohorts of speakers from becoming accepted as part of the wider Gaelic community. For interviewees in the following two extracts, however, lack of personal identity as Gaels is described more in terms of a lack of connectedness to that community per se, rather than any strategic need to keep its boundaries accessible to new speakers:

EDIM2	Tha cànan na Gàidhlig cho cudromach dhomh *The Gaelic language is so important to me*
SD	Mm hmm
EDIM2	Tha mi faireachdainn gu math **emotion**ta a bheil fhios agad? [...] **You know** tha mi a' faireachdainn (.) gu bheil e (.) pàirt den fhèin-eòlas agam um agus (1.2) um:: (0.9) tha e gu math doirbh uaireannan ge-tà (1.0) air sgàth 's nach e (.) nach eil Gàidhlig bho thùs agam

	*I feel quite **emotional** [about it] you know? [...] **You know** I feel (.) that it is (.) part of my sense of self and um and (1.2) um:: (0.9) it's quite hard sometimes though (1.0) because I'm not (.) I don't have Gaelic as a first language*
SD	Mm hmm
EDIM2	Agus cha- chan eil mi anns a' choimhearsnachd ann an dòigh [...] carson a tha iad ag ràdh 'cò às a tha thu?' **You know 'who are you from?'** is mar sin- 'bho thùs' [...] na h-abairtean a th' ann anns a' Ghàidhlig **you know** tha iad (.) um (1.7) tha iad (.) a' sealladh dhomh dè seòrsa (1.8) cultar a tha aig a' Ghàidhlig mu dheidhinn (.) **belonging**
	*And I'm not in the community in a way [...] why do they say 'where are you from?' **You know** ((literal meaning)) 'who are you from?' and so on 'originally' [...] the phrases that exist (for it) in Gaelic you know they're (.) um (1.7) in my view they (.) show what sort of (1.8) culture Gaelic possesses around (.) **belonging***
SD	Hmm
EDIM2	Agus chan eil mi a' faireachdainn gu bheil **belonging** agam
	*And I don't feel I have any **belonging***
SD	So 's ann- bha ceangal pearsanta agus ceangal teaghlaich agad leis a' Ghàidhlig leis gu robh Gàidhlig aig do sheanmhair
	So it was- you had a personal and family connection to Gaelic since your grandmother could speak Gaelic
EDIM4	Aidh ann an dòigh- ann an dòigh
	Yeah in a way- in a way
SD	Ach chan e sin an t-adhbhar as mò gun do dh'ionnsaich thu, no an e?
	But that wasn't the main reason you learned, or was it?
EDIM4	Uill ((sighs)) b' e sin <u>pàirt</u> dheth
	Well ((sighs)) that was <u>part</u> of it
[...]	
SD	Dè tha am facal Gàidheal a' ciallachadh dhut?
	What does the word Gael mean to you?
EDIM4	Uh duine a tha (.) uill (1.8) uill- oh tha sin- tha sin <u>caran</u> doirbh [...ach] mi-fhìn? 'S e Sasannach a th' annam- tha mi duilich!
	Uh a person who (.) well (1.8) well- oh that's- that's quite difficult [...but] personally? I'm an Englishman- I'm sorry!

Both of the above speakers report possessing closer family ties to Gaelic and its speaker community than speaker INVM1. In common with the latter, however, both reject the term 'Gael' as an appellation that reflects their own relationships with Gaelic, on the basis that they do not feel that they belong to the community. Speaker EDIM2 is notably more wistful in noting his lack of a sense of 'belonging' in Gaelic, whilst EDIM4 is rather more bullish, asserting his English identity as one that is implicitly incompatible with being a Gael.

In stark contrast with Nova Scotian interviewees, therefore, the majority of Scottish-based participants rejected the term 'Gael' as a label that adequately reflected their identities in the language. Various reasons were reported for this lack of association, but it is clear that even the minority of speakers with recent family heritage in the language tend, in Scotland, not to view the Gael(ic) identity as one with which they can identify.

It must be noted, however, that a relatively small group of Scottish new speakers described their identities as Gaels in positive and unproblematic terms. When these interviewees reported a feeling of association with the term, a conceptual discussion of its meaning and relationship to other keenly felt identies was generally also involved. For the following speaker, who lacks a heritage connection to Gaelic but received Gaelic-medium education in childhood and now works in the language, her identity as a Gael is clear:

GMEF1	Tha Gàidheil air an sgapadh air feadh an dùthaich [sic] [...] tha an t-uabhas de dh'ìomhaighean Alba a' tighinn às a' Ghàidhealtachd (.) chan eil iadsan ag ràdh gur e ìomhaigh Ghàidhealach a th'ann- ag ràdh gur e ìomhaigh Albannach a th'ann
	Gaels are spread throughout the country [...] loads of symbols of Scotland come from the Highlands (.) that don't purport to be a Highland symbol- but rather a Scottish symbol
SD	Tha sin ceart [...] a bheil a' Ghàidhlig na pàirt chudromach de do chuid fhèin aithne (.) air neo **identity**?
	That's true [...] is Gaelic an important part of your identity?
GMEF1	Dhòmhsa?
	To me?
SD	Aig ìre phearsanta aidh
	Personally yeah
GMEF1	**Yeah**
SD	Tha (.) an e Gàidheal a th'annad?
	Yes (.) are you a Gael?
GMEF1	'S e [...] ach 's e- 's e ceist gu math doirbh a tha sin (.) tha daoine ag ràdh (.) 'uill chan eil Gàidhlig aig do phàrantan' ach: chanainnsa gu bheil- gur e Gàidheal a th'annamsa
	Yes [...] but it's- that's quite a difficult question [...] people say (.) 'well your parents can't speak Gaelic' bu:t I would say so- that I'm a Gael

The interviewee reflects on the prevalence of Highland and Gaelic symbolism in constructions of Scottish national identity. Perhaps reflecting her own childhood, being raised in Highland communities (though without a known family connection to Gaelic), she answers my question clearly in the affirmative, that she is a Gael but that the question is difficult, particulary as others are described as challenging this identity since her parents cannot speak the language. In a similar fashion, the following speaker reflects on the complicated question of Gaelic identity as a 'spectrum', from traditional to new speakers:

SD	Cò na Gàidheil nad bheachdsa?
	Who are the Gaels in your view?
GLAM1	Cò iadsan?
	Who are they?
SD	Cò iadsan?
	Who are they?
GLAM1	Uh (.) na Gàidheil traidiseanta no na Gàidheil ùra no? 'S e **spectrum** a th' ann
	Uh (.) the traditional Gaels or the new Gaels or? It's a **spectrum**
SD	'S e ((laughs)) **spectrum** a th' ann!
	It is ((laughs)) it's a **spectrum***!*
GLAM1	^Yeah!
SD	Uh huh [...] a bheil thu coimhead ort fhèin mar Ghàidheal ùr? (.) An e Gàidheal ùr a th' annadsa?
	Uh huh [...] do you see yourself as a new Gael? (.) Are you a new Gael?
GLAM1	(2.6) Em chan eil mi **really** a' smaointinn [...] a-rithist **you know** ma tha:: ma tha: thusa no (.) fear sam bith ag ràdh 'tha mi nam Ghàidheal' **then aye okay** chan eil mi airson a ràdh nach e
	(2.6) Em I don't **really** *think [so] [...] again* **you know** *if:: if: you or (.) anyone says that 'I am a Gael'* **then aye okay** *I don't want to say I'm not*

This interviewee employs the term 'Gàidheil ùra' ('new Gaels') in his discussion of who the Gaels are, a rather different label with a potentially discrete meaning: he distinguishes 'new' Gaels from 'traditional' Gaels in his explanation of Gael identity. It is notable that while he personally would not self-identify as a 'new' Gael (*Gàidheal ùr*), he would not generally object to others' description of him in those terms. The following account demonstrates how another new speaker, albeit this time one with recent family connections to Gaelic, views herself as a Gael, but children in GME without such a heritage as 'new' Gaels:

SD	Am bi na Gàidheil a' gabhail leat mar Ghàidheal eile?=
	Do the Gaels accept you as another Gael=
GLAF4	=Bidh
	=Yes
SD	Air sgàth 's gu bheil na ceanglaichean san [[teaghlach 's mar sin?]
	Because of the family [[connections and so on?]

GLAF4   [[Uh bidh (.) uh huh] bidh- tha sin a' dèanamh diofar mòr- tha mi smaointinn ma tha thu tighinn gun cheangal sam <u>bith</u> (.) tha e (1.3) nas: duilghe dhut (.) eh a bhith uh fàilte fhaighinn a-steach dhan a' choimhearsnachd

[[Uh yes (.) uh huh] yes- it makes a big difference- I think if you come without <u>any</u> connection at all (.) it's (1.3) harder for you (.) eh to be welcomed into the community

[...]

SD   Dè as ciall dhan fhacal Gàidheal mar sin? An e dìreach cuideigin às a' Ghàidhealtachd le Gàidhlig?=

What does the word Gael mean then? Is it just someone from Highlands who can speak Gaelic=

GLAF4   =Cha chreid mi g'eil- gum feum thu a bhith a' buntainn ri- a' buntainn dhan a' Ghàidhealtachd [...] 's e dòigh- an e dòigh-beatha a th' ann? Chan eil fhios'am – 's e **state of mind** a th' ann [...] tha sinn a' faicinn 'Gàidheil (.) ùra' – mas e sin a thachras – tighinn tro na sgoiltean a-nis (.) luchd-labhairt na Gàidhlig (0.7) nach eil idir Gàidhealach

*=I don't think it is- that you have to belong to- belong to the Highlands [...] it's a way- is it a way of life? I don't know – it's a **state of mind** [...] we see new Gaels – if that's what will happen – coming through the schools now (.) Gaelic speakers who aren't at all connected to the Highlands (((/Gaeldom))*

The above portions of analysis have drawn attention to the various ways in which interview participants in Nova Scotia and Scotland construct and convey their Gaelic identities, their associations with the term Gael or, as was more often the case in Scotland, their tendency to decline or downplay any sense of identity as such. Possible reasons for the disparity between Canadian and Scottish-based interviewees' divergent negotiations of Gaelic identity are discussed in greater detail in the following accounts. Nevertheless, it is clear from the data analysed in the above section that Nova Scotian informants' greater identification with Gael(ic) identity reflects their relatively deeper interest in personal and family heritage as motivating factors for language learning activity.

Culture, community change and linguistic identity

Discourses of Gaelic cultural change and community adaptation are frequently observed in Nova Scotian and Scottish-based interviewees' accounts of ethnolinguistic identity and vitality in the two research settings. In the following accounts, Nova Scotian perspectives on cultural change in that context are juxtaposed with those more typically voiced by Scottish new speakers.

Narratives of advanced language shift in Nova Scotia were nevertheless joined frequently by a strong sense of optimism for the future of Gaelic in Nova Scotia, however – a dimension not frequently observed in Scottish discourses. Nova Scotian new speakers often possessed a sense of wider support for Gaelic revitalisation in the province, which tended to contrast with Scottish participants' descriptions of opposition to Gaelic they have encountered. Among new Gaelic speakers in Nova Scotia, a sense of distinction between the language of local communities of remaining older, L1 Gaelic speakers, and new speakers raising new communities in Gaelic, was frequently conveyed in interviews. In the following account, for instance, the interviewee describes declining numbers locally of the remaining native speakers, but contrasts this with new-speaker parents' attempts to raise children in the language locally:

CBIF1	There's still native speakers in <u>this</u> area- there's only a couple
SD	Yeah
CBIF1	But we also have some <u>new</u> Gaelic native speakers [...] there <u>have</u> been a large group of people my age raising kids in Gaelic
SD	Hmm
CBIF1	And there's been <u>more</u> people [...] there's an ((laughing)) old lady down in um (1.1) xxx ((Cape Breton Island)) a native speaker
SD	Hmm
CBIF1	She calls the learners 'the Gaelickers- the Gaelickers' ((laughing))

The sense of continuity between declining L1 speakers in Nova Scotia and emerging, new speaker parents raising children in the same communities where such elderly Gaelic speakers still live (notwithstanding the relatively limited abilities of some 'Gaelickers') is similarly conveyed in the following two accounts:

CBIF7	Dar a bha mise òg 's e cànan na seann fheadhainn [sic] a bh' ann
	When I was young it was the old people's language
SD	'S e
	Yes
CBIF7	Agus a-<u>niste</u> (.) luchd- luchd-<u>bruidhinn</u> na Gàidhlig tha a' mhòr-chuid (2.3) nas òige na (.) uill (0.8) na an luchd- uh: (0.7) Gàidheil bhon ghlùin mar a chanas iad [...] Ach tha- tha <u>clann</u> ann a-^niste a tha togail- a tha ag [[ionnsachadh]
	And <u>now</u> (.) people- <u>speakers</u> of Gaelic the majority are (2.3) younger than (.) well (0.8) the ones- uh: (0.7) Gaels 'from the knee' as they say [...] But there are- there are <u>children</u> ^now who are picking up- who are [[learning]
SD	[[Hmm:]

CBIF7   Uh (0.6) na Gàidhlig aig an taigh bho am pàrantan [...] 's e rud ùr a th' ann an sin agus tha suim aig <u>iomadh</u> daoine ann an Alba Nuadh- fad na h-<u>ùine</u> bidh- bidh daoine a' tighinn a- a-mach às a' choillidh! ((laughs))

> *Uh (0.6) Gaelic at home from their parents [...] it's a new thing and <u>many</u> people in Nova Scotia- all the <u>time</u> there are- there are people coming out of the wood! ((laughs))*

HALF1   Aon turas bha e ((eòlaiche cànain)) ann thuirt e um: (.) **'It won't be the children of Gaelic speakers who do anything it'll be the grandchildren'** [...] cha chreid mi nach eil e ceart (0.9) tha- tha rudeigin a thaobh (.) um a' chlann [*sic*]

> *One time he ((Scottish language activist)) was over here he said um: (.)* **'It won't be the children of Gaelic speakers who do anything it'll be the grandchildren'** *[...] I really think that's right (0.9) there's- there's something about (.) um the kids*

SD   Hmm bha mi mothachail air an abairt sin [...] A bheil fhios agad cò mheud Gàidheil bho thùs a tha fhathast air fhàgail ann an Albainn Nuaidh?

> *Hmm I was familiar with that phrase [...] Do you know how many native Gaelic speakers are left in Nova Scotia*

HALF1   ^Chan eil fhios'am chan eil <u>mòran</u>! ((sadly)) [...] dh'abrainnsa dà cheud (.) aig a' char as <u>mo</u>

> *I ^don't know- not many! ((sadly)) [...] I would say two hundred (.) at <u>most</u>*

SD   Dè mu dheidhinn luchd-labhairt ùra a tha air Gàidhlig a thogail agus a tha air a h-ionnsachadh?

> *What about speakers who've picked Gaelic up and learned it?*

HALF1   Tha mi smaoineach' mu dhà cheud cuideachd [...] feadhainn a tha siùbhlach fileanta sa Ghàidhlig? Tha mi cinnteach gu bheil mi eòlach orra uileadh agus (.) nam biodh sinn uileadh anns an aon àite lethcheud [...] Dar a bhios feadhainn (.) fileanta siùbhlach agus (.) tha fèin-aithne aca air a thogail tha ceanglaichean aca sa choimhearsnachd chan eil iad airson falbh

> *I think about two hundred as well [...] people who are really fluent in Gaelic? I'm sure that I know them all and (.) if we were all in the same place fifty [...] When people are (.) really fluent and (.) their identity is developed they have connections in the community [and] they don't want to leave*

In the first extract, interviewee CBFI7 contrasts the status of Gaelic in her community during childhood as the language of old people (*'cànan na seann fheadhainn'*) with the reality of its use by a growing group of young parents who have learned Gaelic to fluency and are now raising children to be bilingual speakers of the language. This sense of regeneration in formerly Gaelic-dominant Nova Scotian communities is referred to in rather different terms by HALF1 in the second extract, as she notes a Scottish-based activist's advice that it would not be the children of L1 Gaelic speakers (most of whom are by now relatively elderly) who would reinvigorate the community, but their grandchildren. When I ask about the numbers of fluent speakers with this younger age profile, she estimates around fifty people, but notes that they are the individuals with the best-developed sense of Gaelic identity and community and are thus least likely to leave rural Nova Scotian areas where they might (one day) raise children with the language. In the following extract, my interviewee reflects on how developments of this kind have gathered pace only relatively recently, in tandem with top-down initiatives such as the establishment of the Office of Gaelic Affairs:

HALM2   'S e rud tha mise faicinn tha- 's e 's gu bheil (0.8) um: (.) chan eil fhios'am dh'fhaoidte (.) feumaidh:: cànan agus cultar nan Gàidheal a bhith (1.9) air an togail gu ìre a tha (1.8) uh nas àirde fhathast [...] ach rud a bha mi-fhìn ag ràdhainn nuair a chaidh an oifis a chur air bhonn (.) ann an 2006 cha robh <u>mòran</u> a' tachairt aig ìre na coimhearsnachd
       One thing that I see is- it's that there is (0.8) um: (.) I dunno perhaps (.) the language and culture of the Gaels still have:: to be (1.9) developed together to a greater (1.8) extent [...] but something I myself said when the Office [of Gaelic Affairs] was established (.) in 2006 not <u>much</u> was happening at the community level

SD   Seadh- nach robh?
       Right- wasn't there?

HALM2   Ach bha toll poileataigeach ann
       But there was a political void

Whilst noting that there may still be further work required to develop Gaelic language, culture and community in Nova Scotia, my speaker here implicitly juxtaposes the relative inertia of the Gaelic community when the Office was first instituted with the present-day reality of an active and lively linguistic community in Nova Scotia (as described in the extracts above). In general, therefore, a sense of ongoing decline in the province as the remaining L1 speakers steadily pass away tended in Nova Scotian accounts to be tempered by a sense of positive community change, and of hope for the future.

In Scotland, new speakers often articulated their views regarding the ongoing decline of L1 Gaelic communities in terms of the perceived (relatively urgent) need to develop closer bonds and contacts between new speakers and fluent L1 speakers in the language's heartland areas. This type of discourse is communicated by interviewees in the following two extracts:

EDIM3   Tha sin cudromach um gu bheil daoine a' faireachdainn gu bheil iad pàirt den- pàirt den choimhearsnachd
That's important um that people feel they're part- part of the community
SD   Sin agad e
That's it
EDIM3   Sin e da-rìribh […] Tha mi ag iarraidh turas no dhà eile a dhèanamh ((dha na coimhearsnachdan)) um còmhla ri caraidean aig a bheil Gàidhlig-luchd-ionnsachaidh eile aig a bheil Gàidhlig dìreach um- uill dìreach gum bi cothrom againn bruidhinn ri daoine aig a bheil Gàidhlig bho thùs agus uh **yeah** a bhith sa choimhearsnachd
*That's really it […] I want to make another trip or two ((to Gaelic communities)) um with Gaelic-speaking friends just um- will just so we have a chance to speak to native Gaelic speakers and uh **yeah** to be in the community*

EDIM5   Duine sam bith a tha air Gàidhlig ionnsachadh 's a tha ag obair ann an saoghal na Gàidhlig tha iad ag iarraidh diofar a dhèanadh agus math (dhèanadh) […] can anns na coimhearsnachdan
Anybody who's learned Gaelic and who works in the Gaelic world they want to make a difference and (do) some good […] say in the communities
SD   Sin e=
That's it=
EDIM5   =Gàidhealach a tha seo a <u>tha</u> crìonadh […] 's e aon de na beàrnan as motha a th' againn ann an saoghal na Gàidhlig 's e eadar um luchd-ionnsachaidh agus a' choimhearsnachd Ghàidhlig […] le feadhainn den luchd-ionnsachaidh nuair a tha iad a' bruidhinn 's e- 's e Gàidhlig cho (1.3) neònach, annasach! ((laughing)) […] Dh'ionnsaich mi a' Ghàidhlig airson a bhith bruidhinn ri daoine agus son a bhith conaltradh ri daoine chan ann airson adhbharan uh (.) ideòlach
=Gaelic communities that <u>are</u> declining […] one of the biggest gaps that we have in the Gaelic world is that between um learners and the Gaelic community […] with some learners when they speak it's- it's such a (1.3) strange, weird Gaelic! ((laughing)) I learned Gaelic to speak and communicate with people not for uh (.) ideological reasons

Both research participants in the above extracts observe that the wider Gaelic community in Scotland has a role to play in safeguarding rural communities of native Gaelic speakers, but they do so in rather different terms. Whilst speaker EDIM3 states the importance of the objective that all speakers (regardless of linguistic background) should feel themselves to be part of the Gaelic community, EDIM5 distinguishes L2 learners from the Gaelic community per se. He remarks that the Gaelic they acquire as learners is often strange ('*neònach*, *annasach'*), impeding communication between the two groups. He states that he learned the language for communicative purposes (*'son a bhith conaltradh le daoine'*) rather than being motivated by ideological factors. Furthermore, he regards the communicative disparity between L2 learners and the heartland Gaelic community as one of the biggest gaps (*'aon de na beàrnan as motha'*) in the Gaelic world.

For other Scottish-based participants, the ongoing decline of Gaelic in heartland communities was not perceived in such existentially drastic terms, as the presence of greater numbers of new speakers means that the language will endure in the long term. This dimension is explored further in the following extract:

GLAF1	Tha fios aig daoine gu bheil (1.3) luchd-labhairt ùra ann
	People know that there are (1.3) new speakers
SD	Hmm
GLAF1	**So actually** tha e **okay** [...] tha fios'am gu bheil (1.6) Gàidheil ùra (.) ann
	So actually it [i.e., the language] is okay [...] I know that there (.) are (1.6) new Gaels
SD	Hmm
GLAF1	Agus sin rud eadar-dhealaichte- tha Gàidheil ùra ann agus tha luchd-labhairt ùra ann
	And that's something else- there are new Gaels and there are new speakers
SD	Hmm
GLAF1	Ach tha iadsan eadar-dhealaichte bho (.) na Gàidheil fhèin tha mi a' smaoineachadh [...] **for something to die out because it's been oppressed** (.) **that's unacceptable to <u>me</u>**
	But they're different from (.) the Gaels themselves I think [...] **for something to die out because it's been oppressed** (.) **that's unacceptable to <u>me</u>**

Thus whilst the above interviewee observes that the existence of new speakers (*'luchd-labhairt ùra'*) – and interestingly, new Gaels (*'Gàidheil ùra'*) – means that the current predicament of the language is 'actually... okay', she sees the latter group as distinct from the (traditional) Gaels themselves. Indicating her own possible motivations for learning Gaelic in the first place, she states that the long-term decline of the language and its potential to 'die out' due to past oppression is 'unacceptable' to her, personally. The frequent idiomatic codeswiching speaker GLAF1 deploys acts to emphasise and frame her strength of feeling around the subject. Still other Scottish new speakers viewed the 'gap' between new and traditional speakers described by EDIM5, above, in potentially more problematic terms, however:

GLAF4	Tha: (.) daoine em (1.3) an saoghal na Gàidhlig (.) chan eil fios agam carson- chan eil iad ag iarraidh daoine ùr- chan eil cuid dhiubh ag iarraidh daoine ùra
	There are: (.) people em (1.3) in the Gaelic world (.) I don't know why- they don't want new people- some of them don't want new people
SD	Hmm
GLAF4	Luchd-labhairt ùra a thàladh a-staigh- car<u>son</u>?
	To attract new people in [to the community]- <u>why</u>?
SD	Hmm 's e deagh cheist a th' ann
	It's a good question
GLAF4	Tha e cho neònach (.) rud cultarail a th' ann feumaidh [...] tha mi smaointinn gu <u>bheil</u> sgaradh ann fhathast (1.2) ach (1.3) gu bheil sin a' crìonadh- gu bheil tuigse ann gu bheil- gu bheil <u>feum</u> air luchd-labhairt ùra
	It's so strange (.) it must be a cultural thing [...] I think there <u>is</u> still a split (1.2) but (1.3) that it's weakening- that there is an understanding that- that new speakers are <u>needed</u>

Whilst speaker GLAF4 therefore regards some Gaelic speakers to be against new people becoming part of the wider Gaelic-speaking community, stating that such a stance must be 'a cultural thing' ('*rud cultarail a th' ann feumaidh*'), she regards this split to be lessening as more people appreciate that new speakers will be required to ensure the future existence of Gaelic. As I demonstrate in the following accounts, this appreciation is also now well developed in Nova Scotian communities. For instance, a Cape Breton–based interviewee observes in the following extract that as more people have learned Gaelic in Nova Scotia, more have become mindful that the language still exists in the province, a situation he contrasts with that which prevailed ten years previously:

CBIM1	Tha mi faicinn uh (.) barrachd is barrachd daoine ag ionnsachadh na Gàidhlig
	I see uh (.) more and more people learning Gaelic
SD	Hmm
CBIM1	'S feadhainn aig a bheil <u>suim</u> anns a' Ghàidhlig
	And people who are <u>interested</u> in Gaelic
SD	Sheadh
	Yeah
CBIM1	Agus an fheadhainn (1.4) aig nach <u>eil</u> a' Ghàidhlig (2.1) tha iad (2.8) tha:: (1.2) tha mi a' smaoineach' gu bheil- gu bheil e <u>fada</u> nas fheàrr an-diugh na bha e bho chionn (.) deich bliadhna [...] tha mi ^smaoineach' gu bheil- gu bheil daoine (.) a' chuid as motha dhe na daoine a' <u>tuigsinn</u> (.) um: sna làithean seo gu <u>bheil</u> a' Ghàidhlig ann (.) chan eil e- chan <u>eil</u> e marbh

> And the people (1.4) who <u>can't</u> speak Gaelic (2.1) they are (2.8) are:: (1.2) I think that- that it's <u>far</u> better today than it was (.) ten years ago [...] I ^think that- that people (.) most people <u>understand</u> these days that Gaelic <u>exists</u> (.) it isn't- it's <u>not</u> dead

In a similar fashion, a Halifax-based interviewee remarks in the following extract that the situation of public awareness of Gaelic has only recently changed, and that even in this urban setting, members of the public recognise that Gaelic speakers exist locally – and furthermore, recognise such speakers as Gaels:

SD   A bheil mòran Gàidheil mun cuairt a seo?
> *Are there many Gaels around here?*

HALF3   Um: (0.7) ^tha: (1.0) ^tha: (.) chan eil (1.2) tha mòran luchd-ionnsachaidh ann [...] tha iadsan gu math um (0.7) deònach airson clasaichean a dhèanadh agus um cùrsaichean bogaidh a dhèanadh anns an Àrd-bhaile [...] tha rudeigin air atharrachadh chan eil fhios agam dè a thachair ach anns an Àrd-bhaile tha fhios aig daoine gur e Gàdheil a th' <u>annainn</u>
> *Um: (0.7) ^yes: (1.0) ^yes (.) there aren't (1.2) there are lots of learners [...] they are quite um (0.7) willing to do classes and um immersion courses in Halifax (.) [...] something has changed I don't know what happened but in Halifax people know that <u>we are</u> Gaels*

Positive feeling around Gaelic in Nova Scotia, related to the recent growth and development of Gaelic in the province is described by another Halifax-based speaker in the following account:

HALM2   A-nis tha coimhearsnachd a' dol air adhart [...] chan eil fhios'am- dh'fhaoidte (.) gu bheil san fharsaingeachd car faireachdainn nas fheàrr ann
> *Now there is a community developing [...] I don't know- perhaps (.) there is a slightly better feeling around generally*

SD   Hmm

HALM2   Fhios agad a thaobh na Gàidhlig agus a' chultair agus (.) gu bheil sin a' toirt air daoine a bhith (1.1) a bhith: (1.2) feuchainn ri – fhios agad – a' fàs fileanta [...] bha (1.9) bha sinn a' bruidhinn air- air a (0.6) air a' ghràin a th' aig feadhainn a's an t-seann dùthaich [...] agus (2.2) bidh mise (.) tric gu leòr a' faireachdainn (0.8) um gu bheil a' <u>mhòr</u>-chuid dhe na daoine tha iad (1.8) tha iad toilichte gu bheil rudeigin a' tachairt
> *You know in terms of Gaelic and the cuture and (.) that that inspires people to (1.1) to: (1.2) try to – you know – become fluent [...] we (1.9) we were speaking about- about the (0.6) about the hatred some people have in Scotland ((for Gaelic)) and (2.2) I (.) quite often feel (0.8) um that <u>most</u> people they are (1.8) they are pleased that something is happening*

As more L2 learners become fluent new speakers of the language in Nova Scotia, members of the public are viewed to be mostly pleased that development for Gaelic in the province is being undertaken (*'a' mhòr-chuid dhe na daoine ... tha iad toilichte gu bheil rudeigin a' tachairt'*). This scenario is implicitly contrasted with perceived opposition to Gaelic development in Scotland, a topic on which the speaker had remarked previously in the interview. In Scotland, the matter of public opposition to the language was discussed by several participants. In that context, widespread ignorance concerning the Gaelic language, and public distrust of policy to revitalise it, was a discursive theme that surfaced relatively frequently in interviews, in contrast to Nova Scotia where opposition to the language was rarely described. As the following account demonstrates, such attitudes are often attributed by new speakers in Scotland to right-wing media and its ongoing influence on public opinion:

EDIF5	Air sgàth 's nach ann à seo a tha mi tha daoine an-còmhnaidh a' faighneachd '^O agus ^dè tha thu ^dèanamh an-seo?'
	Because I'm not from here people always ask me '^Oh and ^what are you ^doing here?'
SD	((laughs))
EDIF5	'S bidh mise ag ràdh 'Uill 's e xxx a th' annam agus bidh mi a' teagasg Gàidhlig' agus tha iad dèanamh **double-take** agus tha iad mar '^<u>Dè</u>::?'
	*And I say 'Well I am xxx and I teach Gaelic' and they do a **double-take** and they're like '^Wha::t?'*
SD	((laughs)) Cinnteach gu bheil
	((laughs)) I'm sure
EDIF5	((mimicking stupid voice)) 'Chan eil Gàidhlig agamsa agus 's ann à ^Alba a tha mi!' [...] Agus an uair sin tha iad ag <u>innse</u> ^dhut a h-<u>uile</u> rud a tha iad a' smaoineachadh mu dheidhinn na Gàidhlig! [...] 'O: <u>uill</u> (.) fhios agad dè tha gam bhodraigeadh mu dheidhinn na Gàidhlig?'
	'I don't speak Gaelic and I'm from ^Scotland!' [...] And then they <u>tell</u> ^you everything they think about Gaelic! [...] 'Oh: <u>well</u> (.) do you know what bothers me about Gaelic?'
SD	Dìreach! ((laughs))
	Exactly ((laughs))
EDIF5	Like 'O: ^**yeah** <u>innis</u> dhomh (.) bidh seo <u>cho</u> inntinneach ((sarcastic)) fhios agad (.) air sgàth 's gu bheil mi <u>cinnteach</u> gu bheil barrachd fios <u>agadsa</u> na tha <u>agamsa</u> air a' <u>chùis</u> seo!' (.) <u>no::t</u>! [...] Dh'ionnsaich mi leasan- na bruidhinn mu dheidhinn na Gàidhlig ma tha rudeigin **stressful** agad ri dhèanamh an dèidh làimh air sgàth 's gum bi daoine (.) **predictably** (.) ag ràdh tòrr (0.9) <u>cac</u> (.) a thog iad bhon **Daily Mail**
	*Like 'Oh: ^**yeah** <u>tell</u> me (.) this will be <u>so</u> interesting ((sarcastic tone)) you know (.) because I'm <u>sure you</u> know more than <u>I know</u> about this!'(.)*

> no::t! *[...] I learned a lesson- don't speak about Gaelic if you have some-*
> *thing* stressful *to do afterward because people (.)* predictably *(.) talk a*
> *lot of (0.9)* shit *(.) they picked up from the* Daily Mail

The combination of the above interviewee's origins outside of Scotland and her occupation teaching Gaelic is thus viewed to elicit comment and discussion from strangers in the urban Lowlands around personal bugbears and reservations about Gaelic. She likens such comments to a lot of 'shit' that they are assumed to have 'predicably' picked up from the right-wing tabloid press (*'tòrr cac a thog iad bhon* Daily Mail*'*). For the following speaker, opposition to Gaelic development in the eastern Lowlands, and ignorance around the language generally, are seen as things that need to change:

SD An canadh tu gu bheil iomairtean leasachaidh na Gàidhlig cudromach air feadh na h-Alba, no a bheil iad nas cudromaiche ann an sgìrean sònraichte?
Would you say Gaelic development is important throughout Scotland or more important in particular areas?

GMEF1 Tha iad gu h-àraid cudromach ann an Gàidhea- sa Ghàidhealtachd ann an- agus ann an Glaschu chionn 's nach (.) faigh sinn cho mòr- an t-uabhas de (.) **opposition** anns na h-àiteachan sin [...] Airson daoine nach eil (.) an-sàs ann chan eil- chan eil (.) càil a dh'fhios aca air (.) feumaidh sinn smaoineach- faighinn na daoine seo sgur a ràdh **'oh that G[ei]lic thing'** feum aca 'g ràdh **'oh yeah G[a:]elic, yeah wish I had (x) that- that's cool eh?'**
They're particularly important in the Highl- in the Highlands in- and in Glasgow as we don't (.) get as much- a load of (.) **opposition** *in those places [...] For people who aren't (.) involved it's not- they don't know anything (.) we need to think- get those people to stop saying* **'oh that G[ei]lic thing'** *instead they need to say* **'oh yeah G[a:]elic, yeah wish I had (x) that- that's cool eh?'**

I have indicated in square parentheses a point of linguistic interest in GMEF1's constructed dialogue of opposition to Gaelic in urban Lowland communities such as Edinburgh. The particular pronunciation of the word Gaelic as [geilik] in Scotland has become (rightly or wrongly) increasingly ideologically associated with criticism of the language and its community, and particularly with public spending on it. This stands in stark contrast with Nova Scotia, where similar pronunciations of the word – in English – are in general usage, and are not enregistered or otherwise ideologically imbued with anti-Gaelic sentiment. As speaker GMEF1 indicates with the two constructed dialogues she produces at the end of the above extract, however, the pronunciations [ga:]lic and [gei] lic are now often interpreted to index pro- and anti-Gaelic feeling respectively. Criticism of the language – and of public spending on it – is often equated by speakers of Gaelic with a wider lack of public understanding around the historical and contemporary presence of Gaelic in various communities (cf. Dunmore 2017). In the following extract, ignorance of Gaelic's relevance to a particular area in the mainland Highlands in which he works is likened by my interviewee to 'funnel vision' and the film *The Matrix*:

GMEM3   Trì càirteal de dhaoine san sgìre aig an robh Gàidhlig [gu h-eachdraid-heil...] 's chan eil daoine sam bith eile a' tuigsinn neo a' faicinn sin **you know**? 'S e Gàidhlig air an taobh eile a tha seo
*Three quarters of people spoke Gaelic in this area [historically...] and nobody understands or sees that **you know**? It's Gaelic on the other side here*

SD   Hmm

GMEM3   'S chan eil- 's e seòrsa **Matrix** a th'ann – 's e **funnel vision almost** (x) air **you know**
*And it's not- it's a kind of **Matrix** – it's **funnel vision almost** (x) **you know***

SD   Dìreach
Exactly

GMEM3   **Awareness** a bheil fhios agad – aithneachadh [...] airson a' mhòr-chuid de dhaoine tha e follaiseach nuair a tha mise a' faicinn a-nise chan eil sin cudromach idir dhaibh
***Awareness** do you know – awareness [...] for most people it's obvious when I see (them) now that it's not at all important to them*

SD   Hmm

GMEM3   'S dòcha gu bheil mise dìreach beagan gòrach ((laughs)) 's e sin an duilgheadas a th' agam – beagan gòrach – ach 's e seòrsa **Matrix** a th'ann mar a tha mi (ga fhaicinn)
*Perhaps I'm just a bit silly ((laughs)) that's the trouble I have – I am a bit silly – but it's a sort of **Matrix** as I (see it)*

The final speaker's observation, in the last extract above, that awareness of the cultural importance of Gaelic locally is akin to the *Matrix* highlights the quasi-secretive presence of the language in twenty-first-century Scotland. Gaelic is, on one hand, more visible in public life, signage and media than has ever previously been the case, yet widespread appreciation of the language's cultural significance in many areas remains limited, a situation analogised here to the alternative, parallel reality of computer simulation in the film *The Matrix*. In this metaphor, it is as if the Gaelic world is somehow imperceptible unless one is able to understand the language itself.

This section has therefore addressed discourses of Gaelic cultural change and community adaptation in Nova Scotian and Scottish-based interviewees' accounts of ethnolinguistic identity and vitality in the two contexts. Once again, Nova Scotia new speakers' views surrounding the revitalisation of Gaelic in the province tend to contrast with those expressed more typically by Scottish new speakers. Narratives pertaining to advanced language shift in Nova Scotia are nevertheless joined frequently by a strong sense of optimism for the future in Nova Scotia, a dimension not frequently observed in Scottish discourses. Similarly, Nova Scotian new speakers' sense of wider support existing for Gaelic revitalisation in the province has been shown to contrast with most Scottish participants' descriptions of opposition to Gaelic they have encountered.

Gaelic learning motivations: heritage and language socialisation

As shown previously, Nova Scotian and Scottish interviewees' accounts of their motivations for having learned Gaelic were discussed frequently, pertaining in the former context most often to personal and family heritage in the language. Certain discourses illustrate speakers' limited exposure to Gaelic at home in childhood; in all cases, such exposure was insufficient for full acquisition of the language but was regarded by many participants as a major motivating factor in learning it later in life. As I show below, many Nova Scotian participants without such direct family connections to Gaelic nevertheless viewed their (relatively more distant) Gaelic heritage as a motivating factor for acquiring the language. In Scotland, by contrast, a substantial majority generally described lacking any family socialisation or heritage connection to Gaelic and reported other motivations for learning it. A smaller, but still significant, subsection of Scottish participants described some childhood experiences of Gaelic language socialisation in community and school as informing their decision to learn and use Gaelic.

For many Nova Scotian participants in the research, motivation to acquire Gaelic in adolescence and adulthood was informed not just by heritage as an abstract notion, but by immediate family connection to and socialisation in Gaelic during childhood. In this sense, such individuals may be placed along a spectrum of heritage speakerhood, in the sense more generally associated with the term heritage language in applied (socio)linguistics (e.g., Brinton, Kagan and Bauckus 2008; Valdés et al. 2008). In the following two extracts, interviewees describe their (more or less) successful attempts to learn Gaelic as stemming from family exposure to the language:

SD   Bha Gàidhlig aig d'athair nach robh?
Your father could speak Gaelic couldn't he?
HALM2 Bha- bha
Yes- yes

SD	Uill tha fhathast
	Well he still can
HALM2	Tha tha e fhathast gu math beò! [...] Chuala mise Gàidhlig nuair a bha mi: nuair a bha mi glè òg (.) agus bhiodh esan a' bruidhinn ri- ri a bhràthair (1.1) agus bhruidhinn a pheathraichean uh (.) dìreach beagan sa Ghàidhlig
	Yes yes he's still very much alive! [...] I heard Gaelic when I was: when I was young (.) and he would speak to- to his brother (1.1) and his sisters would speak uh (.) just a little in Gaelic
ANTM2	Dar a bha mi beag (0.9) leig m' athair a' bruidhinn na Gàidhlig rium
	When I was small (0.8) my father spoke Gaelic to me
SD	Seadh
	Yes
ANTM2	Ach cha robh ann ach abairtean [...] bha fhios againn riamh gur i- gur i a' Ghàidhlig am prìomh chànan a bh' againne ach gu robh Beurla againn cuideachd [...] thuirt mi '<u>sin</u> an cànan againne (.) tha a' Bheurla againn cuideachd ach sin an cànan againn'
	But it was only odd phrases [...] we always knew that- that Gaelic had been our main language but that we had English as well [...] I said '<u>that</u> is our language (.) we can speak English too but that's our language'

Both above speakers were raised in homes in which their fathers were able to speak Gaelic (albeit to varying degrees), but only did so to a limited degree. For both, however, the fact of having had such close parental connections to Gaelic motivated them to acquire the language through different means. For speaker HALM2, this entailed requesting that his great uncle converse with him in the language to aid his acquisition, whilst in the second extract, ANTM2 describes developing an awareness that Gaelic was 'our' language (*'an cànan againne'*) through his father's occasional use of words and phrases. More frequently in Nova Scotia, interviewees would identify one or more grandparents whom they remembered using occasional Gaelic words, as in the following account:

ANTF3	^I was <u>always</u> interested in it uh: because like uh: my parents named me xxx which is a Gaelic name [...] my grandmother would say like little Gaelic words to us all the time and stuff [...] my mom and my grandmother is who I <u>am</u> like really connected to cos they really love all that stuff
SD	Hmm
ANTF3	Uh: my mom like <u>tries</u> ((laughing)) to learn Gaelic but hasn't really put a whole lot of time into it ((laughs)) [...] they've never like none of them have every really like <u>tried</u> to learn them<u>selves</u>

Other speakers referred to their grandparents' having spoken substantially more Gaelic during their own childhoods, and to this having impacted directly on their motivations to acquire speaking ability:

CBIF7	Chan eil Gàidhlig aig mo phàrantan ach tha Gàidhlig aig mo ^sheanmhair
	My parents can't speak Gaelic but my ^grandmother speaks Gaelic
SD	Glè mhath
	Very good
CBIF7	'S bha: ^beagan Gàidhlig aig mo sheanair air an taobh <u>sin</u> agus bha (.) beagan de Ghàidhlig aig mo sheanair air an taobh eile cuideachd **so** (.) **so** bha Gàidhlig san <u>teaghlach</u> agamas [[dar a bha mi òg]
	*And my: grandfather on <u>that</u> side could speak a ^little Gaelic and (.) my grandfather on the other side could speak a little bit of Gaelic too **so** (.) **so** there was Gaelic in my <u>family</u> [[when I was young]*
SD	[[Bha]
	[[Yes]
CBIF7	Chuala mi rudan mar 'O m' eudail' 's (x) […] agus chan eil Gàidhlig aig mo <u>mhàthair</u> (0.8) uh ach bidh ise (.) ^speuradh sa Ghàidhlig uaireannan!
	I heard things like 'Oh my darling' and (x) […] and my <u>mother</u> can't speak Gaelic (0.8) uh but she (.) ^swears in Gaelic some times!
SD	Dìreach ((laughs))
	Exactly ((laughs))
CBIF7	Bidh i ag ràdhainn 'Ìosa Ìosa Mhuire (x)' cha robh i <u>cinnteach</u> dè bha i ag ràdhainn […] dh'fhuirich mise còmhla ri mo sheanmhair airson (.) bliadhna agus leth agus 's e Gàidhlig an cànan a bh' againn san taigh
	She says 'Jesus Jesus son of Mary (x)' she wasn't <u>certain</u> of what she was saying […] I lived with my grandmother for (.) a year and a half and Gaelic was the language we spoke at home

In this extract, my interviewee describes a number of formative socialisation experiences in Gaelic during her childhood, including her parents' and grandparents' use of Gaelic for affective and emotional purposes (with notable references to endearment and swearing, sometimes without the interviewee's family members knowing exactly what they were saying). Furthermore, having been motivated through such early experiences to undertake Gaelic acquisition activities, speaker CBIF7 even reports having lived with her grandmother for eighteen months, in which time she had learned sufficient Gaelic to maintain the language as the medium of household interaction. Grandparents thus play an extremely important role in the linguistic biographies of various Nova Scotian new speakers. In the following account, my interviewee describes opportunities she and her grandmother had to visit and interact in Gaelic with her great-grandmother:

CBIF2   Ann an <u>dòigh</u> bha fhios agam gur e a' Ghàidhlig a' chiad chànan a bh' aig mo sheanmhair ach ^chan eil fhios'am **like it <u>didn't</u> register or something** [...] cha robh Beurla aig mo sheanmhair nuair a chaidh i dhan sgoil aig còig bliadhna a dh'aois
    In a <u>way</u> I knew that Gaelic was my grandmother's first language but I ^don't know **like it <u>didn't</u> register or something** *[...] my grandmother coul- couldn't speak English when she went to school at five years of age*
SD   Hmm
CBIF2   Agus nist chan eil Gàidhlig aice tuilleadh- <u>uill</u> tha mise an dùil gu bheil Gàidhlig aice [...] chan eil <u>mòran</u> Gàidhlig aice ach bha barrachd na bh' agamsa is thigeadh sinne- uh: rachadh sinne a chèilidh air mo shinn sheanmhair [...] tha mise <u>cho</u>:: fortanach gu robh- bha ùine gu <u>leòr</u> agam còmhla rithe is dh'ionnsaich mi an t-<u>uabhas</u> bhuaipe
    And now she can't speak Gaelic any more- well I suspect that she can [...] she can't speak <u>much</u> Gaelic- she knew more than me and we would come- uh: we would go to visit my great-grandmother [...] I am so:: lucky that- I spent so much time with her and learned <u>so much</u> from her

In each of the interview extracts discussed above, participants describe experiences of language socialisation by family members in Gaelic during childhood – albeit generally to rather limited degrees. Experiences of Gaelic socialisation later in life are seen to a much greater degree to have impacted on speakers' acquisition of the language as an L2, and upon their motivation to improve their abilities in it. Whilst opportunities for such direct exposure to Gaelic by close family members were only reported by a small group of Nova Scotian participants, they nevertheless constitute an important subset of new speakers in that context (in contrast, generally speaking, to Scotland).

More frequently in Nova Scotia, family connections to Gaelic, whilst still strong, were more historic than in the cases of the five speakers above. A more substantial subgroup of Nova Scotian new speakers thus conveyed motivations for learning Gaelic in relation to family heritage, but not direct socialisation in the language by family members. Interestingly, in the following extract my interviewee describes not having been socialised at all in Gaelic during childhood, in spite of having lived with her two Gaelic-speaking grandmothers (a likely consequence of attitudes to Gaelic transmission internalised by their generation):

CBIF5   Dh' eug m' athair ach bha (.) a mhàthair agus (.) màthair mo mhàthar- thàinig iadsan a dh'fhuireach còmhla rinn- bha iad a' fuireach anns a- sa **bhasement**
    My father had died but (.) his mother and (.) my mother's mother- they came to live with us- they lived in the- in the **basement**

SD	Seadh!
	Really!
CBIF5	Bha iad a' fuireach an-siud agus bha Gàidhlig aig an dithis aca
	They lived there and they could both speak Gaelic
SD	Uh huh
CBIF5	Agus cha robh fios agams' gu dè bh' anns a' chànan sin <u>idir</u> [...] tha mi smaointinn gu robh mi dh'fhaoidte dusan bliadhna a dh'aois aig an <u>àm</u> sin uh ach aig an <u>aon</u> àm air sàilleabh 's nach do dh'fhàs mise suas (.) um: (1.2) <u>anns</u> a' chultar siud- dh'fhàs ann an ^dòigh
	And I didn't know what language that was <u>at all</u> [...] I think I was maybe twelve at the <u>time</u> uh but at the <u>same</u> time because I didn't grow up (.) um: (1.2) <u>in</u> that language- I did in a ^way
SD	Dh'fhàs ann an dòigh [[nach do dh'fhàs?]]
	You did in a way [[didn't you?]]
CBIF5	[[Dh'fhàs ann an] dòigh ach nuair a bha- can (.) mus robh mi dusan bliadhna a dh'aois (.) cha robh fios'am gu dè a bh' <u>ann</u> an Gàidhlig
	[[I did in] a way but when I was- say (.) before I was twelve years old (.) I didn't even know what Gaelic <u>was</u>

Other Nova Scotia–based interviewees foregrounded their grandparents' negative experiences of using Gaelic in official domains, and their internalised negative attitudes to speaking Gaelic to their own (grand)children. Such discourses are exemplified in the following two accounts:

HALF1	Bha Gàidhlig aig mo sheanair (1.2) agus: mar as minig a thachair cha robh cead aca Gàidhlig a bhruidhinn aig an sgoil agus mar sin chuir sin stadtha- tha <u>facal</u> no dhà aig m' athair- tha blas (.) aige nas fheàrr na th' agam fhìn
	My grandfather could speak Gaelic (1.2) an:d as often happened they weren't permitted to speak Gaelic in school and so that stopped- it- my father can still speak a <u>word</u> or two- his accent (.) is better than my own
SD	Uh huh [...] an ann air sgàth nan ceanglaichean sin a thog thu ùidh sa Ghàidhlig sa chiad dol-a-mach?
	[...] was it because of those [family] connections that you became interested in Gaelic in the first place?
HALF1	'S ann- 's ann agus bha ^mise caran (mothachail) um:: (1.8) gur e siud an naidheachd a bh' aig a' chuid as motha dhe na daoine [...] coltach ri m' athair fhèin (1.1) tha- tha tuilleadh 's a chòir
	Yes- yes and ^I was somewhat (mindful) um: (1.8) that that was the same history that most of the people shared [locally] [...] there- there are more than there should be (1.1) who are similar to my own father

CBIF11	Uill bha Gàidhlig aig mo sheanmhair- cha robh i ga bruidhinn rinne
	Well my grandmother could speak Gaelic- she didn't speak it to us
SD	Seadh
	Okay
CBIF11	Ach bha i gabhail na h-òrain gun teagamh so thog mi òrain Gàidhlig [...] 's e rud a bh' ann airson na cloinne chan ann dìreach son nan seann daoine
	But she would sing the songs for sure so I learned Gaelic songs [...] it was a thing for children not just the old people
[...]	
SD	Agus tha dithis cloinne agad a bheil?
	And you have two children do you?
CBIF11	Tha
	Yes
SD	Tha agus ciamar a tha iadsan em (.) tighinn air adhart a thaobh na Gàidhlig?
	And how are they em (.) coming on in terms of their Gaelic?
CBIF11	^Glè ^glè mhath em tha mo mhac dol a bhith còig air an ath mhìos [...] on a bha mi òg thuirt mi 'Dar a bhios clann agam tha mi dol a bhruidh-tha mi dol a theagasg Gàidhlig dhaibh'
	^Very ^very well em my son will be five next month [...] since I was young I said 'When I have children I will speak- I'm going to teach them Gaelic'

In spite of the inability of their grandparents' generation to transmit Gaelic within the home domain, therefore, both above interviewees relate their own decision to acquire fluent Gaelic to the L1 linguistic and wider cultural practices of particular grandparents. For the second speaker, a sense of connection to a Gaelic heritage was profound enough to motivate her to raise children through the language. It is particularly noteworthy that only a small minority of new speakers whom I interviewed in Nova Scotia had no known, direct family connection to the language. The following extract exemplifies the types of family history typical of these relatively few individuals. Whilst Gaelic family heritage is not reported per se, a wider association with Scottish culture and heritage was generally reported by this subset of speakers, and the possibility that Gaelic was historically present in the speaker's heritage thereby (implicitly) entertained:

SD	An robh Gàidhlig ga labhairt nad theaghlach fhèin- an robh ceanglaichean ann?
	Was Gaelic spoken in your own family- were there any connections?
CBIF4	Chan eil ^fhios'am
	I don't ^know
SD	Nach eil?
	Don't you?

CBIF4	So:: 's e: (.) xxx ((Scottish surname)) an t-ainm a th' air mo mhàthair-maiden name
	So:: (.) xxx ((Scottish surname)) is my (.) mother's name- **her maiden name**
SD	Seadh
	Okay
CBIF4	So (1.1) dh' fhàs mi suas- dh' fhàs mi suas gu math eòlach air a- air a' (.) chultar Albannach a bh' againn anns an teaghlach [...] chan eil mi buileach cinnteach a bha Gàidhlig san teaghlach agam ach cha robh Gàidhlig aig duine sam bith eile
	So (1.1) I grew up- I grew up quite aware of the- of the (.) Scottish culture we had in the family [...] I'm not entirely sure Gaelic was in my family but certainly no one else could speak Gaelic

Contrasting with the Nova Scotian interview extracts discussed above, a substantial majority of Scottish new speakers professed no known family connection to Gaelic, and heritage tended not to feature in accounts of motivations for having learned the language in general. Nevertheless, some speakers described Gaelic language acquisition by parents who had also learned the language as an L2, as exemplified by speakers in the following two extracts:

SD	Tha gu leòr Gàidhlig aig d' athair cuideachd nach eil?
	Your father can speak plenty of Gaelic as well can't he
EDIF1	Tha agus aig mo mhàthair cuideachd
	Yes and my mother can too
SD	Sheadh? Sin glè mhath
	Really? That's very good
EDIF1	Tha an dithis aca air ionnsachadh (.) tha an dithis aca air an cùrsa comais a dhèanadh [...] bha mise ann bho '98–'99 (.) uh agus am bliadhna- an ath bhliadhna chaidh mo mhàthair ann oir bha ise- mhothaich i an adhartas a rinn mi [...ach] is glè ainneamh a-nist **actually** gum bi sinn a' bruidhinn Gàidhlig (x)
	Both of them have learned (.) they've both done the cùrsa comais ((Sabhal Mòr Ostaig intensive course)) I was there from [19]98–'99 (.) uh and the year- the following year my mother went because she was- she noticed the progress I made [...but] now it's very seldom that we **actually** *speak Gaelic [together] (x)*
SD	An robh Gàidhlig aig duine no tè na do theaghlach?
	Could anyone in your family speak Gaelic?
GMEF4	Cha robh- cha robh aig an àm eh dh'ionnsaich mo mhàthair ach e:m
	No- not at the time ((in school)) eh my mother learned but e:m

SD	An do dh'ionnsaich?
	Did she?
GMEF4	Bha mi fhìn (.) sa bhun-sgoil tha mi smaointinn
	I was (.) in primary school I think
SD	Uh huh
GMEF4	Dh'ionnsaich i ach chan eil aig m'athair- eh chan eil esan ga cleachdadh idir idir
	She learned but my father can't- eh he doesn't use it at all
SD	Nach eil?
	No?
GMEF4	Eh tha Mam fhathast
	Eh Mum still does

In general, however, experiences of partial socialisation in Gaelic by family members, or of strong motivation to acquire Gaelic stemming from family heritage and identity were largely absent among the great majority of Scottish interviewees. The dominant overall position on questions of heritage conveyed by Scottish new speakers is exemplified in the following interviewee's rejection of (rather distant) connections to Gaelic heritage as 'not really important' (*'chan eil sin really cudromach'*):

SD	An ann à baile Ghlaschu fhèin a tha thu bho thùs?
	Are you from Glasgow itself originially?
GLAM4	Tha aidh (x) **yeah** ann an Glaschu no na **suburbs** [...] **so** chan eil buntain- neas agam ris a' chànan- uill a-staigh- a-staigh em (1.2) **you know living memory** co-dhiù
	*Yeah aye (x) **yeah** in Glasgow or the **suburbs** [...] **so** I don't have any family relationship to the language- well within- within em (1.2) **you know living memory** anyway*
SD	Seadh [...] dol air ais pìos beag 's dòch'
	Yeah [...] going back a bit perhaps
GLAM4	Ach cha robh- chan eil- chan eil sin **really** cudromach chan e sin an [sic] adhbhar a thòisich mi
	*But that wasn't- that isn't- that isn't **really** important that's not the reason I started*

Whilst the above excerpt exemplifies the majority view concerning Gaelic heritage among Scottish new speakers in my dataset, a notable subset of participants nevertheless described experiences of family heritage or community to explain their acquisition of Gaelic language. In Scotland, new speakers with direct family ties to Gaelic were a marked minority, but those with such heritage generally reported this background as being highly relevant to their initial motivations for having acquired the language. Interviewees in the following two accounts describe such experiences in explaining their language learning motivations. Notably, however, both report having been born and raised for the early part of their lives in England. For these two speakers, therefore, the possession of recent family heritage in Gaelic, the importance of this detail as a motivating factor in acquiring the language and the experience of having lived for a period in a diasporic context are all points of commonality with the majority of Nova Scotia–based interviewees. Indeed, two other participants in Scotland reported growing up in England. Further research on this subset of new speakers with connections to the Scottish Gaelic diaspora in England would clearly be beneficial.

SD	An robh Gàidhlig na do theaghlach idir?=
	Was Gaelic in your family at all?=
GLAF4	=Bha: bha: **so** tha i aig mo mhàthair 's mo sheanair 's mo sheanmhair 's: **uncles aunties** a h-uile duine uh (1.2) taobh mo mhàthar […] an uair sin nuair a bha sinn ann am ((Galltachd)) (0.9) bha **Mum-** on a bha i air a bhith ann an Sasainn is gun chothrom (.) idir aice ga bruidhinn le duine sam bith shìos an-sin (.) bha i ag iarraidh cothrom fhaighinn a bhith ga bruidhinn is mar sin thòisich sinn ann an clasaichean còmhraidh còmhla
	=*Yes: yes:* **so** *my mother can speak it and my grandfather and grandmother an:d* **uncles aunties** *everyone uh (1.2) on my mother's side […] then when we were living in ((Lowlands)) (0.9)* **Mum** *was- since she'd been in England without any (.) opportunity to speak to anyone down there (.) she wanted the opportunity to speak it so we started conversation classes together*
GMEM1	Rugadh mi ann an Lunainn
	I was born in London
SD	An do rugadh? Uh huh
	Were you?
GMEM1	Ach 's ann uill 's ann à xxx is na h-eileanan a tha an teaghlach againn- 's ann à xxx ((Eilean)) a tha mo sheanmhair […] ach rugadh mo mhàthair ann an Dùn Èideann […] chan eil cuimhne agam ro mhòr air an ùine ann an Lunnainn co-dhiù ach
	But well our family is from xxx in the Hebrides- my grandmother is from xxx ((island)) […] but my mother was born in Edinburgh […] I don't remember our time in London too well anyway but
SD	So a bheil Gàidhlig aig do mhàthair mar sin?
	So can your mother speak Gaelic then?
GMEM1	Uill (.) tha tuigse aice ach (.) cha bhi i ga bruidhinn aig an taigh (.) 's ann dìreach le mo sheanmhair a tha mise a' bruidhinn Gàidhlig
	Well (.) she has an understanding but (.) she doesn't speak it at home (.) I only speak Gaelic to my grandmother

Both of the above speakers thus experienced no substantial language socialisation in Gaelic from family members while living in England, and learned the language in Scotland subsequently. The combination of close family connection to the language and living away from Scotland appear for both to have informed their decision to learn Gaelic to fluency, however. For participant GLAF4, the experience of learning Gaelic initially through conversation classes with her mother in the Lowlands, and for GMEM1 of re-establishing a linguistic relationship in Gaelic with his grandmother after learning the language, are relatively unusual in new speaker biographies generally. A more frequently encountered situation was that of former GME students sharing their educational experiences in Gaelic with siblings, as exemplified in the following extract:

SD	An robh Gàidhlig aig do theaghlach bho thùs?
	Could your family speak Gaelic?
GMEF3	Bha em tha Gàidhlig aig Granaidh em
	Yes em Granny can speak Gaelic em
SD	Seadh
	Yes
GMEF3	Agus chaidh mi tro foghlam tro mheadhan na Gàidhlig agus tha dà bhràthair agam chaidh iadsan ann cuideachd **so** 's e dìreach Granaidh 's na bràithrean agam [...] thòisich mi eh anns a' chròileagan agus cha robh facal agam
	*And I went through Gaelic-medium education and I have two brothers they went as well **so** it's just Granny and my brothers [...] I started eh in the cròileagan ((toddler group)) and didn't have a word*

In total, six of the thirty Scottish-based interviewees had first acquired Gaelic ability through immersion in the language in GME. Although such new speakers, who continue to speak the language with frequency and commitment following immersion schooling, constitute a marked minority of graduates of past-GME classes generally (cf. Dunmore 2017, 2019) they are clearly an extremely important subset of new speakers, both in terms of national language policy ambitions and of demographics.

GMEM3	Rugadh 's thogadh mi ann am xxx ((Eilean)) [...ach] ghluais mo phàrantan a-steach dhan a sgìre anns na seachdadan agus 's ann air sgàth gu robh uill bha obair aca an-sin anns an sgoil [...] bha Gàidhlig san sgìre- 's e sin an rud as cudromaiche ann an dòigh- 's e àite gu math Gàidhealach- gu math Gàidhlig a bh'ann
	I was born and raised in the Isle of xxx [...but] my parents moved into the area in the seventies and it was because of- well they had jobs in the school

there [...] Gaelic was present in the area- that was the most important thing in a way- it was quite a Gaelic place ((culturally)) – quite a Gaelic place ((linguistically)

SD   'S e 's e
         Yes yes
GMEM3   Aig an àm a bha siud
         At that time

Two speakers out of the thirty interviewed for the current research reported the combination of exposure to Gaelic in Gaelic-medium education, and in the community in which they were raised, as instructive in their motivation to learn and use the language beyond the immersion classroom setting. In spite of the fact that his parents did not speak Gaelic, interviewee GMEM3 observes in the final extract above that the presence of Gaelic in the wider community when he was growing up was 'the most important thing' (*'an rud as cudromaiche'*) in inspiring his continued desire to acquire and use Gaelic after school. Whilst experiences such as this were decidedly unusual, both among participants in the present study and among leavers of GME in previous research (see Dunmore 2019), it is a likely consequence of present language planning priorities that GME leavers will form an increasingly important and sizeable demographic in Gaelic Scotland in years to come.

This chapter has drawn attention to the various ways in which interview participants in Nova Scotia and Scotland construct and convey their identities as Gaels – or, as was more often the case in Scotland, decline or downplay any identity as such. The possible reasons for the disparity between Canadian and Scottish-based interviewees' negotiations of Gaelic identity were discussed in greater detail in the subsequent sections. It is clear from the data analysed above that Nova Scotian informants' greater identification with Gael(ic) identity reflects their relatively deeper interest in personal and family heritage as a motivating factors for language learning activity. Discussion then addressed discourses of Gaelic cultural change and community adaptation in Nova Scotian and Scottish-based interviewees' accounts of ethnolinguistic identity in the two contexts. Once again, Nova Scotian new speakers' views concerning the revitalisation of Gaelic in the province tend to contrast with those expressed more typically by Scottish new speakers. Narratives pertaining to advanced language shift in Nova Scotia are nevertheless joined frequently by a strong sense of optimism for the future in Nova Scotia, a dimension not so frequently observed in the Scottish discourses outlined in this chapter. Similarly, this chapter has demonstrated Nova Scotian new speakers' sense of wider support for Gaelic revitalisation in the province, which tends to contrast with Scottish participants' descriptions of opposition to Gaelic they have encountered.

Finally, analysis in the later parts of the chapter demonstrated how the majority of new speakers' limited experiences of Gaelic language socialisation by family members contrasts in the Nova Scotian context with the high degree of salience attached to family heritage in motivating Gaelic acquisition. Scottish new speakers were distinguished once again from their Nova Scotian counterparts in the sense that relatively few attached significance to family ties to the Gaelic community; for the majority of Scottish speakers, such ties were either non-existent or were not deemed to be in any way significant. Overall, this chapter has once again emphasised key distinctions in relation to new speakers' cultural identities as Gaels in the two contexts under investigation. In order to consider from a different perspective issues of language use, acquisition and identity that the last two chapters have examined qualitatively, the following chapter draws on survey data as a means of triangulating findings across the book's key themes.

SIX

Quantitative Perspectives on New Gaelic Speakerhood in Scotland and Nova Scotia

This chapter summarises the quantitative research findings from an online survey of new speaker language practices, attitudes and identities, which elicited eighty responses between January 2018 and January 2019. The results of the descriptive statistical analysis presented are described in relation to qualitative observations recorded in the previous three chapters, in order to triangulate between the various datasets and make methodologically and empirically grounded conclusions in respect of Gaelic language use and new speaker identities.

Online survey: Sample method and sociodemographic characteristics

A bilingual (Gaelic–English), online survey of language use, socialisation, acquisition and attitudes was designed and piloted in 2017, and uploaded using the Jisc online survey tool in January 2018. Over the course of the twelve months during which the survey was live, links to the survey were circulated and retweeted at regular intervals on Twitter/X using my personal handle (@Dun_Mor) and were shared through various Gaelic learners' groups and pages on Facebook. By the end of the twelve-month period, eighty-two complete responses were received, two of which were found on closer scrutiny to be duplicate responses by participants who had previously completed the questionnaire. These two responses were disaggregated and removed from the dataset. Locations of the eighty unique respondents are displayed in Figure 6.1, below.

As shown in Figure 6.1, forty-nine of the eighty questionnaire respondents were based in Scotland (61 per cent), twenty-five in Nova Scotia (31 per cent) and six individuals were based elsewhere in the world (8 per cent). As the online survey was specifically designed for and circulated among networks of new speakers in Scotland and Nova Scotia, the six respondents who reported living in neither location were disaggregated and excluded from the descriptive

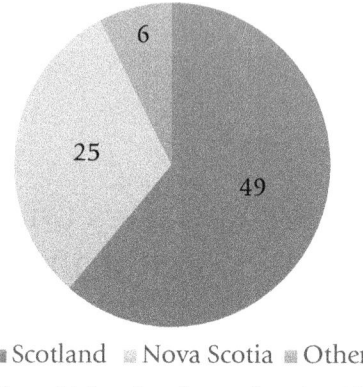

Figure 6.1 Location of respondents (n = 80)

statistical analysis. An important research question in future investigations of new speaker motivations, language practices and attitudes will be the degree to which growing and digitally interconnected networks of Gaelic speakers in other locations concur or contrast with those of Scotland- and Nova Scotia-based speakers. Among the six individuals excluded from the present analysis, respondents' reported locations included Australia, continental Europe, the United States and two other Canadian provinces. It is likely that these four major zones are prevalent sites for the emergence of new networks of Gaelic speakers beyond Scotland and Nova Scotia. In that sense, the data they provided will be useful for informing subsequent case study research. For the present analysis, however, excluding such respondents, it will suffice to note that two-thirds of the final dataset of seventy-four responses were received from participants in Scotland (66 per cent), and one-third from speakers in Nova Scotia (34 per cent).

In terms of age, broadly comparable populations were recorded in Scotland and Nova Scotia. Among Scotland-based respondents, an average (mean) age of 47.2 was recorded, with a standard deviation of 13.7; Nova Scotia-based respondents' mean age was slightly younger at 45.6, with a standard deviation of 12.8. Survey respondents' distribution by broad age groups is displayed by percentage below.

As illustrated in Figure 6.2, below, respondents' age groups in Scotland and Nova Scotia were largely comparable, but were more concentrated within the 30–40 and 41–50 age brackets in Nova Scotia, accounting for 64 per cent of participants there (as opposed to 48 per cent in Scotland). By contrast, Scotland-based survey respondents were more evenly spread across the five broad age brackets. It is particularly notable that very few survey respondents in either location were aged under thirty (just six in Scotland, and two in Nova Scotia).

In terms of Scottish and Nova Scotian respondents' gender, striking differences are observable between the two research settings. In Scotland, 74 per cent

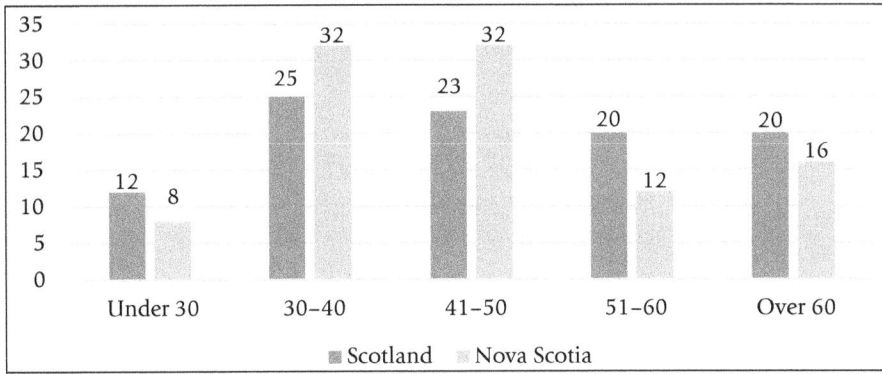

Figure 6.2 Age of respondents (%)

of survey participants indicated their gender was male, 24 per cent female and 2 per cent non-binary; in Nova Scotia, by contrast, almost inverse proportions are recorded, with 28 per cent reporting their gender as male and 72 per cent as female. This clear disparity will have important implications for other considerations that will be described below.

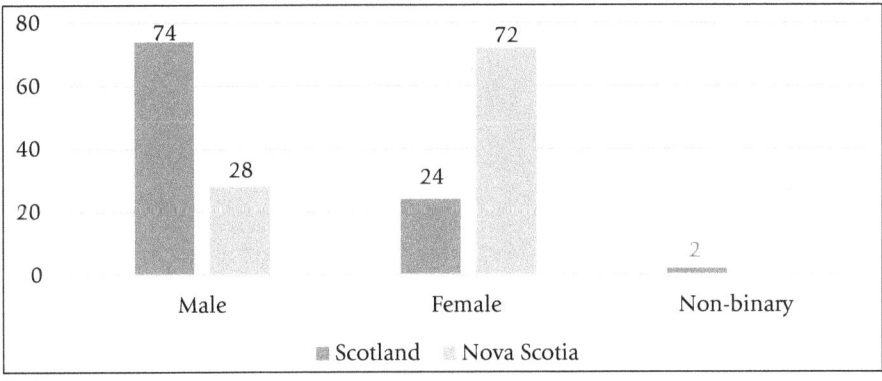

Figure 6.3 Gender (%)

A broad measure of socioeconomic class was attained by means of grouping survey respondents' reported occupations according to established NS-SEC conventions, such as those employed by the UK Office for National Statistics in analysing national census data (see, for example, ONS 2022). As can be seen in Figure 6.4, below, socioeconomic classifications recorded in Scotland and Nova Scotia were largely comparable. Sixty per cent of Scottish-based respondents indicated higher or lower professional occupations, whilst 64 per cent of Nova Scotia-based participants did so. Twenty-two per cent of participants based in Scotland indicated intermediate or routine occupations, whilst 20 per cent of those based in Nova Scotia did so. Eighteen per cent of Scottish-based participants and 16 per cent of Nova Scotian respondents were in full-time education,

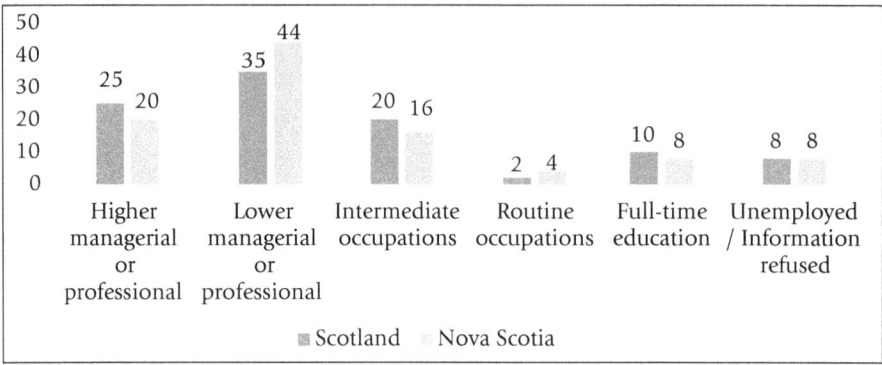

Figure 6.4 Socio-economic class (%)

were otherwise economically inactive or declined to state their occupation. Overall, therefore, self-report bias indicating disproportionately higher levels of professional class membership was visible in the sample from both contexts, compared to national averages in both the UK and Canada. It is not possible to say with any degree of certainty, however, whether or not such proportions are reflective of Gaelic learners and new Gaelic speakers in Scotland and Nova Scotia as a whole.

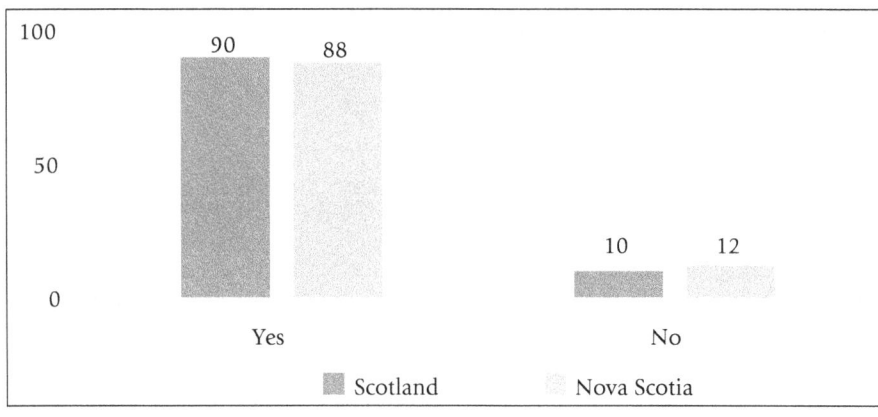

Figure 6.5 University attendance (%)

As Figure 6.5 illustrates, rates of university attendance in both research contexts were very high, again likely reflecting self-report bias in the sample. It is possible that such high proportions of participants from higher socioeconomic classes are reflective of wider populations of Gaelic language learners and L2 users, but relevant data are currently lacking to either confirm or disprove this suggestion.

As Figure 6.6 indicates (below), reported overall ability in Gaelic was relatively high among new speakers in both research contexts, though the proportion

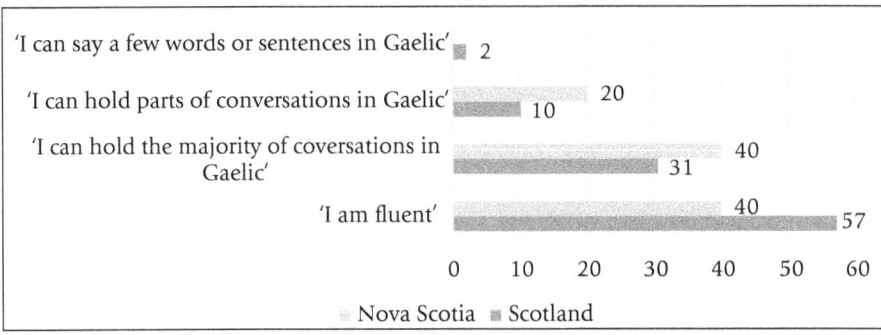

Figure 6.6 Ability in Gaelic (%)

reporting fluency in Gaelic in Scotland (57 per cent) was notably higher than in Nova Scotia (40 per cent). Conversely, proportions reporting an ability to hold the 'majority' or 'parts' of conversations in Gaelic were notably higher in Nova Scotia than Scotland (40 per cent versus 31 per cent, and 20 per cent versus 10 per cent, respectively). The finding that three-fifths of Scottish-based participants (57 per cent) reported fluency in Gaelic, with the same proportion of Nova Scotian informants (60 per cent) reporting less than fluent competency, seems particularly striking. In practice, of course, the distinction between regarding oneself as 'fluent' in a language, as opposed to being able to 'hold the majority of conversations' in it, may be rather slight, and more reflective of opportunities and confidence to speak the language in question. Nevertheless, the possibility of genuinely lower levels of Gaelic proficiency among Nova Scotian new speakers cannot be ruled out. In order to throw further light on the issue, survey participants were next asked to indicate their language proficiencies, on a scale of 0 to 10, in both Gaelic and English with regard to various linguistic skills. The results of these aptitude matrices are displayed in Table 6.1, below.

On an ordinal scale of 0–10, we see that average (mean) professed Gaelic abilities were uniformly higher in Scotland than Nova Scotia, with differences of 2.0, 2.1, 0.6 and 0.6 reported between Scotland and Nova Scotia–based participants' abilities in reading, writing, speaking and understanding the language, respectively. By contrast, divergences between mean professed abilities in English among the two cohorts were notably slight, at 0, 0.2, 0.2 and 0.1 respectively. It is thus telling that, on one hand, differences in reported levels of Gaelic literacy were higher between the two cohorts than in relation to Gaelic oracy, and that more advanced English language skills were reported across both subgroups. The former finding may of course reflect the divergent approach to Gaelic language instruction that has tended to be prioritised in Nova Scotia, with emphasis on speech and comprehension rather than reading and writing. Very high levels of English language ability across both the Scottish

Table 6.1 Reported linguistic abilities in Gaelic and English

	Gaelic ability: Reading	Gaelic ability: Writing	Gaelic ability: Speaking	Gaelic ability: Understanding	English ability: Reading	English ability: Writing	English ability: Speaking	English ability: Understanding
Scotland Mean	8.9	8.2	8.3	8.7	10	9.9	9.9	9.9
Standard deviation	1.4	2	1.6	1.4	0.1	0.4	0.4	0.3
Nova Scotia Mean	6.9	6.1	7.7	8.1	10	9.7	9.7	9.8
Standard deviation	2.5	2.6	1.8	1.6	0.2	0.7	0.6	0.4

and Nova Scotian cohorts, conversely, are suggestive of that language's greater role in participants' childhood language socialisation, education and daily linguistic practice.

Informants' Gaelic acquisition, language socialisation and use

The next portion of the survey invited participants to indicate their first exposure to Gaelic language acquisition in different domains. As part of this exercise it was also possible to attain a broad measure of Gaelic language socialisation during childhood in the important contexts of school, home and community.

As Figure 6.7, below, indicates, respondents' first age of exposure to Gaelic language acquisition was notably younger in Nova Scotia than in Scotland. Whilst there are limitations to what we may infer from these data in terms of statistical significance and generalisability, due to the small and self-selected nature of the sample, divergences in earliest reported Gaelic acquisition between Nova Scotian and Scottish subgroups are striking. Over half of Nova Scotia-based respondents (52 per cent) indicated having first started to learn Gaelic under the age of eighteen, compared to just 28 per cent of participants in Scotland. Conversely, over twice the proportion of Scottish-based participants reported having first acquired Gaelic over the age of thirty (45 per cent) as was true of informants in Nova Scotia (20 per cent). Whilst the total numbers of participants within each category are small, particularly in the Nova Scotian subgroup, these distinctions are particularly noteworthy. As discussed in light of Figure 6.2, above, the rather advanced average ages of new Gaelic speakers in either context (forty-seven in Scotland, forty-six in Nova Scotia) may play some role in explaining the apparent disparity in age of first Gaelic acquisition visible in Figure 6.7. On one hand, Scottish-based respondents would for the most part have been too old to have benefited from the introduction of Gaelic-medium

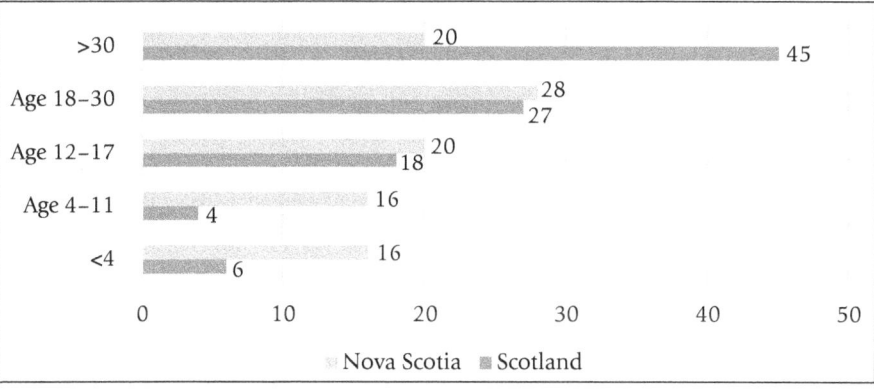

Figure 6.7 Age of first Gaelic acquisition (%)

education in that context in 1985, while it is possible that some of the Nova Scotian cohort experienced exposure to Gaelic in formerly Gaelic-dominant communities at home or school in Cape Breton as recently the 1970s.

In order to throw further light on these potential explicating factors, respondents were next asked to indicate their exposure to Gaelic in the domains of school, home and community during childhood. As Figure 6.8, below, demonstrates, a large majority of informants from each context received no exposure at all to Gaelic within the formal education system during childhood (72 per cent Nova Scotia; 82 per cent Scotland). Whilst similar proportions in both contexts reported some exposure to Gaelic education at secondary school (16 per cent Nova Scotia; 12 per cent Scotland), twice the proportion of Nova Scotia–based participants (12 per cent) encountered some Gaelic at primary school as was the case in Scotland (6 per cent). Tellingly, however, 4 per cent of Scottish-based informants (that is, two individuals) reported having received Gaelic-medium education at primary school. Overinterpreting these percentage disparities would be unwise in light of the small and self-selected sample under analysis, and it is likely that the exposure to Gaelic at school that 28 per cent of the twenty-five Nova Scotia–based respondents reported was rather limited.

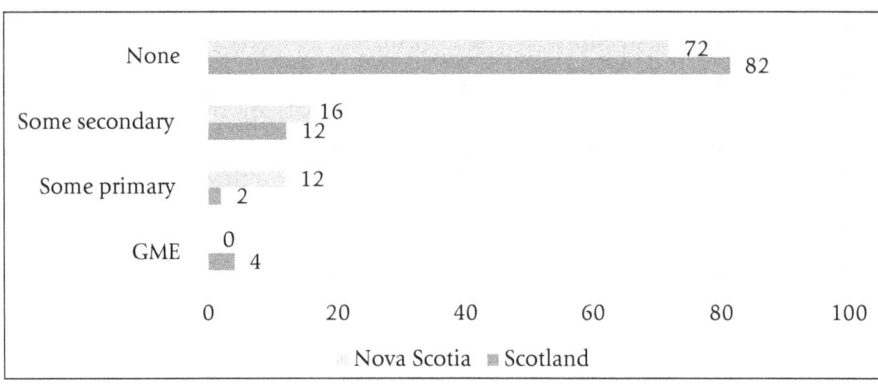

Figure 6.8 School exposure to Gaelic in childhood (%)

Large majorities of both Scottish (74 per cent) and Nova Scotian (80 per cent) participants reported that only English was used in the homes in which they were raised, as Figure 6.9, below, demonstrates. Whilst 8 per cent and 4 per cent of respondents from Scotland respectively reported 'mostly English' and 'mostly Gaelic' use in their childhood homes (as against 16 per cent and 4 per cent in Nova Scotia), 12 per cent in Scotland reported the use of 'other' languages (compared to none in Nova Scotia). This finding is potentially reflective of cultural and linguistic diversity in contemporary networks of new Gaelic speakers, particularly in Scotland's cities (see McLeod, O'Rourke and Dunmore 2014). No single respondent in either context reported 'equal' use of English and Gaelic, or of 'Gaelic only' in the homes in which they grew up.

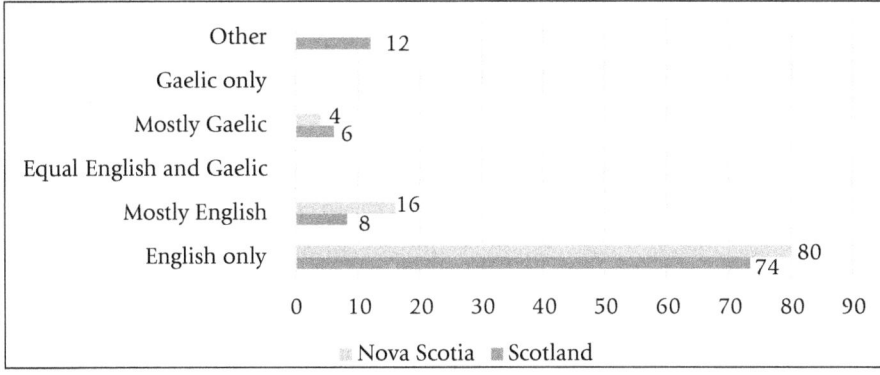

Figure 6.9 Language use in childhood home (%)

Whilst large majorities of survey respondents indicated use of 'only' or 'mostly' English within the communities in which they were raised (71 per cent Scotland; 92 per cent Nova Scotia), nuanced distinctions between the two contexts are nevertheless visible in Figure 6.10, below. The finding that over half (57 per cent) of Scottish-based participants grew up in communities where 'only English' was used (compared to 40 per cent in Nova Scotia) perhaps reflects the greater extent of officially supported multilingualism in the Canadian context. Fifty-two per cent of Nova Scotia–based participants reported that English was 'mostly' used in their childhood community (as against 40 per cent reporting 'English only'). This finding is likely suggestive of the presence, if only marginal, of the French (in particular) and possibly Mi'kmaq languages as minority varieties within communities where most Nova Scotia-based participants were raised.

The finding that 10 per cent of the forty-nine Scottish-based participants reported that at least some Gaelic was used in their childhood communities

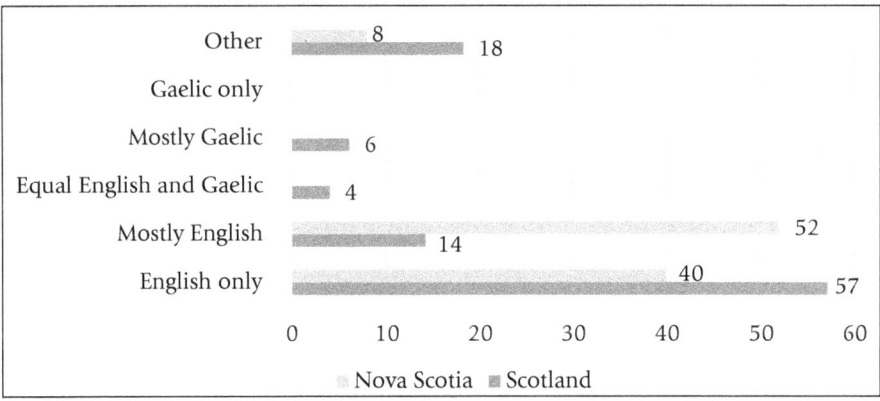

Figure 6.10 Language use in community (%)

is likely reflective of the respondents' average age (forty-seven; compare Figure 6.2, above). Conversely, the finding that 18 per cent in Scotland reported use of other languages at a community level during childhood is likely to reflect the urban, Lowland background of many participants in this setting. Distinctions between first language acquisition experiences and childhood exposure to Gaelic in the school, home and community are thus notable between the Scottish and Nova Scotian subgroups. In general, however, childhood Gaelic language socialisation was extremely limited among large majorities of participants, reflective of the 'new' speakerhood of participants in both research contexts.

The next portion of the online survey asked respondents to indicate the overall frequency of their Gaelic language use at present. As can be seen in Figure 6.11, below, large majorities of survey participants in both contexts reported using Gaelic on a daily basis (Nova Scotia 64 per cent; Scotland 73 per cent) or weekly basis (Nova Scotia 20 per cent; Scotland 21 per cent) at present. Only small proportions in either setting reported using Gaelic more seldom than weekly (note in particular that the 8 per cent of respondents from Nova Scotia who reported using Gaelic less frequently than monthly amount to just two individuals).

In order to quantify the specific extent of respondents' Gaelic language use compared to English, the next section of the survey invited indications of linguistic usage in various contexts and with different types of interlocutor. As Figure 6.12 demonstrates, similar proportions of survey respondents in both settings reported using 'only' English in the home setting, with 18 per cent of Scottish-based and 24 per cent of Nova Scotia-based informants doing so. Forty per cent in Nova Scotia and 52 per cent in Scotland reported 'mostly' English use at home, with 16 per cent of Nova Scotian respondents reporting 'equal' English and Gaelic use, compared to 18 per cent of their Scottish counterparts.

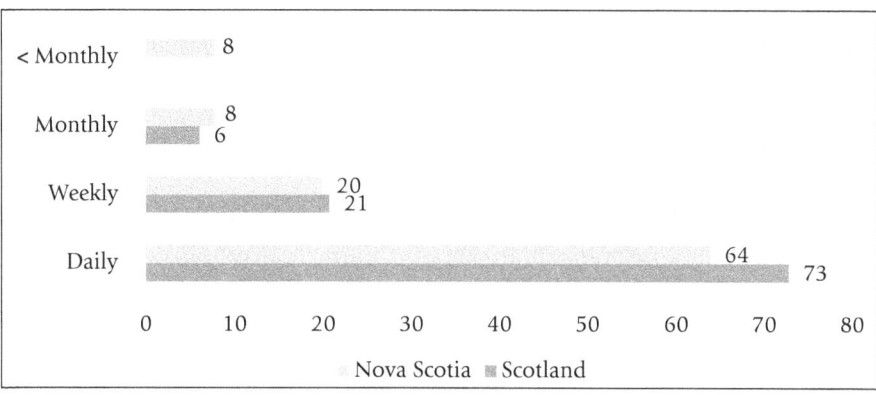

Figure 6.11 Overall frequency of Gaelic use (%)

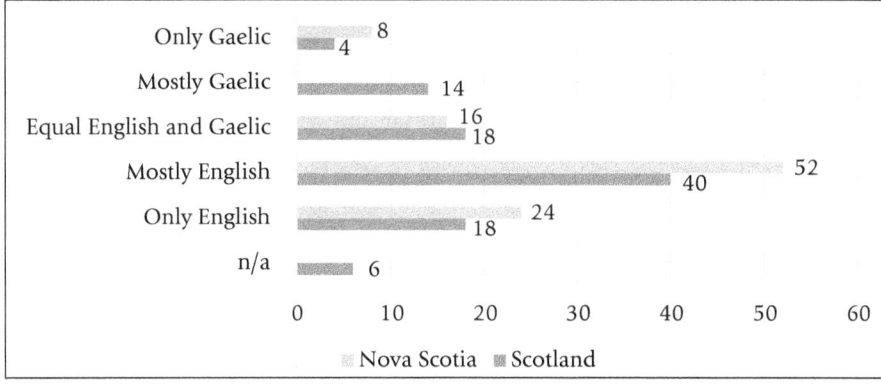

Figure 6.12 Language use at home (%)

Eighteen per cent of Scottish participants reported 'only' or 'mostly' Gaelic use at home, compared to 8 per cent of Nova Scotians who reported using 'only' Gaelic (with none indicating 'mostly' Gaelic). Proportionally, therefore, home use of English appears to dominate to a greater degree in Nova Scotia (with 76 per cent reporting at least 'mostly' English-speaking homes) than in Scotland, where the corresponding proportion is 58 per cent. Whilst a quarter of Nova Scotian informants (26 per cent) reported at least 'equal' use of Gaelic as of English at home, over one third of Scottish respondents (36 per cent) did so. Three individuals in Scotland (6 per cent) responded that this question was not applicable to them.

In relation to language use in the context of work (see Figure 6.13), 46 per cent of Scotland-based respondents reported using 'only' or 'mostly' Gaelic (half of whom use 'only' Gaelic). This very high level of Gaelic use in employment in the Scottish context compares with just 12 per cent (n = 3) of Nova Scotian respondents who reported using 'mostly' Gaelic at work. By contrast, however, 28 per cent of Nova Scotian informants indicated 'equal' use

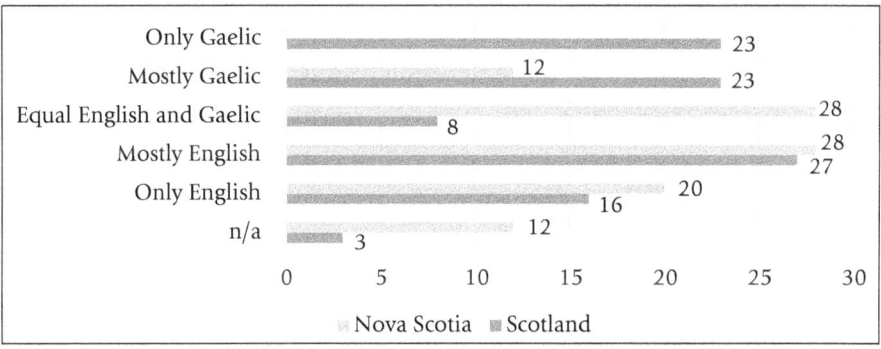

Figure 6.13 Language use at work (%)

of Gaelic and English in the domain of work (compared to 8 per cent of Scots). Proportions indicating 'mostly' or 'only' English use in their working lives are thus broadly comparable across the two contexts, at 48 per cent in Nova Scotia and 43 per cent in Scotland. At least 'equal' use of Gaelic in employment, as reported by 40 per cent of Nova Scotian and 54 per cent of Scottish informants, thus highlights the importance of this domain for new speakers' regular use of the language in both research settings.

In terms of social use of Gaelic with friends, Figure 6.14 (below) displays informants' responses in the two research contexts. Sixty per cent of Nova Scotia-based participants reported at least 'equal' use of Gaelic as English with friends, compared to 55 per cent of respondents from Scotland. Thirty-two per cent and 35 per cent of Nova Scotian and Scottish informants reported using 'mostly' English with friends, implying that fully 92 per cent and 90 per cent of respondents from Nova Scotia and Scotland, respectively, use Gaelic to at least some degree in their social interactions with friends. These high rates of Gaelic usage outside of the domains of home and work life likely reflect the importance of new Gaelic speakers' social networks for their frequent usage of Gaelic.

By contrast, Gaelic use with romantic partners or spouses is relatively more unusual (Figure 6.15, below). Eighteen per cent of Scottish-based respondents indicated at least 'equal' Gaelic use with their partner or spouse, the same proportion as of who reported this question did not apply to them. Although twice the proportion of Nova Scotian respondents (36 per cent) indicated this question was not applicable, clear majorities in both contexts (64 per cent in Scotland; 60 per cent in Nova Scotia) claimed to use 'only' or 'mostly' English with partners. Prospects for using Gaelic in domestic contexts would thus be understandably limited for most participants (as verified in Figure 6.12, above) with implications for potential rates of intergenerational transmission of the language at home.

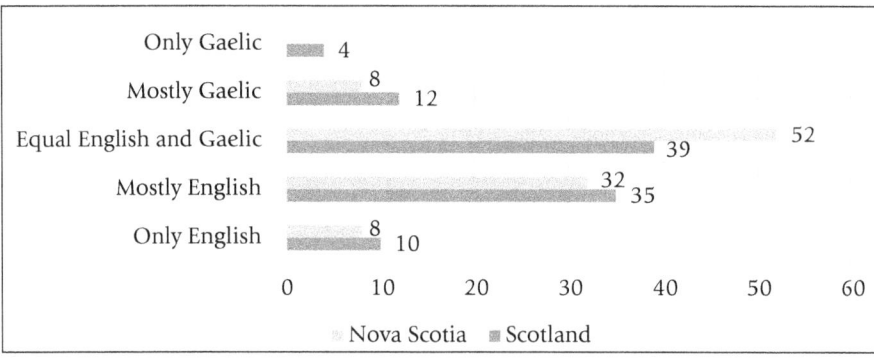

Figure 6.14 Language use with friends (%)

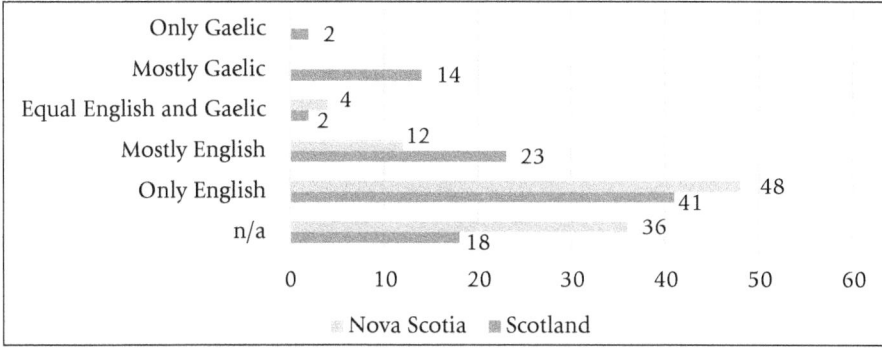

Figure 6.15 Language use with partner/spouse (%)

Although majorities of participants indicated that the question of language use with a child did not apply to them (55 per cent in Scotland; 60 per cent in Nova Scotia), twice the proportion of those with children in Scotland reported at least 'equal' use of Gaelic with a son or daughter (36 per cent) as of those who reported using 'mostly' or 'only' English (18 per cent). In Nova Scotia this pattern was essentially reversed, with equivalent percentages of 12 per cent and 28 per cent. Proportionally lower levels of language transmission may thus tentatively be interpreted from the Nova Scotian setting, though the total numbers of relevant respondents in each context (twenty-two in Scotland; ten in Nova Scotia) are too small to effectively support this explanation with confidence. A further complicating factor in comparing the two settings is the gender disparity across subgroups in the two contexts (74 per cent male in Scotland, 72 per cent female in Nova Scotia; cf. Figure 6.3, above).

As Figure 6.17 (below) shows, whilst over half of Scottish informants (51 per cent) responded that the question of language use with their mother was not applicable, nine tenths of the remainder reported using 'only' English

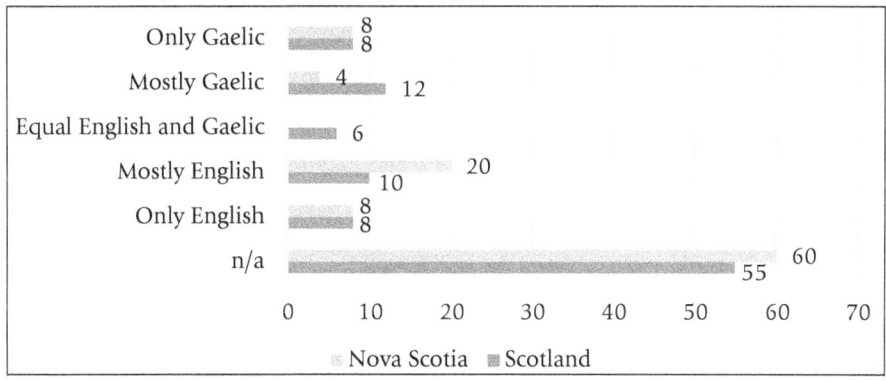

Figure 6.16 Language use with son/daughter (%)

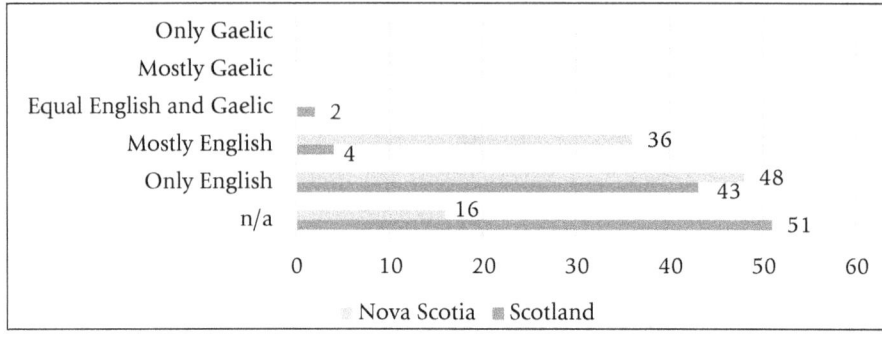

Figure 6.17 Language use with mother (%)

with their mothers. One further individual in Scotland (2 per cent) reported speaking 'equal' Gaelic and English, while two others (4 per cent) reported 'mostly' English. In Nova Scotia, subtly different patterns are apparent: whilst 16 per cent answered that the question didn't apply to them, almost half (48 per cent) reported 'only' using English with their mothers, while 36 per cent used 'mostly' English with them.

As Figure 6.18 shows, survey respondents reported fractionally more Gaelic use with fathers than with mothers, though use of English still dominated in both contexts. Although half of participants from Scotland (49 per cent) responded that this question did not apply to them, the vast majority of the remainder spoke 'only' English with their father, with two individuals reporting using 'mostly' English (4 per cent) and the same number reporting either 'equal' or 'only' Gaelic. Among Nova Scotian respondents, a quarter (24 per cent) responded that the question was not applicable, with over twice as many of the remainder (48 per cent) using 'only' English as 'mostly' English (20 per cent). One individual in Nova Scotia (4 per cent) reported using 'equal' Gaelic and English with their father, and one claimed to use 'only' Gaelic.

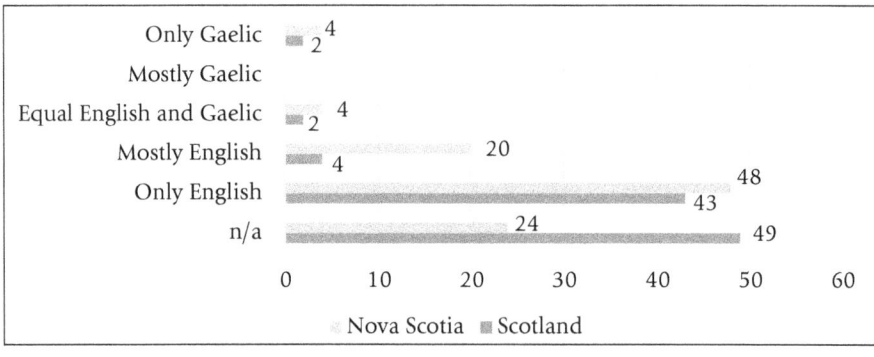

Figure 6.18 Language use with father (%)

Figure 6.19 (below) displays participants' responses in each context concerning language use with siblings. In Scotland, almost a quarter of informants indicated the question was not applicable (23 per cent), and four-fifths of the remainder reported speaking 'only' English with their sibling(s). Five individuals in Scotland (10 per cent) reported 'mostly' English use with a brother or sister, while two (4 per cent) reported 'equal' English and Gaelic use. In Nova Scotia, fractionally more Gaelic use was reported, with just over two-thirds of informants to whom the question was applicable reporting 'only' English use with their sibling(s), five individuals (20 per cent) using 'mostly' English with them, and two (8 per cent) reporting 'mostly' Gaelic use.

As shown in Figure 6.20 (below), clear majorities of respondents from both Scotland (65 per cent) and Nova Scotia (56 per cent) indicated that the question of language use with grandparents no longer applied to them. Amongst the minority of respondents with surviving grandparents, similar proportions of participants in each context indicated 'only' English use (23 per cent in Scotland; 28 per cent in Nova Scotia) and 'mostly' English use (10 per cent in Scotland; 8 per cent in Nova Scotia) with grandparents. Nevertheless, one individual in Scotland

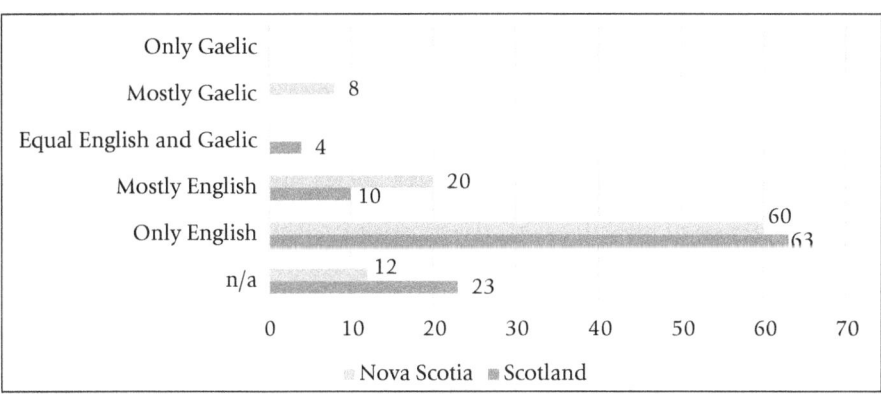

Figure 6.19 Language use with brother/sister (%)

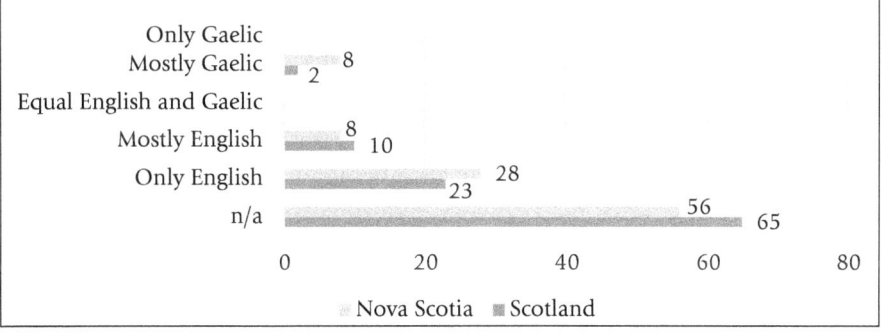

Figure 6.20 Language use with grandparents (%)

(2 per cent) and two in Nova Scotia (8 per cent) reported speaking 'mostly' Gaelic with their grandparents. Whilst we should be careful not to overinterpret the significance of such small numbers, the importance of intergenerational opportunities for Gaelic language use among minorities of survey respondents was described clearly by several Nova Scotian interviewees in Chapter 4.

Whilst, proportionally speaking, respondents reported using substantially more English than Gaelic within the various domains and with different interlocutors displayed in Figures 6.11–6.20 in this section, the importance of Gaelic language use – especially in the domain of work (Figure 6.13) and, to some extent, with friends (Figure 6.14) – was clearly apparent in questionnaire responses in both research settings. For small but not inconsequential minorities of respondents in both contexts, use of Gaelic professionally and socially was bolstered by use of the language to varying degrees in the home (Figure 6.12), with partners and spouses (particularly in Scotland, Figure 6.15) and children (Figure 6.16). New speakers' usage of Gaelic with such key interlocutors and in such crucial domains as home and family was thus generally limited among survey respondents (as was largely true in interviewees' responses in Chapter 4). The importance of professional and social opportunities for Gaelic use is again highlighted in the quantitative survey analysis, although in light of the small and self-selected sample on which responses are based, the analysis should be regarded as indicative rather than definitive.

Language attitudes and social identities

The next section of the survey asked participants to indicate the extent to which they agreed or disagreed with five attitudinal statements regarding the Gaelic language as an element of personal, regional, and national or provincial identity. Following convention in language attitudes research, a five-point Likert scale was employed to quantify respondents' extent of agreement with each proposition.

With regard to the suggested importance of Gaelic to the regions of the Highlands and Islands (Scotland) and Cape Breton (Nova Scotia), total agreement with the relevant attitudinal statements was extremely high, as Figure 6.21 (below) indicates. Ninety-six per cent of Scottish-based respondents agreed that with the proposition, whilst 91 per cent in Nova Scotia agreed with the equivalent statement in that context. In Scotland, one single individual (2 per cent) disagreed that 'Gaelic is important to the Highlands and Islands', whilst three respondents (6 per cent) held no view. Agreement with statements suggesting the importance of Gaelic to all of Scotland and Nova Scotia were similarly high. Ninety-two per cent of participants in Nova Scotia agreed that 'Gaelic is important to Nova Scotia as a whole', with 8 per cent (two individuals) neither agreeing or disagreeing. Ninety-six per cent of respondents from Scotland

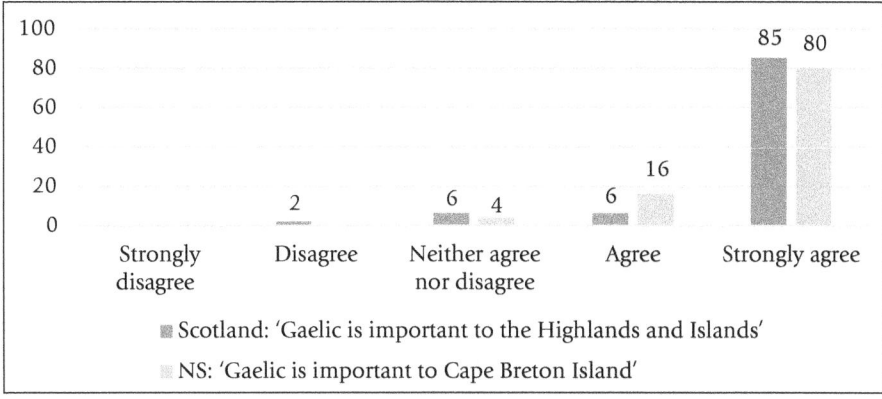

Figure 6.21 Attitudes to the regional importance of Gaelic (%)

agreed that 'Gaelic is important to Scotland as a whole', with one individual disagreeing with the proposition (2 per cent) and one expressing no view (2 per cent). Very high levels of support for both attitudinal statements were therefore found in both research contexts. The views of new Gaelic speakers in the present research thus outstrip levels of support for the language as a facet of national or regional identity among a nationally representative sample of Scottish citizens consulted as part of the 2022 Scottish Survey of Social Attitudes, for example (ScotCen Social Research 2022).

Similarly, in relation to personal identity, agreement with the suggestion that Gaelic is important to individual respondents' (see Figure 6.23, below) sense of self was substantially higher among new speaker informants in the present research than was true in the 2022 Scottish Social Attitudes Survey (ScotCen Social Research 2022). As Figure 6.23 shows, below, 92 per cent of Nova Scotian

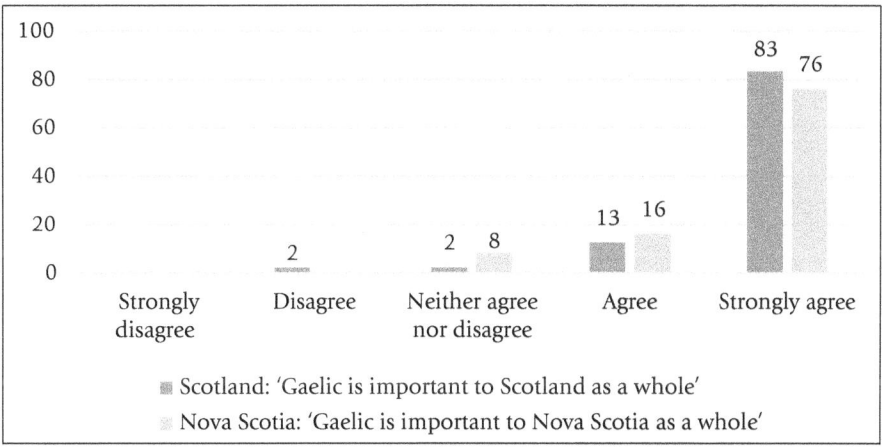

Figure 6.22 Attitudes to the national/provincial importance of Gaelic (%)

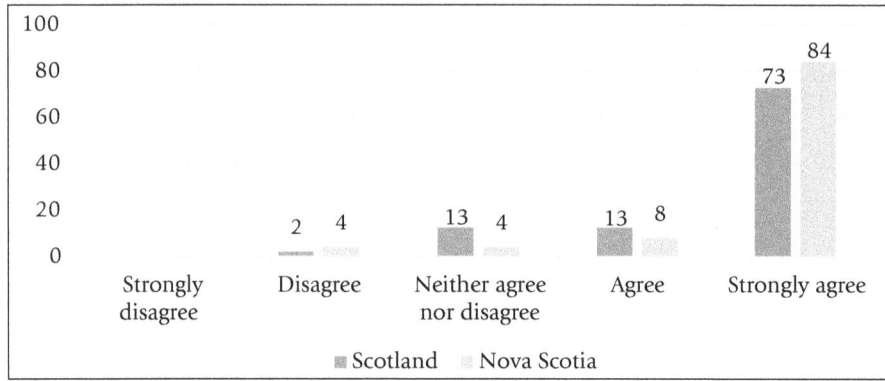

Figure 6.23 Responses to 'Gaelic is important to my personal identity' (%)

and 86 per cent of Scottish-based respondents agreed that 'Gaelic is important to my personal identity', with just one informant in each location disagreeing (2 per cent in Scotland; 4 per cent in Nova Scotia). A greater degree of ambivalence was apparent in Scotland with regard to this attitudinal statement than was true of previous propositions, however, with six individuals (13 per cent) expressing no view (compared to one single respondent in Nova Scotia).

Figure 6.24, below, shows high overall levels of support for the suggestion that the loss of Gaelic would entail the loss of distinctive identity at a national or provincial level, though strength of agreement in both contexts is relatively less than in relation to previous statements. Overall 98 per cent of Scottish-based participants agreed that 'Scotland would lose its distinctive identity without Gaelic', whilst 84 per cent of Nova Scotian participants agreed that 'Nova Scotia would lose its distinctive identity' without the language. In total, four Nova Scotian informants (16 per cent) either disagreed with this statement or expressed no view, while just one individual in Scotland expressed no view.

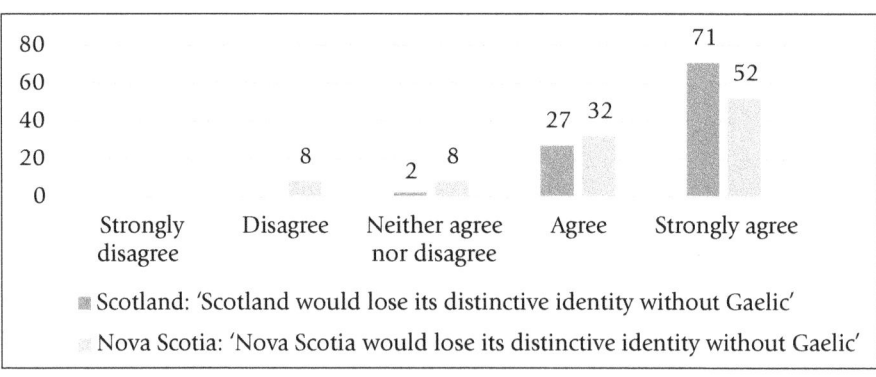

Figure 6.24 Attitudes to potential language and identity loss (%)

Proportionally stronger support for this statement in Scotland than Nova Scotia is likely reflective in part of subtle divergences in the nature of (provincial) Nova Scotian distinctiveness, and (national) identity in Scotland. Although further detailed research on the importance attached to Gaelic in the expression of Nova Scotia's identity would be beneficial, the finding that such large proportions of Gaelic users in the province regard the language as an important facet of its distinctive identity is a significant outcome in its own right. This finding is particularly noteworthy in light of the greatly more advanced stage of language shift that Gaelic is currently undergoing in Nova Scotia compared to Scotland. In this connection, Figure 6.25 (below) shows degrees of agreement with the suggestion that 'Gaelic is dying out'. In total, 32 per cent in Nova Scotia agreed with this statement, whilst the same proportion again disagreed (32 per cent), and the largest proportion (44 per cent) expressed no view either way. Thirty-five per cent in Scotland agreed with the statement, with 42 per cent disagreeing and 23 per cent declining to express a view. It is thus likely that the greater degree of ambivalence surrounding the prospect of Gaelic in Nova Scotia reflects the substantially smaller size of the Gaelic community in the province compared to that in Scotland. It is nevertheless notable that over a third of Scottish new speakers in the survey sample were of the view that Gaelic is indeed dying out in that context.

Overall, survey respondents exhibited remarkably high levels of agreement with expressions of attitudinal support for Gaelic – particularly as a facet of personal, regional, and national or provincial identity – in both research contexts. The final portion of the survey invited participants to indicate the various categories of cultural identities that they felt themselves to possess and express. Divergences in responses among participants in the two settings, as suggested, are likely reflective of idiosyncratic distinctions between the nature of Nova Scotia's distinctive identity as a Canadian province, and Scotland's national identity, albeit within the wider constitutional context of the United Kingdom.

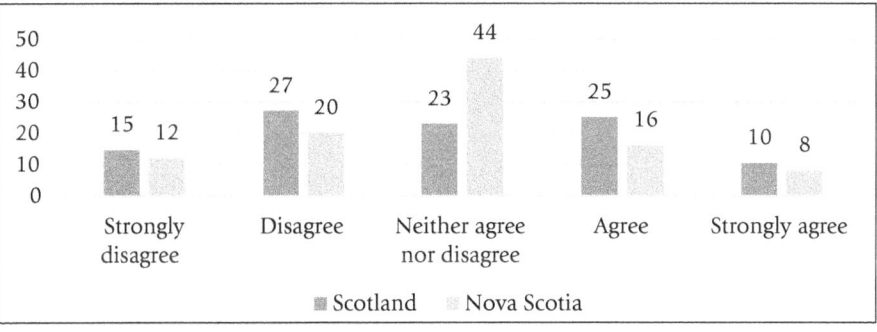

Figure 6.25 Responses to 'Gaelic is dying out' (%)

Figures 6.26 and 6.27 (below) display survey respondents' reported cultural and national identities. The questionnaire permitted participants to select any number of identity categories that they wished from a provided selection. A choice of 'European', 'British', 'Scottish', 'Gael' and 'Other' was available to Scottish-based participants, with respondents who selected 'Other' invited to indicate which additional identities they felt. As Figure 6.26 illustrates, thirty individuals in Scotland reported an identity as 'Scottish' (61 per cent of all respondents in that context). The next most widely reported identities were 'European' (reported by 45 per cent), 'Gael' (41 per cent), 'Other' (18 per cent) and 'British' (8 per cent). Of the nine individuals who indicated an 'Other'

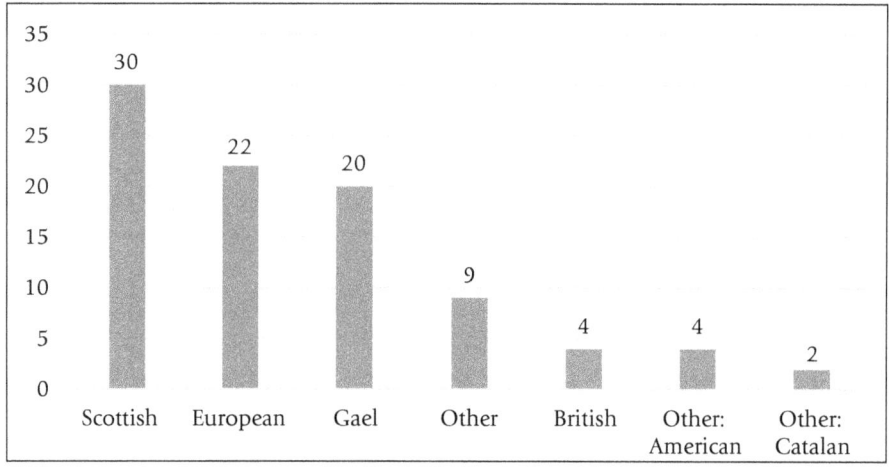

Figure 6.26 Reported identities in Scotland (n)

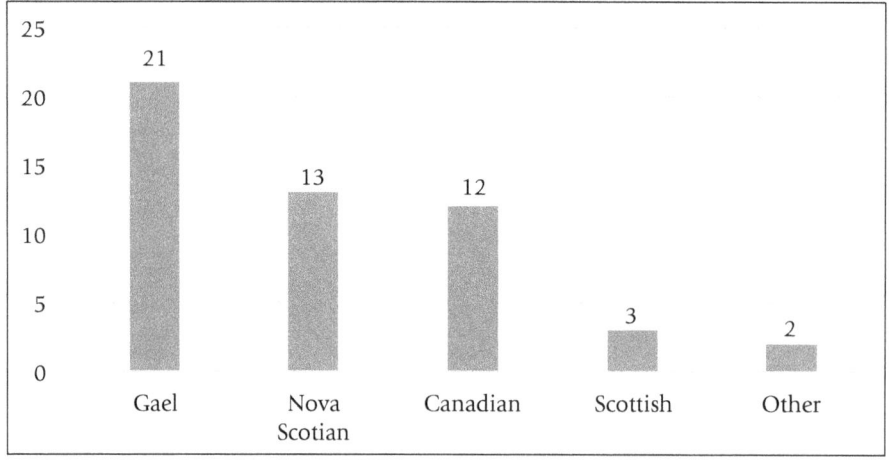

Figure 6.27 Reported identities in Nova Scotia (n)

identity, four stated 'American' (or '*Ameireaganach*') and two stated 'Catalan' (or '*Catalanach*'). The remaining identities that three participants reported within this 'Other' category were so specific as to potentially compromise the respondents' anonymity; they are thus not reported here.

In the Nova Scotian context, by contrast, twenty-one respondents (84 per cent of participants from that setting) indicated a sense of identity as a 'Gael', by far the most widely reported identity in that setting. The next most widely reported identities were 'Nova Scotian' (52 per cent), 'Canadian' (48 per cent), 'Scottish' (12 per cent) and 'Other' (8 per cent). Identities specified within the last category were, again, precise enough to potentially compromise respondents' anonymity.

The most striking finding from the comparison of Figures 6.26 and 6.27 is the relative frequency of Nova Scotian respondents' reporting of a sense of identity as Gaels. Importantly, the proportion of respondents reporting such an identity in Nova Scotia (84 per cent) was over twice the percentage recorded in Scotland (41 per cent). Whilst care should clearly be taken not to overinterpret the significance of this statistic in light of the small and self-selected sample under investigation, the relative strength of Nova Scotian new speakers' sense of identity as Gaels, compared to their Scottish-based counterparts, clearly resonates with the qualitative analysis of interview material discussed in the previous chapter.

The descriptive statistical analysis of survey responses this chapter presents tends to lend substantial support to the conclusions outlined in Chapters 4 and 5. Although the numbers of responses – especially in the Nova Scotian context – are too limited to facilitate more detailed, inferential statistical analysis, the degree of triangulation permitted by comparing quantitative survey results and the qualitative, ethnographic findings in the foregoing chapters of the book lends theoretical and empirical depth to conclusions deriving from interview-based and ethnographic material. In particular, proportionally higher levels of language socialisation in Gaelic during childhood and adolescence among Nova Scotian new speakers in the survey concord with interviewees' narratives concerning relatively more extensive exposure to the language and its community in Chapter 4. In general, however, childhood Gaelic language socialisation was limited among large majorities of participants, reflective of the 'new' speakerhood of participants in both research contexts. In the present day, conversely, clear majorities of participants in both contexts use Gaelic on either a daily (Nova Scotia 64 per cent; Scotland 73 per cent) or weekly basis (Nova Scotia 20 per cent; Scotland 21 per cent).

In the home domain, English appears to dominate to a rather greater degree in Nova Scotia (with 76 per cent reporting at least 'mostly' English-speaking homes) than in Scotland (where the corresponding proportion was 58 per cent). At work, at least 'equal' use of Gaelic was as reported by 40 per cent of

Nova Scotian and 54 per cent of Scottish informants, highlighting the importance of this domain for new speakers' regular use of the language. This finding particularly concords with mixed methods research on former Gaelic-medium students' continued use of the language after school (cf. Dunmore 2019). In terms of social use of the language, similar findings were reported in both research contexts for linguistic practice with friends and family; it was particularly noteworthy that clear majorities in both contexts (64 per cent in Scotland; 60 per cent in Nova Scotia) claimed to use 'only' or 'mostly' English with partners or spouses (again, see Dunmore 2019).

Lastly, remarkably similar patterns of language attitude were recorded in the two contexts in relation to the importance of Gaelic for local, (sub)national and personal identities. The relative strength of Nova Scotian new speakers' sense of identity as Gaels outlined above stands in close agreement with the qualitative analysis presented in Chapter 5; tellingly, the proportion of respondents reporting an identity as Gaels in Nova Scotia (84 per cent) was over twice that recorded in Scotland (41 per cent). The relative strength of Nova Scotian new speakers' sense of identity as Gaels thus clearly resonates with the qualitative analysis of interview material discussed in the qualitative analytic chapters.

In the final chapter, I draw together some of the overarching conclusions that the qualitative and quantitative analyses presented in this book.

SEVEN

New Worlds: Transatlantic Gaeldom and Twenty-first-century Linguistic Practice

This final chapter draws together the principal research findings of the study, providing a synthesis of key conclusions in respect of the overarching research questions: namely, the reported linguistic practices of new Gaelic speakers on both sides of the Atlantic, and the role that ethnolinguistic and heritage identities appear to play in determining these practices. The discussion presented will relate these findings to previously formulated theories of language revitalisation, and the possible role of new speakers in reversing language shift (as discussed in Chapters 1–2) as well as the overarching language ideologies observed to operate in both research contexts (as outlined in Chapter 3).

The chapter initially addresses the study's principal conclusions in respect of language use and acquisition among the sixty interviewees and eighty survey respondents, suggesting what likely prospects for language maintenance can be inferred from this investigation. It then presents the book's overarching conclusions with reference to participants' language ideologies and attitudes in relation to their cultural identities (as discussed in Chapter 5) and examines how these subjectivities appear to underlie research informants' current linguistic practices and future aspirations in respect of Gaelic culture and community. Lastly, the chapter considers the interrelationship of new speakers' Gaelic language use, ideology and identity from a sociolinguistic perspective, before providing a series of recommendations for policymakers in the Scottish and Nova Scotia governments who are currently attempting to revitalise Gaelic in each context.

Numerous important distinctions, but also commonalities, were observed between the linguistic practices of Scottish and Nova Scotian participants in Chapters 4 and 6 of this book. Firstly, a key disparity was demonstrated in relation to (potential and present) new speakers' opportunities to interact with first-language Gaelic speakers in the two contexts. Analysis in Chapter 4 demonstrated that, in spite of the substantially smaller size of Nova Scotia's Gaelic community, language policy in that context emphasises the importance of providing opportunity for learners of Gaelic to interact with remaining L1 speakers. This policy objective is foregrounded in order to inform both new speakers' language socialisation more generally, and language acquisition specifically. Yet, whilst immersion opportunities that explicitly connect learners to native speakers for purposes of Gaelic acquisition are not widely funded by Scottish policymakers at present, seeking out such opportunities voluntarily was described by many new speakers in that context as having been crucial to their learning Gaelic. Encouraging the development of programmes in Scotland similar to the *Bun is Bàrr* master-apprentice scheme will likely become an important objective for increasing Gaelic language socialisation for new speakers in coming years.

The sociolinguistic mudes and key life stages to have had significant consequences for new speakers' Gaelic language learning in both contexts ranged from accounts of family socialisation in Nova Scotia to Gaelic-medium immersion education in Scotland. These two contexts of language socialisation in turn form a key distinction between Nova Scotian and Scottish participants. Conversely, extracurricular immersion experiences in the language, formal adult study and, in particular, enrolment on courses at Sabhal Mòr Ostaig each form sociolinguistic experiences that were common to substantial numbers of interviewees in both contexts. The significance of Sabhal Mòr, especially, for informing new speakers' learning and socialisation experiences on both sides of the Atlantic, is a relatively understudied area of Gaelic language policy and planning.

In general, it is noteworthy that sociolinguistic mudes in (post-)adolescence and adulthood were recounted by majorities of participants in both Nova Scotia and Scotland as being particularly formative for their own Gaelic acquisition as new speakers. In spite of this, it is also instructive to consider the (admittedly rather few) instances of individuals who acquired some Gaelic in childhood through community interaction and formal (non-Gaelic-medium) education. The descriptive statistical analysis of survey responses presented in Chapter 6 lends substantial support to the conclusions outlined in Chapter 4. Although numbers of responses were too limited to facilitate more fine-grained, inferential statistical analysis, the degree of triangulation with qualitative analyses that comparison with these responses facilitates is instructive for our understanding of new Gaelic speaker practices. In particular, proportionally higher levels of language socialisation in Gaelic during childhood and adolescence among Nova Scotian new speakers in survey responses concord closely with Nova Scotian interviewees' narratives of exposure to the language and its community in childhood.

In general, however, childhood Gaelic language socialisation was limited for large majorities of participants in both contexts, reflective of the 'newness' of participants' Gaelic speakerhood in both research contexts. Quantitative analysis in Chapter 6 demonstrated that, in the present day, clear majorities of participants in both contexts use Gaelic on either a daily basis (Nova Scotia 64 per cent; Scotland 73 per cent) or a weekly basis (Nova Scotia 20 per cent; Scotland 21 per cent).

In the home domain, quantitative survey responses indicated that use of English dominated to a greater degree in Nova Scotia (with 76 per cent of respondents reporting at least 'mostly' English-speaking homes) than in Scotland (where the corresponding proportion was 58 per cent). At work, at least 'equal' use of Gaelic was as reported by 40 per cent of Nova Scotian and 54 per cent of Scottish informants respectively, highlighting the importance of this domain for new speakers' regular usage of the language. This finding tallies particularly closely with mixed methods research on former Gaelic-medium students' continued use of the language after school (Dunmore 2019). In terms of the use of Gaelic as the language of social and informal interaction, similar findings were reported in both research contexts. This is, for instance, borne out in findings concerning linguistic practice with friends and family; it was particularly noteworthy that clear majorities in both contexts (64 per cent in Scotland; 60 per cent in Nova Scotia) claimed to use 'only' or 'mostly' English with partners or spouses (see also Dunmore 2019).

In relation to new speakers' reported linguistic practices, a number of key additional observations were made on the basis of the interview data. Among Nova Scotian interviewees, the importance of acquiring a distinctive accent, or employing characteristically local dialect features, was a theme emphasised in many interviews. In Scotland, by contrast, a large majority of interviewees dismissed the importance of learning a particular Gaelic dialect or acquiring an accent of a particular area as generally impractical, inauthentic or undesirable for other reasons. The scholarly importance and general interest that new speakers in Scotland attached to Gaelic dialects, on one hand, tended on the other hand not to be matched with any sense of commitment to acquiring dialectal forms of the language, as aiming to acquire such forms was generally regarded as inauthentic or unnatural. This contrasts quite clearly with new speaker orientations towards spoken L1 dialects in Nova Scotia. Such clear distinctions are similarly apparent in relation to speakers' attitudes concerning opportunities for using Gaelic after having acquired an initial competence in the language.

In this regard, Chapter 4 highlighted key contrasts in understandings of opportunities for target language use in the two research contexts, with Nova Scotian participants frequently highlighting the importance of their own agency in creating such opportunities within their social networks. In Scotland, new speakers often expressed awareness of their agency in such decisions, but observed more frequently that other aspects of their lives (whether within the domains of work or home) had sometimes led them to deprioritise using

Gaelic. Possible exceptions to this general pattern were exemplified in accounts of home life after starting a family, though such descriptions featured less prominently than was the case in the Nova Scotia data.

Whilst important discrepancies in language acquisition trajectories, current linguistic practices and ideologies concerning opportunity were key to conclusions presented in the analysis in Chapters 4 and 6, commonalities and areas of shared sociolinguistic experience also came frequently to the fore. Possible reasons for shared and divergent experiences across the two research settings were explored in greater detail in Chapter 5, which presented emergent themes concerning interviewees' conceptions of heritage and identity. As the analysis demonstrated, understandings of the salience of ethnolinguistic identity and heritage as motivations for acquiring and using Gaelic contrasted sharply between contexts, and contrasting sociolinguistic ideologies were presented across the two settings.

Analytic attention turned from practical issues of linguistic acquisition and use to address new speakers' sociolinguistic subjectivities (after Kramsch 2004, 2013) in terms of their language ideologies and identities. To this end, Chapter 5 initially drew attention to the various ways in which interview participants in Nova Scotia and Scotland construct and convey their Gaelic identities, and their sociocultural association, or lack thereof, with the term 'Gael'. The possible reasons for the disparity between Canadian and Scottish-based interviewees' negotiations of Gaelic identities were explored in further depth in following sections of that chapter. Data analysed in interview extracts throughout Chapter 5 demonstrated that Nova Scotian informants' greater identification with Gael(ic) identity reflects their relatively deeper interest in personal and family heritage as motivating factors for (past) language learning activities. Revisiting Norton's (2013, 2019) concept of L2 investment, we may consider that an 'imagined' identity as a Gael might have initially informed such Nova Scotian speakers' decisions to learn Gaelic to high levels of oracy. For such individuals in the present day, however, there appeared to be nothing imagined about this aspect of their sociocultural and ethnolinguistic identities. New speakers in the Nova Scotia setting overwhelmingly considered themselves to be Gaels and to experience their worlds largely via that identity. In that sense, Norton's model of investment, which pertains chiefly to L2 learners rather than bilingual speakers who may no longer be 'invested' in the language learning process, may only apply in contexts of new speakerhood to a certain point.

The discussion then addressed discourses of Gaelic cultural change and community adaptation in interviewees' accounts of ethnolinguistic identity and vitality in the two contexts. Once again, Nova Scotia new speakers' views surrounding the revitalisation of Gaelic in the province tended to contrast with those expressed more typically by Scottish new speakers. Narratives pertaining to advanced language shift in Nova Scotia were nevertheless frequently accompanied in that setting by a strong sense of optimism for the future of Gaelic in the province, a dimension not so frequently observed in Scottish discourses. Similarly, analysis of interview data demonstrated Nova Scotian new speakers' sense of wider public support for Gaelic revitalisation in the province, a sentiment which clearly contrasted with most Scottish participants' descriptions of public opposition to Gaelic which they encountered in that context.

The final sections of Chapter 5 demonstrated how the majority of new speakers' limited Gaelic language socialisation by family members contrasts, in the Nova Scotian context, with the high degree of salience attached to family heritage as a motivating factor for Gaelic acquisition. By contrast, Scottish new speakers were distinguished once again from their Nova Scotian counterparts in the sense that only relatively few attached any significance to family ties (past or present) within the Gaelic community. For the majority of Scottish speakers, such ties were either non-existent or were not deemed to be significant. Triangulation of qualitative data from the interview corpus and numerical data from the online survey provides clear confirmation of the patterns described above. From a quantitative perspective, the analysis in Chapter 6 demonstrated remarkably similar patterns of language attitude to those reflected in the above summary of language ideologies that were conveyed within interviews in the two contexts.

Firstly, closely parallel patterns of language attitudes were recorded between the two contexts in relation to the importance of Gaelic for local, (sub)national and personal identities. Interestingly, however, remarkably similar attitudes reflecting uncertainty over the future prospects for Gaelic were recorded across the two research settings in the quantitative analysis. This finding stands in contrast to the notably greater level of optimism for the future of Gaelic in Nova Scotia in comparison to Scotland identified in the qualitative analysis. Finally in Chapter 6, survey responses demonstrated the relative strength of Nova Scotian new speakers' sense of identity as Gaels, in close agreement with the qualitative analysis presented in Chapter 5. Tellingly, the proportion of respondents reporting an identity as Gaels in Nova Scotia (84 per cent) was over twice that recorded in Scotland (41 per cent). The high level of salience attached by Nova Scotian new speakers to their own sense of identity as Gaels thus clearly resonates with the qualitative analysis of interview material.

Discussion: contrast and commonality in new Gaelic speakerdom

Amongst other objectives, the foregoing analyses have sought to demonstrate that whilst the linkage envisaged between language and ethnolinguistic identity in Fishman's (1991, 2001, 2013) RLS model is largely sidestepped or overtly rejected by research participants in Scotland, the term 'Gael' has substantially greater currency among new speakers in Nova Scotia. The traditional 'Xian' ethnolinguistic community indexed by the term 'Gael(s)' seems not to be one with which Scottish new speakers readily associate as part of their 'ideal' L2 selves (after Dörnyei and Ushioda 2009; Ushioda 2011, 2019). Neither does the notion appear to have been instructive for such new speakers' past acquisition of Gaelic as an 'imagined identity' that may have directed their past language learning motivations (Norton 2013, 2019).

The apparent degree of 'stigma' currently attached to the term 'Gael' for new speakers in Scotland, though rarely explicitly clarified by interviewees in their discussion of Gael(ic) identity, appears to contribute to this patterning of linguistic ideology in the Scottish context. This dynamic of course clearly recalls Mertz's (1982) seminal research on Nova Scotian Gaelic decline historically. It is equally clear that the former sense of stigma that Nova Scotian Gaelic speakers attached to their identities as Gaels a century ago has largely been overcome. Nevertheless, it is noteworthy that, in the extracts from Scottish-based interviews in Chapter 5, conceptions and definitions of the term that privilege a direct ancestral connection to the language in the negotiation of Gael(ic) identity are viewed very differently in Scotland and Nova Scotia. In Scotland, the ideological association of the 'Gael' identity with rurality, tradition and the past appears to contribute to its perception as a stigmatised social category with which new speakers do not readily identify.

The relative enthusiasm with which Nova Scotian new speakers of Gaelic appear to construct and negotiate their ethnolinguistic identities as Gaels thus stands in stark contradistinction to the Scottish speakers' apparent disillusionment with the term. The definition of the Gael(ic) identity that Nova Scotian participants convey in discourses discussed in chapter 5 does seem chiefly pertain to ancestry and ethnolinguistic socialisation within 'authentically', historically Gaelic communities. In that sense, the definition of what it means to be a 'Gael', and which Nova Scotian speakers embrace so readily, is not so far removed from that which Scottish new speakers overwhelmingly shun (see also Dunmore 2017, 2018a). Whilst the evidence from Scotland tends to corroborate the view that supposedly essentialist conceptions of language and ethnolinguistic identity fail to capture new speakers' identifications with minority languages, the Nova Scotian evidence clearly challenges this thesis.

Thus, whilst the feasibility of positing a straightforward relationship between a minority language and its traditional speakers as a strategy for revitalising minority varieties has been problematised by authors such as Jaffe (2007a, 2007b), Edwards (2010), and Duchêne and Heller (2012), most Nova Scotian participants' clear desire to embrace an ethnolinguistic identity as Gaels, and to privilege their ethnic heritage in negotiating this identity, does lend support to Fishmanian conceptions of the language-identity nexus. Yet, as noted in

Chapter 2, Fishman's models of language and ethnicity often sit uneasily with contemporary conceptions which problematise essentialism (see Bucholtz and Hall 2004, 2005; Jaffe 2007a). Jaffe (2007a: 70) famously advocated approaches to language and identity 'that acknowledge the political and social character of all identity claims and that leave room for the multiple forms of language practice', without positing any direct relationship between the two. This stance was informed by many years of ethnographic research within the Corsican context, in which 'an essential relationship between language, culture and identity is posited as a given' (Jaffe 2007a: 70).

In such cases, Bucholtz and Hall (2004: 376) argue, essentialist perspectives should not be altogether dismissed, since they continue to possess salience and meaning for the speakers whom linguists study. As observed previously, Bourdieu (1991: 221) commented that contested definitions of ethnic identity and the nature of its 'reality' can be understood only if one includes within conceptions of reality 'the representation of reality'. Jaffe (2007a: 56) similarly advises against interpreting essentialist outlooks as entirely separable from meaningful representation; where essentialist positions are reflected in informants' language ideologies, they frequently constitute socially meaningful constructions. Appreciating the social reality of essentialist perspectives does necessitate assuming such a perspective in one's own theoretical approach, but as Dorian (2010: 89) repeatedly emphasised on the basis of her celebrated research in East Sutherland, the situated realities linking language and identity are in fact rarely as straightforward as essentialist conceptions would envisage.

From such a perspective, neither Nova Scotian speakers' somewhat essentialist outlook on Gaelic nor Scottish new Gaelic speakers' apparent lack of a clear identity as Gaels need be viewed as problematic in or of itself. For Nova Scotian new Gaelic speakers, ethnic identities are constructed within a wider Canadian and North American context in which perceived heritage often forms the basis of cultural identity claims in general. In Scotland, on the other hand, if new speakers' principal identification with and use of the Gaelic language derives from their professional lives, it is clear no such heritage-oriented ethnic identity should be expected to develop.

Yet without a strong social identity in the language outside of the less personal spheres of everyday life, it would similarly seem unlikely that substantial proportions of new speakers will take the language forward as a vital aspect of their domestic and family lives, and transmit it to children in the home-community context in future (see Chapter 6). On the other hand, whilst Nova Scotian new speakers may well possess the requisite ethnolinguistic commitment to Gaelic to desire that their own children acquire a sense of heritage and identity as Gaels, the relative paucity of support mechanisms for intergenerational transmission in the province, combined with the fast-dwindling network of native speakers, provides clear challenges for the socialisation of young people in the language itself.

The practical language policy questions that considerations of this kind pose for language advocates and policymakers also provide some challenging conclusions for theory in second language acquisition and motivation more widely. As MacIntyre, Baker and Sparling (2017) have previously observed, Gardner and Lambert's (1959, 1971; Gardner 2019) notion of integrativeness and Dörnyei (2005) and Ushioda's (2011, 2019; Dörnyei and Ushioda 2009) L2 self model appear to be embodied among learners of Gaelic in Nova Scotia in terms of their 'rooted' L2 selves. The notion of rootedness in L2 motivation can be theorised more generally here as impacting on such heritage-motivated learners' successful L2 acquisition, but also, more widely, on their socialisation and expression of an identity they feel themselves already to possess. In that sense, the notion of rootedness that successful new Gaelic speakers frequently already feel within communities prior to acquiring competence in Gaelic, tends not to sit easily with Norton's (2019) concept of imagined identity. Rather than an imaged identity, therefore, Nova Scotian new speakers overwhelmingly claim an affiliation as Gaels as an aspect of their lived and embodied selves, even prior to becoming proficient speakers of Gaelic.

This development of rootedness as a theoretical notion for conceptualising ethnocultural connections within Gaelic communities can also be seen to impact on contrasting realisations of 'authenticity' among Scottish and Nova Scotian new speakers. Whilst Nova Scotians regard their identities as Gaels to be an authentic expression of their rootedness in that context, Scottish participants appear to regard claiming such an identity as a potentially inauthentic act in contemporary Scotland. Notwithstanding the foregoing issues of cultural rootedness, however, we may observe that since the use of Gaelic by new speakers is comparable across the two contexts – both in terms of frequency and commitment – the lack of a developed 'rooted' identity among new speakers in Scotland need not after all necessarily be viewed as problematic. However, if it is hoped that new Gaelic speakers in each context will attain fluency, and then progress to using the language in the home-community sphere, whilst simultaneously developing a strong identity in the language, additional attention and resources should be focused on that specific objective in Scotland, as is the case in Nova Scotia. Whilst Nova Scotians often look enviously at current provision for GME in Scotland, it is clear in that respect that policymakers in Edinburgh and Inverness would benefit from ongoing dialogue with language teachers and advocates in Halifax and Cape Breton. As a response, Scottish children currently in GME schools and classes should be encouraged to socialise in the language outside of class as much as possible, to interact with fluent speakers wherever possible and to better understand the relevance of Gaelic to their (keenly felt) civic identities as Scots in a modern, multicultural Scotland.

In terms of speakers' bilingual development, issues of linguistic practice, ideology and identity are central to much research that has already been produced on the phenomenon of new speakers of minority languages (see for example McLeod, O'Rourke and Dunmore 2014; O'Rourke, Pujolar and Ramallo 2015; O'Rourke and Walsh 2020). The findings presented in this monograph are indicative of Scottish and Nova Scotian new speakers' cultural identifications with Gaelic, although they are by no means exhaustive. In Scotland, most new speakers' rejection of the label 'Gael' is significant inasmuch as it does not distinguish them from the majority of former GME students, who tend to make only limited use of Gaelic in the present day. (For further analysis and discussion of this important demographic see also Dunmore 2017, 2019.) As noted above, these new Gaelic speakers' lack of identification as Gaels need not be viewed as problematic for language policy objectives as such. If, as contemporary policy statements suggest, however, new speakers with strong ideological commitment to the language and to passing it on to children are among the intended outcomes of GME and Gaelic learning activity generally, additional resources should be directed specifically at encouraging students' development of concomitant practices and identities in school and at home.

In Nova Scotia, by contrast, developing the ethnolinguistic identity component of new speakers' Gaelic language acquisition appears to be foregrounded in efforts both to instruct students' linguistic practices and to secure a future for the language in the province. Yet even notwithstanding such explicit objectives in language policy, heritage and ancestry appear from interviewees' own accounts to form the principal motivations of Nova Scotian new speakers' attempts to acquire and use the language. As a consequence, their expressions of identity as Gaels are notably stronger than those of the majority of their Scottish counterparts, who tend to problematise or reject the term as a facet of their own identities.

Table 7.1 Key to transcription conventions

[[words]	overlapping speech
(.)	perceivable pause <1s duration
(2.0)	perceivable pause >1s duration
(word)	uncertain transcription
(x)	unintelligible
((word))	analyst's comments
[…]	material omitted
wo::	elongation
word	emphatic speech
word=	latched speech, no pause
words	codeswitch
^	high, rising intonation
xxx	name or identifier removed

The clear contrasts between the two settings reflect the divergent histories and social geographies of Scotland and Nova Scotia, and in turn represent an intriguing source of diversity within the twenty-first-century transatlantic Gaelic community. Greater numbers of new speakers in both countries are an increasingly important part of that diverse community, as my analysis has considered in this book. Crucially, it is clear that language advocates, speakers and policymakers throughout this transatlantic community will continue to have a great deal to learn from one another in coming decades, even as long-term prospects remain precarious.

Bibliography

Al-Hoorie, A. H., and P. MacIntyre, eds. 2019. *Contemporary Language Motivation Theory: 60 Years Since Gardner and Lambert (1959)*. Bristol: Multilingual Matters.
Anderson, B. R. O. 1991. *Imagined Communities: Reflections on the Origin and Spread of Nationalism*. 2nd edn. London: Verso.
Baker, C. 2011. *Foundations of Bilingual Education and Bilingualism*. 5th edn. Bristol: Multilingual Matters.
Ball, M., and N. Müller, eds. 2009. *The Celtic Languages*. 2nd edn. Abingdon: Routledge.
Barrow, G. W. S. 1989. 'The lost Gàidhealtachd of medieval Scotland.' In *Scotland and Gaelic/Alba agus a' Ghàidhlig*, edited by W. Gillies, 67–88. Edinburgh: Edinburgh University Press.
Bayley, R., and S. R. Schecter. 2003. 'Introduction: Toward a dynamic model of language socialization.' In *Language Socialization in Bilingual and Multilingual Societies*, edited by R. Bayley and S. R. Schecter, 1–8. Clevedon: Multilingual Matters.
Bòrd na Gàidhlig. 2014. 'Gaelic education helps reverse decline of the Gaelic language.' Accessed 9 July 2020. http://www.gaidhlig.org.uk/bord/en/news/article.php?ID=474.
Bòrd na Gàidhlig. 2018. *The National Gaelic Language Plan, 2018–2023*. Inverness: Bòrd na Gàidhlig.
Bòrd na Gàidhlig. 2022. *Draft National Gaelic Language Plan, 2023–28*. Inverness: Bòrd na Gàidhlig. Accessed 8 September 2022. https://www.gaidhlig.scot/en/national-gaelic-language-plan-2023-28.
Bòrd na Gàidhlig. 2023. *The National Gaelic Language Plan, 2023–2028*. Inverness: Bòrd na Gàidhlig.
Boudreau, A., and L. Dubois. 2007. 'Français, Acadien, Acadjonne: Competing discourses on language preservation along the shores of the Baie Sainte-Marie.' In Duchêne and Heller, *Discourses of Endangerment*, 99–120.
Bourdieu, P. 1991. *Language and Symbolic Power*. Translated by G. Raymond and M. Adamson. Cambridge: Polity Press.
Brinton, D., M. O. Kagan, and S. Bauckus, eds. 2008. *Heritage Language Education: A New Field Emerging*. New York: Routledge.
Bucholtz, M., and K. Hall. 2004. 'Language and identity.' In Duranti, *A Companion to Linguistic Anthropology*, 369–94.
Bucholtz, M., and K. Hall. 2005. 'Identity and interaction: A sociocultural linguistic approach.' *Discourse Studies* 7: 585–614.
Campbell, D., and R. MacLean. 1974. *Beyond the Atlantic Roar: A Study of the Nova Scotia Scots*. Toronto: McClelland and Stewart.
Cavanaugh, J. 2013. 'Language ideologies and language attitudes.' In *Language Variation: European Perspectives IV*, edited by P. Auer, J. Caro Reina, and G. Kaufmann, 45–55. Amsterdam: John Benjamins.

Cavanaugh, J. 2020. 'Language ideology revisited.' *International Journal of the Sociology of Language* 263: 51–7.

Clancy, Thomas O. 2011. 'Gaelic in medieval Scotland: Advent and expansion.' *Proceedings of the British Academy* 167: 349–92.

Costa, J. 2017. *Revitalising Language in Provence: A Critical Appraoch.* Oxford: Blackwell and Philological Society.

Cox, L. V. 1994. 'Gaelic and the schools in Cape Breton.' *Nova Scotia History Review* 14: 20–40.

Crago, M. B., B. Annahatak, and L. Ningiuruvik. 1993. 'Changing patterns of language socialization in Inuit homes.' *Anthropology and Education Quarterly* 24: 205–23.

Dean, L., F. O'Hanlon, S. Hinchliffe1, A. Scholes, J. Curtice, R. Whitford, V. Wilson, C. Standing-Tattersall, and A. Daniels-Creasey. 2022. 'Scottish Social Attitudes Survey 2021 public attitudes to Gaelic in Scotland – Main report.' Report for Bòrd na Gàidhlig. Inverness: Bòrd na Gàidhlig.

Dembling, J. 1997. *Joe Jimmy Alec Visits the Mod and Escapes Unscathed: The Nova Scotia Gaelic Revivals.* Unpublished PhD thesis. Halifax, NS: St Mary's University.

Devine, T. M. 1994. *Clanship to Crofter's War.* Manchester: Manchester University Press.

Dorian, N. 1981. *Language Death: The Life Cycle of a Scottish Gaelic Dialect.* Philadelphia: University of Pennsylvania Press.

Dorian, N. 2010. 'Linguistic and ethnographic fieldwork.' In Fishman and García, *Handbook of Language and Ethnic Identity (Vol. 1),* 89–106.

Dorian, N. 2011. 'The ambiguous arithmetic of language maintenance and revitalization.' In Fishman and García, *Handbook of Language and Ethnic Identity (Vol. 2),* 461–71.

Dörnyei, Z. 2005. *The Psychology of the Language Learner: Individual Differences in Second Language Acquisition.* Mahwah, NJ: Lawrence Erlbaum.

Dörnyei, Z., and E. Ushioda, eds. 2009. *Motivation, Language Identity and the L2 Self.* Bristol: Multilingual Matters.

Duchêne, A., and M. Heller, eds. 2007. *Discourses of Endangerment: Ideology and Interest in the Defence of Languages.* London: Continuum.

Duchêne, A., and M. Heller. 2012. *Language in Late Capitalism: Pride and Profit.* London: Routledge.

Duff, P. A. 2010. 'Language socialization into academic discourse communities.' *Annual Review of Applied Lingustics* 30: 169–92.

Dumville, David N. 2002. 'Ireland and North Britain in the earlier Middle Ages: Contexts for Míniugud Senchasa Fher nAlban.' In *Rannsachadh na Gàidhlig 2000,* edited by Colm Ó Baoill and Nancy R. McGuire, 185–212. Aberdeen: An Clò Gaidhealach.

Dunbar, R. 2006. 'Gaelic in Scotland: The legal and institutional framework.' In McLeod, *Revitalising Gaelic in Scotland,* 1–23.

Dunbar, R. 2008. 'Minority language renewal: Gaelic in Nova Scotia, and lessons from abroad.' Report for NS Govt Office of Gaelic Affairs. Halifax, NS: Office of Gaelic Affairs.

Dunmore, S. 2015. *Bilingual Life After School? Language Use, Ideologies and Attitudes Among Gaelic-Medium Educated Adults.* Unpublished PhD thesis. University of Edinburgh.

Dunmore, S. 2017. 'Immersion education outcomes and the Gaelic community: Identities and language ideologies among Gaelic-medium educated adults in Scotland.' *Journal of Multilingual and Multicultural Development* 38: 726–41.

Dunmore, S. 2018a. 'New Gaelic Speakers, New Gaels? Language ideologies and ethnolinguistic continuity among Gaelic-medium educated adults.' In Smith-Christmas et al., *New Speakers of Minority Languages,* 23–44.

Dunmore, S. 2018b. 'Bilingual life after school? Opportunity, choice and ideology among former Gaelic-medium students.' *Transactions of the Gaelic Society of Inverness* 63: 287–316.

Dunmore, S. 2019. *Language Revitalisation in Gaelic Scotland: Linguistic Practice Ideology.* Edinburgh: Edinburgh University Press.

Duranti, A., ed. *A Companion to Linguistic Anthropology.* Oxford: Blackwell.

Durkacz, V. E. 1983. *The Decline of the Celtic Languages.* Edinburgh: John Donald.

Dwelly, E. 1994 [1901]. *Illustrated Gaelic to English Dictionary.* 12th edn. Glasgow: Gairm Publications.
Edwards, J. R., ed. 1984. *Linguistic Minorities, Policies and Pluralism.* London: Academic Press.
Edwards, J. R. 1991. 'Gaelic in Nova Scotia.' In Williams, *Linguistic Minorities, Society and Territory,* 269-97.
Edwards, J. R. 2009. *Language and Identity.* Cambridge: Cambridge University Press.
Edwards, J. R. 2010. *Minority Languages and Group Identity: Cases and Categories.* Amsterdam: John Benjamins.
Edwards, J. R. 2013. 'Bilingualism and Multilingualism: Some Central Concepts.' In Bhatia and Ritchie, *Handbook of Bilingualism and Multilingualism,* 5-25.
Fishman, J. A. 1972. *Language in Socio-Cultural Change.* Stanford, CA: Stanford University Press.
Fishman, J. A. 1991. *Reversing Language Shift: Theoretical and Empirical Foundations of Assistance to Threatened Languages.* Clevedon: Multilingual Matters.
Fishman, J. A., ed. 2001a. *Can Threatened Languages Be Saved? Reversing Language Shift Revisited: A 21st Century Perspective.* Clevedon: Multilingual Matters.
Fishman, J. A. 2001b. 'From theory to practice (and vice versa): Review, reconsideration, and reiteration.' In Fishman, *Can Threatened Languages Be Saved?,* 451-83.
Fishman, J. A. 2010. 'Sociolinguistics: Language and Ethnic Identity in Context.' In Fishman and García, *Handbook of Language and Ethnic Identity (Vol. 1),* xxiii-xxxv.
Fishman, J. A. 2013. 'Language maintenance, language shift, and reversing language shift.' In Bhatia and Ritchie, *Handbook of Bilingualism and Multilingualism,* 466-94.
Fishman, J. A., and O. García, eds. 2010. *Handbook of Language and Ethnic Identity: Disciplinary and Regional Perspectives (Vol. 1).* 2nd edn. Oxford: Oxford University Press.
Fishman, J. A., and O. García, eds. 2011. *Handbook of Language and Ethnic Identity: The Success-Failure Continuum in Language and Ethnic Identity Efforts (Vol. 2).* 2nd edn. Oxford: Oxford University Press.
Gal, S., and K. Woolard. 1995. 'Constructing languages and publics: Authority and representation.' *Pragmatics* 5: 129-38.
García, O. 2009. *Bilingual Education in the 21st Century: A Global Perspective.* Oxford: Blackwell.
Gardner, R. C. 2019. 'Looking back and looking forward.' In Al-Hoorie and MacIntyre, *Contemporary Language Motivation Theory,* 5-16.
Gardner, R. C., and W. E. Lambert. 1959. 'Motivational variables in second language acquisition.' *Canadian Journal of Psychology* 13: 266-72.
Gardner, R. C., and W. E. Lambert. 1972. *Attitudes and Motivation in Second Language Learning.* Rowley, MA: Newbury House.
Garrett, P. 2007. 'Language socialization and the (re)production of bilingual subjectivities.' In Heller, *Bilingualism: A Social Approach,* 233-56.
Garrett, P., and P. Baquedano-López. 2002. 'Language socialization: Reproduction and continuity, transformation and change.' *Annual Review of Anthropology* 31: 339-61.
Gellner, E. 2006. *Nations and Nationalism.* 2nd edn. Oxford: Blackwell.
Glaser, K. 2007. *Minority Languages and Cultural Diversity in Europe: Gaelic and Sorbian Perspectives.* Clevedon: Multilingual Matters.
Globe and Mail. 2022. 'A small Cape Breton schoolhouse offers hope for the future of Gaelic in Canada.' 3 January 2002. https://www.theglobeandmail.com/canada/article-a-small-cape-breton-schoolhouse- offers-hope-for-the-future-of-gaelic.
Harley, B. 1994. 'After Immersion: Maintaining the Momentum.' *Journal of Multilingual and Multicultural Development* 15: 229-44.
Heller, M. 2006. *Linguistic Minorities and Modernity: A Sociolinguistic Ethnography.* 2nd edn. London: Continuum.
Heller, M., ed. 2007a. *Bilingualism: A Social Approach.* London: Palgrave Macmillan.
Heller, M. 2007b. 'Bilingualism as ideology and practice.' In Heller, *Bilingualism,* 1-24.

Heller, M. 2010. *Paths to Postnationalism: A Critical Ethnography of Language and Identity.* Oxford: Oxford University Press.

Hobsbawm, E. J. 1992. *Nations and Nationalism since 1780: Programme, Myth, Reality.* 2nd edn. Cambridge: Cambridge University Press.

Hroch, M. 1985. *Social Preconditions of National Revival in Europe.* Cambridge: Cambridge University Press.

Hunter, J. 1976. *The Making of the Crofting Community.* Edinburgh: John Donald.

Hymes, D. 1974. *Foundations in Sociolinguistics: An Ethnographic Approach.* London: Tavistock.

Irvine, J. T. 1989. 'When talk isn't cheap: Language and political economy.' *American Ethnologist* 16: 248–67.

Jaffe, A. 1999. *Ideologies in Action: Language Politics on Corsica.* Berlin: Mouton de Gruyter.

Jaffe, A. 2007a. 'Discourses of endangerment: Contexts and consequences of essentializing discourses.' In Duchêne and Heller, *Discourses of Endangerment*, 57–75.

Jaffe, A. 2007b. 'Minority language movements.' In Heller, *Bilingualism*, 50–95.

Johnstone, R. 2001. *Immersion in a Second or Additional Language at School: Evidence from International Research.* Stirling: Scottish Centre for Teaching and Research.

Jones, R., and C. Williams. 2009. 'The sociolinguistic context of Welsh.' In Ball and Müller, *The Celtic Languages*, 650–711.

Joseph, J. 2010. 'Identity.' In Llamas and Watt, *Language and Identities*, 9–17.

Kehoe, S. Karly. 2021. 'Jacobites, Jamaica, and the establishment of a Highland Catholic community in the Canadian Maritimes.' *Scottish Historical Review* 10: 199–217.

Kehoe, S. Karly. 2022. *Empire and Emancipation: Scottish and Irish Catholics at the Atlantic Fringe, 1780–1850.* Toronto: University of Toronto Press.

Kennedy, M. 2002. 'Gaelic Nova Scotia: An economic, cultural, and social impact study.' Report for Nova Scotia Government. Halifax, NS: Nova Scotia Museum.

King, K. A. 2000. 'Language ideologies and heritage language education.' *International Journal of Bilingual Education and Bilingualism* 3: 167–84.

Kramsch, C. 2004. 'Language, thought, and culture.' In *The Handbook of Applied Linguistics*, edited by A. Davies and C. Elder, 235–61. Oxford: Blackwell.

Kramsch, C. 2013. *The Multilingual Subject.* Oxford: Oxford University Press.

Krombach, H. 1995. 'The dialectic of identity: From individual to nation.' *ASEN Bulletin* 10, 42–4. London: London School of Economics.

Kroskrity, P. V., ed. 2000. *Regimes of Language: Ideologies, Polities, and Identities.* Santa Fe, NM: School of American Research Press.

Kroskrity, P. V. 2004. 'Language ideologies.' In Duranti, *Companion to Linguistic Anthropology*, 496–517.

Kulick, D., and B. B. Schieffelin. 2004. 'Language socialization.' In Duranti, *Companion to Linguistic Anthropology*, 349–68.

Kumar, K. 2003. *The Making of English National Identity*, Cambridge: Cambridge University Press.

La Fontaine, J. S. 1985. 'Person and individual: Some anthropological reflections.' In *The Category of the Person*, edited by M. Carrithers, S. Collins and S. Lukes, 123–40. Cambridge: Cambridge University Press.

Llamas, C., and D. Watt, eds. 2010. *Language and Identities.* Edinburgh: Edinburgh University Press.

MacCaluim, A. 2007. *Reversing Language Shift: The Social Identity and Role of Scottish Gaelic Learners.* Belfast: Cló Ollscoil na Banríona.

McCrone, D. 1998. *The Sociology of Nationalism: Tomorrow's Ancestors.* London: Routledge.

McCrone, D. 2001. *Understanding Scotland: The Sociology of a Nation.* 2nd edn. London: Routledge.

Macdonald, S. 1997. *Reimagining Culture: Histories, Identities and the Gaelic Renaissance.* Oxford: Berg.

Macdonald, S. 1999. 'The Gaelic renaissance and Scotland's identities.' *Scottish Affairs* 26: 100–18.

MacEachen, F. 2008. 'Am blas againn fhìn: Community Gaelic Immersion Classes in Nova Scotia – An evaluation of activities in 2006–2007.' Report for Office of Gaelic Affairs. Halifax, NS: Office of Gaelic Affairs.
McEwan-Fujita, E. 2003. Gaelic in Scotland, Scotland in Europe: Minority Language Revitalization in the Age of Neoliberialism. Unpublished PhD thesis. University of Chicago.
McEwan-Fujita, E. 2010a. 'Ideology, affect, and socialization in language shift and revitalization: The experiences of adults learning Gaelic in the Western Isles of Scotland.' Language in Society 39: 27–64.
McEwan-Fujita, E. 2010b. 'Ideologies and experiences of literacy in interactions between adult Gaelic learners and first-language Gaelic speakers in Scotland.' Scottish Gaelic Studies 26: 87–114.
McEwan-Fujita, E. 2010c. 'Sociolinguistic ethnography of Gaelic communities.' In Watson and Macleod, Edinburgh Companion to the Gaelic Language, 172–217.
McEwan-Fujita, E. 2020. Gaelic Revitalization Concepts and Challenges. Halifax, NS: Bradan Press.
MacFarlane, A., and M. Wesche. 1995. 'Immersion Outcomes: Beyond Language Proficiency.' Canadian Modern Language Review 51, 250–74.
MacGregor, M. D. 2006. 'The statutes of Iona: Text and context.' Innes Review 57: 111–81.
MacGregor, M. D. 2009. 'Gaelic barbarity and Scottish identity in the later Middle Ages.' In Mìorun Mòr nan Gall, 'The Great Ill-Will of the Lowlander'? Lowland Perceptions of the Highlands, Medieval and Modern, edited by D. Broun and M. D. MacGregor, 7–48. Glasgow: Centre for Scottish and Celtic Studies, University of Glasgow.
MacIntyre, P., S. Baker, and H. Sparling. 2017. 'Heritage passions, heritage convictions and the rooted L2 self: Music and Gaelic language learning in Cape Breton, Nova Scotia.' Modern Language Journal 101: 501–516.
MacKinnon, K. 1977. Language, Education and Social Processes in a Gaelic Community. London: Routledge and Kegan Paul.
MacKinnon, K. 1991. Gaelic: A Past and Future Prospect. Edinburgh: Saltire Society.
MacKinnon, K. 1996. 'Cape Breton – Western Isles: Transatlantic resonance of language and culture.' In Language Contact across the North Atlantic, edited by P. Sture Ureland and I. Clarkson, 363–86. Tübingen: Max Niemeyer Verlag.
MacKinnon, K. 2001. 'Gaelic in Canada: Haki and Hekja's inheritance in "The Land of Promise".' In Global Eurolinguistics: European languages in North America – Migration, Maintenance and Death, edited by P. Sture Ureland, 19–47. Tübingen: Niemeyer.
MacKinnon, K. 2009. 'Scottish Gaelic today: Social history and contemporary status.' In Ball and Müller, The Celtic Languages, 587–649.
MacLean, R. 1978. 'The Scots: Hector's cargo.' In Banked Fires:The Ethnics of Nova Scotia, edited by D. Campbell, 51–72. Port Credit, ON: Scribblers' Press.
MacLeod, D. J. 2007. 'Sùil air ais.' In Foghlam tro Mheadhan na Gàidhlig, edited by M. NicNeacail and M. Maclomhair, 1–15. Edinburgh: Dunedin Academic Press.
Macleod, M. 2010. 'Language in society: 1800 to the modern day.' In Watson and Macleod, Edinburgh Companion to the Gaelic Language, 22–45.
McLeod, W. 2005. 'Gaelic in Scotland: The impact of the Highland Clearances.' In *Creating Outsiders: Endangered Languages, Migration and Marginalisation: Proceedings of the Ninth Conference of the Foundation for Endangered Languages*, edited by N. Crawhill and N. Ostler, 176–83. Bath: Foundation for Endangered Languages.
McLeod, W., ed. 2006. *Revitalising Gaelic in Scotland: Policy, Planning and Public Discourse*. Edinburgh: Dunedin Academic Press.
McLeod, W. 2014. 'Gaelic in contemporary Scotland: Contradictions, challenges and strategies', *Europa Ethnica*, 2014: 3–12.
McLeod, W. 2020. *Gaelic in Scotland: Policies, Movements, Ideologies*. Edinburgh, Edinburgh University Press.
McLeod, W., B. O'Rourke, and S. Dunmore. 2014. *New Speakers of Gaelic in Edinburgh and Glasgow: Soillse Research Report*. Sleat, Isle of Skye: Soillse.

McLeod, W., and B. O'Rourke. 2015. *Irish Parents and Gaelic-Medium Education in Scotland: Soillse Research Report*. Sleat, Isle of Skye: Soillse.

Makihara, M. 2010. 'Anthropology.' In Fishman and García, Handbook of Language and Ethnic Identity (Vol. I), 32–48.

Makoni, S., and A. Pennycook. 2007. *Disinventing and Reconstituting Languages*. Clevedon: Multilingual Matters.

May, S. 2012. *Language and Minority Rights: Ethnicity, Nationalism and the Politics of Language*. 2nd edn. Abingdon: Routledge.

Mendoza-Denton, N., and D. Osborne. 2010. 'Two languages, two identities?' In Llamas and Watt, *Language and Identities*, 113–22.

Mertz, E. 1982. *'No Burden to Carry': Cape Breton Pragmatics and Metapragmatics*. Unpublished PhD thesis. Duke University.

Mertz, E. 1989. 'Sociolinguistic creativity. Cape Breton Gaelic's linguistic "tip".' In *Investigating Obsolescence. Studies in Language Contraction and Death*, edited by N. C. Dorian, 103–16. Cambridge: Cambridge University Press.

Mill, J. S. 1991 [1861]. *On Liberty and Other Essays*. Edited by J. M. Gray. Oxford: Oxford University Press.

Moïse, C. 2007. 'Protecting French: The view from France.' In Duchêne and Heller, *Discourses of Endangerment*, 216–41.

Nairn, T. 1997. *Faces of Nationalism: Janus Revisited*. London: Verso.

Nance, C. 2015. '"New" Scottish Gaelic speakers in Glasgow: a phonetic study of language revitalisation.' *Language in Society* 44: 553–79.

Nance, C., W. McLeod, B. O'Rourke, and S. Dunmore. 2016. 'Identity, accent aim, and motivation in second language users: new Scottish Gaelic speakers' use of phonetic variation.' *Journal of Sociolinguistics* 20: 164–91.

National Records of Scotland. 2013. *Statistical Bulletin: 2011 Census – Key Results on Population, Ethnicity, Identity, Language, Religion, Health, Housing and Accommodation in Scotland – Release 2A*. Accessed 26 September 2017. www.scotlandscensus.gov.uk/documents/censusresults/release2a/StatsBulletin2A.pdf.

National Records of Scotland. 2024. *Scotland's Census 2022. National Records of Scotland Table UV208a – Gaelic language skills*. Accessed 31 May 2024. https://www.scotlandscensus.gov.uk/webapi/jsf/tableView/tableView.xhtml.

Nettle, D., and S. Romaine. 2000. *Vanishing Voices: The Extinction of the World's Languages*. Oxford: Oxford University Press.

Newton, M. 2014. 'The Gaelic diaspora in North America.' In *The Modern Scottish Diaspora: Contemporary Debates and Perspectives*, edited by M. S. Leith and D. Sims, 136–52. Edinburgh: Edinburgh University Press.

NicLeòid, S., and S. Dunmore. 2019. 'Sòisealachadh cànain agus leantainneachd dhà-chànanach am measg cloinne agus inbhich a rinn FMG.' *Scottish Gaelic Studies* 31.

Norton, B. 2013. *Identity and Language Learning: Extending the Conversation*. 2nd edn. Bristol: Multilingual Matters.

Norton, B. (2019), 'Motivation, Identity and Investment: A Journey with Robert Gardner.' In Al-Hoorie and MacIntyre, *Contemporary Language Motivation Theory*, 153–68.

Ó Baoill, Colm. 2010. 'A history of Gaelic to 1800.' In Watson and Macleod, *Edinburgh Companion to the Gaelic Language*, 1–21.

Ochs, E. 1993. 'Constructing social identity: A language socialization perspective.' *Research on Language and Social Interaction* 26: 287–306.

Ó hIfearnáin, T. 2002. 'Doimhne an dúchais: éagsúlacht san aistriú teanga i gCeap Breatainn na hAlban Nua.' *Taighde agus teagasc* 2: 62–91.

O'Rourke, B., and F. Ramallo. 2013. 'Competing ideologies of linguistic authority amongst new speakers in contemporary Galicia.' *Language in Society* 42: 287–305.

O'Rourke, B., J. Pujolar, and F. Ramallo (2015), 'New speakers of minority languages: The challenging opportunity – Foreword.' *International Journal of the Sociology of Language* 231: 1–20.
O'Rourke, B., and J. Walsh. 2020. *New Speakers of Irish in the Global Context: New Revival?* Abingdon: Routledge.
Office of Gaelic Affairs. 2018. *Our Community*. Accessed 15 October 2018. https://gaelic.novascotia.ca/ community.
Office for Nationa Statistics. 2022. *National Statistics Socioeconomic Classifications*. Accessed 15 December 2022. https://www.ons.gov.uk/methodology/classificationsandstandards/otherclassifications/thenationalstatisticssocioeconomicclassificationnssecrebasedonso c2010.
Oliver, J. 2002. *Young People and Gaelic in Scotland: Identity Dynamics in a European Region*. Unpublished PhD thesis. University of Sheffield.
Oliver, J. 2005. 'Gaelic and identities in Scotland: Contexts and contingencies.' *Scottish Affairs* 51: 1–24.
Oliver, J. 2006. 'Where is Gaelic? Revitalisation, language, culture and identity.' In McLeod, *Revitalising Gaelic in Scotland*, 155–68.
Oliver, J. 2010. 'The predicament? Planning for culture, communities and identities.' In *Coimhearsnachd na Gàidhlig an-diugh/Gaelic Communities Today*, edited by G. Munro and I. Mac an Tàilleir, 73–86. Edinburgh: Dunedin Academic Press.
Paterson, L., F. O'Hanlon, R. Ormston, and S. Reid. 2014. 'Public attitudes to Gaelic and the debate about Scottish autonomy.' *Regional and Federal Studies* 2014: 1–22.
Pujolar, J. 2007. 'Bilingualism and the nation-state in the post-national era.' In Heller, *Bilingualism*, 71–95.
Pujolar, J. and Gonzàlez, I. 2013. 'Linguistic "Mudes" and the De-Ethnicization of Language Choice in Catalonia.' *International Journal of Bilingual Education and Bilingualism* 16: 138–52.
Pujolar, J., and M. Puigdevall. 2015. 'Linguistic mudes: how to become a new speaker in Catalonia.' *International Journal of the Sociology of Language* 231: 167–87.
Reicher, S., and N. Hopkins. 2001. *Self and Nation*. London: Sage.
Romaine, S. 2000. *Language in Society: An Introduction to Sociolinguistics*. 2nd edn. Oxford: Oxford University Press.
Richards, E. 2007. *Debating the Highland Clearances*. Edinburgh: Edinburgh University Press.
Rogerson, J., and A. Glover. 1995. 'Gaelic cultural revival or language decline?' *Scottish Geographical Magazine* 111: 46–52.
Romaine, S. 2006. 'Planning for the survival of linguistic diversity.' *Language Policy* 5: 441–73.
Romaine, S. 2008. 'Linguistic diversity, sustainability, and the future of the past.' In *Sustaining Linguistic Diversity Endangered and Minority Languages and Varieties*, edited by K. King, N. Schilling-Estes, L. Fogle, J. Lou, and B. Soukup, 7–21. Washington, DC: Georgetown University Press.
Romaine, S. 2013. 'The bilingual and multilingual community.' In Bhatia and Ritchie, *Handbook of Bilingualism and Multilingualism*, 445–65.
Rosa, J. 2019. *Looking Like a Language, Sounding Like a Race: Raciolinguistic Ideologies and the Learning of Latinidad*. Oxford: Oxford University Press.
Sapir, E. 1962. *Culture, Language, and Personality: Selected Essays*. Edited by D. Mandelbaum. Berkeley: University of California Press.
Schieffelin, B. B., and E. Ochs. 1986a. 'Language socialization.' *Annual Review of Anthropology* 15: 163–91.
Schieffelin, B. B., and E. Ochs, eds. 1986b. *Language Socialization across Cultures*. Cambridge: Cambridge University Press.
Schieffelin B. B., K. A. Woolard, and P. Kroskrity, eds. 1998. *Language Ideologies: Practice and Theory*. Oxford: Oxford University Press.
Schiffrin, D. 1996. 'Narrative as self-portrait: Sociolinguistic constructions of identity.' *Language in Society* 25: 167–203.
Schilling-Estes, N. 2004. 'Constructing ethnicity in interaction.' *Journal of Sociolinguistics* 8: 163–95.

Schmidt, R. 2007. 'Defending English in an English-dominant world: The ideology of the "Official English" movement in the United States.' In Duchêne and Heller, *Discourses of Endangerment*, 197–215.

ScotCen Social Research. 2022. *Scottish Social Attitudes Survey 2021: Public Attitudes to Gaelic in Scotland – Main report*. Accessed 3 March 2023. http://www.gaidhlig.scot/en/news/SSAS.

Scottish Government. 2014. *Consultation Paper on a Gaelic Medium Education Bill*. Edinburgh: Scottish Government.

Scottish Parliament. 2023. *Scottish Languages Bill*. Edinburgh: Scottish Parliament. Accessed 29 November 2023. https://www.parliament.scot/bills-and-laws/bills/scottish-languages-bill/introduced.

Sellers, D., and N. Carty. 2019. *Inbhich a tha ag ionnsachadh Gàidhlig – 2018/Adults Learning Gaelic – 2018*. Inverness: Bòrd na Gàidhlig.

Shaw, J. 1977. 'Bithidh iad a' moladh na Gàidhlig, ach 'sann anns a' Bheurla.' *West Highland Free Press*, 23 September.

Silverstein, M. 1979. 'Language structure and linguistic ideology.' In *The Elements: A Parasession on Linguistic Units and Levels*, edited by R. Cline, W. Hanks, and C. Hofbauer, 192–247. Chicago: Chicago Linguistic Society.

Silverstein, M. 2000. 'Whorfianism and the linguistic imagination of nationality.' In Kroskrity, *Regimes of Language*, 85–138.

Smith, A. 2010. *Nationalism*. 2nd edn. Cambridge: Polity Press.

Smith-Christmas, C., N. Ó Murchadha, M. Hornsby, and M. Moriarty, eds. 2018. *New Speakers of Minority Languages: Linguistic Ideologies and Practices*. London: Palgrave.

Statistics Canada. 2015. *National Household Survey Profile: Nova Scotia 2011*. Accessed 13 December 2021. https://www12.statcan.gc.ca/nhs-enm/2011/dppd/prof/details/page.cfm?Lang=E&Geo1=PR&Code1=12&Data=Count&SearchText=Canada&SearchType=Begins&SearchPR=01&A1=Non-official%20language&B1=All&Custom=.

Statistics Canada. 2022. *2021 Census of Population – Nova Scotia*. https://www12.statcan.gc.ca/census-recensement/2021/dp-pd/prof/index.cfm?Lang=E.

Taigh Sgoile na Drochaide. 2021. *Our Learning Method*. Accessed 6 March 2023. https://taighsgoile.ca/learn.

Trudgill, P. 1974. *Sociolinguistics: An Introduction*. Harmondsworth: Penguin.

Ushioda, E. 2011. 'Language learning motivation, self and identity: current theoretical perspectives.' *Computer Assisted Language Learning* 24: 199–210.

Ushioda, E. 2019. 'Rerearching L2 motivaton: Re-evaluating the role of qualitative inquiry, or the "wine and conversation" approach.' In Al-Hoorie and MacIntyre, *Contemporary Language Motivation Theory*, 194–211.

Valdés, G., S. V. Gonzàlez, D. L. García, and P. Márquez, P. (2008), 'Heritage languages and ideologies of language.' In Brinton et al., *Heritage Language Education*, 107–30.

Walsh, J., and W. McLeod. 2008. 'An overcoat wrapped around an invisible man? Language legislation and language revitalisation in Ireland and Scotland.' *Language Policy* 7: 21–46.

Watson, M., and M. Macleod, eds. 2010. *The Edinburgh Companion to the Gaelic Language*. Edinburgh: Edinburgh University Press.

Watson, S., and M. Ivey. 2016. 'Nàisean cultarach nan Gàidheal: Ath-chruthachadh tìr- dhùthchasaich ann an Albainn Nuaidh.' In *Rannsachadh na Gàidhlig 8*, edited by W. McLeod, A. Gunderloch, and R. Dunbar, 183–94. Edinburgh: Dunedin Academic Press.

Watson-Gegeo, K. A., and D. W. Gegeo. 1986. 'Calling-out and repeating routines in Kwara'ae children's language socialization.' In Schieffelin and Ochs, *Language Socialization across Cultures*, 17–49.

Wenger, E. 1998. *Communities of Practice: Learning, Meaning, and Identity*. Cambridge: Cambridge University Press.

Whorf, B. L. 1956 [1940]. *Language, Thought, and Reality: Selected Writings of Benjamin Lee Whorf.* Edited by J. B. Carroll. Cambridge, MA: MIT Press.

Will, V. 2012. *Why Kenny Can't Can: The Language Socialization Experiences of Gaelic-Medium Educated Children in Scotland.* Unpublished PhD thesis. University of Michigan.

Williams, C. H. 2008. *Linguistic Minorities in Democratic Context.* Basingstoke: Palgrave Macmillan.

Williams, C. H. 2013. *Minority Language Promotion, Protection and Regulation: The Mask of Piety.* Basingstoke: Palgrave Macmillan.

Williams, C. H. 2023. *Language Policy and the New Speaker Challenge: Hiding in Plain Sight.* Cambridge: Cambridge University Press.

Withers, C. W. J. 1984. *Gaelic in Scotland 1698–1981: The Geographical History of a Language.* Edinburgh: J. Donald.

Withers, C. W. J. 1988. *Gaelic Scotland: The Transformation of a Culture Region.* London: Routledge.

Woolf, A. 2007. *From Pictland to Alba: 789–1070.* Edinburgh: Edinburgh University Press.

Index

Acadians, 8, 14, 37, 46
accent aim, 73–82, 95, 165
Alba, 1, 70, 83, 99, 109, 116, 127
  Kingdom of, 1–2
  see also Scotland
Anderson, Benedict, 26–7, 35
Antigonish County, 8, 12, 40, 47, 83, 100
attitudes *see* language attitudes
Australia, 3, 142

bilingualism, 4, 7, 14, 17, 21, 23, 33, 35, 121, 166, 171; *see also* education: bilingual
Bòrd na Gàidhlig, 5, 7, 15, 17, 48; *see also* National Gaelic Language Plan
Bourdieu, Pierre, 26, 32, 169
Bucholtz, Mary, 24, 26, 34, 169

Canada, 7–10, 15, 34, 42, 144
  Maritime, 7–8
Cape Breton, 1, 7–8, 10–11, 14, 17, 31, 37, 44–9, 52–5, 62, 73–7, 83–6, 89, 99–101, 106, 119, 124, 148, 156–7, 170
Catholics, 9
Ceap Breatainn see Cape Breton
children, 6, 10–12, 14, 17, 32, 37, 44, 80, 85–7, 94, 117, 119, 134, 153, 156, 169–71; *see also* intergenerational transmission; family
clans, 2–3, 46
clearances *see* Highland clearances
Comunn na Gàidhlig, 4
communication, 2–3, 13, 24, 26, 28, 39, 71, 79, 123
community, 6, 15, 24, 26, 28, 32, 35–6, 51
  Anglophone, 10
  bilingual, 23

Francophone, 37 *see also* Acadians
Gaelic, 1, 4, 6–19, 23–8, 32–40, 42–53, 60, 64, 68, 72–4, 85–7, 92–7, 99–102, 106, 112–15, 118–29, 136, 139–40, 147–50, 159–72
  imagined, 26–7, 35; *see also* Anderson, Benedict
  language, 33
  Xian, 16, 23, 26; *see also* Fishman, Joshua; culture: Xian
competence, 82, 96, 106, 165, 170
communicative, 32
culture, 2, 20–1, 23–34, 38, 42–4
  Gaelic, 2–8, 13–15, 42–9, 52, 54, 60, 62–3, 67, 86, 92, 97–106, 108–15, 118, 121, 124, 128–9, 134, 139, 148, 163, 170
  Indigenous, 10
  Irish, 68
  Scottish, 5, 44, 134
  Xian, 16; *see also* Fishman, Joshua

Dál Ríata, 1
diaspora
  Gaelic 7, 15, 48, 137
  Nova Scotia *see* diaspora: Scottish
  Scottish, 7
  see also migration
diglossia, 15, 33
discourse, 31, 34, 40, 51, 65, 68, 73, 77, 80–3, 97–8, 104 107–8, 112, 119–21, 129, 133, 139, 166–8
Dörnyei, Zoltán, 34–5, 170

Edinburgh, 39, 41–2, 64, 127, 137, 170
education, 4, 10, 15, 23, 31, 43, 48, 59, 61, 72–3, 143–4

INDEX

bilingual 5, 7, 14–15,17, 33, 35, 72, 95
Core Gaelic
French immersion, 15
Gaelic learner, 56
Gaelic-medium, 7, 9–12, 14–15, 17, 19, 31, 36–7, 41, 48, 56, 59–60, 111–12, 138–9, 147–8, 164
higher, 50–1, 66
immersion *see* education: bilingual
primary, 55
secondary, 55
Education Scotland, 48
employment, 36, 39, 41, 59, 143–4, 151–2
Enlightenment, 2–3
essentialism, 20, 22, 26, 33, 168–9
ethnicity, 6, 20, 23, 25, 28
Gaelic, 44, 108, 111, 169
Scottish, 9, 44
see also identities: ethnic
ethnography, 6, 18, 30, 38–40, 161, 169

family, 9, 12, 36, 38–9, 42–3, 49, 51–8, 64, 72, 76, 84–5, 93–100, 106–9, 115–18, 129–40, 153–6, 162–9
Fishman, Joshua, 15–16, 23–9, 33–5

Gaelic language acquisition, 14–19, 32–5, 37–8, 45, 49–51, 53–5, 57–61, 63, 65–7, 69–95, 103, 129– 36, 140–1, 147, 150, 163–4, 166–8, 170–1
Gaelic Language (Scotland) Act 2005, 4–5
Gaels 1–2, 9–13, 18, 31, 36, 40–4, 46–8, 63–4, 77–8, 88, 97–8, 100–14, 116–19, 121–5, 139–40, 160–2; *see also* identities: Gaelic
Gàidhealtachd, 52, 111; *see also* Highlands and Islands
Gàidheil see Gaels; identities: Gaelic
García, Ofélia, 20, 24
Gemeinschaft 6, 28; *see also* community
Gesellschaft 6, 28; *see also* society
Glasgow, 7, 44, 80, 111–12, 136

Hall, Kira, 24, 26, 34–5, 169
heritage, 3, 19, 34–6, 40, 42, 97, 99, 107, 129, 132, 140, 169–71
cultural, 5–6, 18, 27, 36, 40
ethnic *see* heritage: cultural; *see also* ethnicity; identities: ethnic
ethnolinguistic, 39, 163; *see also* ethnicity; identities: ethnic

Gaelic, 13, 37–9, 45–9, 70, 97, 101, 116–18, 129, 134–9, 166–71
Halifax, 12, 40, 47–8, 83, 125, 170
Highland Clearances, 3, 9, 39
Highlands and Islands, 1–9, 97, 101, 109–11, 116–18, 127–8, 156–7; *see also* Gàidhealtachd

ideal self *see* L2 motivational self system
identities, 1, 5, 6, 20–38, 89, 136, 141, 169
British, 3, 10, 27, 160
Canadian, 160
cultural, 34, 43–4, 96, 140, 169
English, 28, 116
ethnic *see* identities: ethnolinguistic
ethnolinguistic, 14–15, 25, 33–4, 37, 129, 163, 166–8
Gaelic, 6–7, 13, 19, 38, 40, 43–8, 51, 70, 88–9, 97–114, 116–18, 120–1, 139–40, 160–3, 166–9, 171
heritage, 18, 32, 42, 70, 97, 157, 163
imagined, 35, 166, 170
national, 26–8, 141, 159–60
Scottish, 6–7, 31, 44, 116, 118, 157, 160, 171
social, 5, 21–2, 35, 51, 169; *see also* social identity theory; identities: cultural
Xian, 168 *see also* Fishman, Joshua
improvement *see* Enlightenment; Highland Clearances
indexicality, 28, 31, 102–4
Inglis, 2, 28; *see also* Scots language
intergenerational transmission, 9, 11, 15, 33–4, 43, 51–3, 85, 152, 156, 170; *see also* Fishman, Joshua

Jaffe, Alexandra, 26, 28, 30–1, 33, 168–9

Kroskrity, Paul, 30

L2 motivational self system, 14, 20, 34–5
language attitudes, 5–6, 10–11, 19–20, 23, 30, 46, 49, 63, 82, 92, 95, 109, 132–3, 156–9, 162, 165, 167
language ideologies, 3, 11, 17–19, 29–34, 38, 163
Gaelic, 40, 43, 45, 49, 59, 91, 97–9, 109, 111, 122–7, 163–9, 171
language policy, 13, 19, 33, 35; *see also* language revitalisation
Gaelic, 13, 15, 17, 35, 43, 51, 65, 72, 95, 126, 138, 164, 170–1

language policy (*cont.*)
  Nova Scotian, 36, 48, 163–4
language revitalisation, 1, 14, 26, 33–5
  Gaelic, 4, 6–7, 13–19, 36–7, 47–9, 103, 107, 119, 126–7, 129, 139, 163, 166–8
language shift, 14–15, 21, 23–5, 30, 33
  Gaelic, 1–3, 9–12, 32, 53, 94, 119, 129, 139, 159, 163, 167
language socialisation, 8, 12, 18, 20–1, 29, 32, 37
  Gaelic, 19, 33, 50, 51–5, 57, 59–60, 64, 69–72, 85, 95, 97, 107, 129–32, 136–41, 147, 150, 161, 164, 167–8, 170
linguistic anthropology, 20, 21–3, 29; *see also* sociolinguistics
linguistic practices, 5, 7–8, 13, 20–6, 29–32, 34, 38, 45, 49–51, 65, 83, 85, 93, 95, 141–2, 147, 163–6, 169–71

MacDonald, Sharon, 4, 6
McLeod, Wilson, 3–5, 18, 35–6
media, 23, 126, 128; *see also* communication
migration, 23
  Gaelic, 3, 7–9, 12, 99
  see also diaspora: Gaelic
Mi'kmaq, 8, 14, 37, 149
Mill, John Stuart, 3, 28
modernity, 12, 26, 27, 34, 171
motivation, 1, 13, 18–19, 30, 34–6, 38, 41–2, 53–4, 59, 68–70; 73; 97, 107, 118, 123, 129–32, 134–7, 139–40, 142, 166–8, 170–1; *see also* L2 motivational self system
mudes, 50–4, 56, 59–62, 65–72, 95, 164

National Gaelic Language Plan, 5, 17
nationalism, 20, 26–8, 31, 67–8; *see also* identities: national; Romanticism

New England, 12
new speakers, 6–7, 13–19, 33–8, 40–4, 49–59, 63–75, 77–80, 82–99, 104, 107–14, 116–26, 129–71
Norton, Bonnie, 35, 166, 170

Office of Gaelic Affairs, 13, 17, 48, 61, 121
Oliver, James, 6
oracy, 59, 145, 166; *see also* competence
O'Rourke, Bernadette, 6, 18, 35
ought-to self *see* L2 motivational self system

Pictish, 1
Protestants, 9, 106, 109

Romaine, Suzanne, 20, 23
Romanticism, 2, 26–8, 31; *see also* identities: national; nationalism
rooted L2 self *see* rootedness; L2 motivational self system
rootedness, 14, 25, 35, 170

Sabhal Mòr Ostaig, 19, 50, 68–72, 91, 95, 105, 110–11, 135, 164
Sapir-Whorf Hypothesis, 22
Scots language, 2; *see also* Inglis
Scottish Government, 5
second language acquisition *see* Gaelic language acquisition; motivation
Silverstein, Michael, 29, 34
social identity theory, 21; *see also* identities: social
sociolinguistics, 16, 20–1, 23, 31, 33–4, 37, 72, 89, 95, 163–4, 166; *see also* linguistic anthropology
Statutes of Iona, 2

Ushioda, Ema, 34–5, 170

EU representative:
Easy Access System Europe
Mustamäe tee 50, 10621 Tallinn, Estonia
Gpsr.requests@easproject.com

www.ingramcontent.com/pod-product-compliance
Lightning Source LLC
Chambersburg PA
CBHW051127160426
43195CB00014B/2374